JAMES JOYCE
and
ITALO SVEVO

The Story of a Friendship

For Judy – as always

Also by Stanley Price

NOVELS
Crusading for Kronk
A World of Difference
Just for the Record
The Biggest Picture

NON-FICTION
Somewhere to Hang My Hat
The Road to Apocalypse (with Munro Price)

PLAYS
Horizontal Hold
The Starving Rich
The Two of Me
Moving
Why Me?

(for television)
All Things Being Equal
Star Quality
Close Relations
Genghis Cohn
A Royal Scandal

JAMES JOYCE
and
ITALO SVEVO
The Story of a Friendship

STANLEY PRICE

SOMERVILLE PRESS

Somerville Press Ltd,
Dromore, Bantry,
Co. Cork, Ireland

© Stanley Price 2016

First published 2016

Designed by Jane Stark
Typeset in Adobe Garamond Pro
seamistgraphics@gmail.com

ISBN: 978 0 9927364 84

Printed and bound in Spain
by GraphyCems, Villatuerta, Navarra

Contents

ACKNOWLEDGEMENTS

To THOSE WHO HAVE GONE BEFORE – the first full biography of James Joyce, an authorised one, was written by Herbert Gorman, a *New York Times* journalist and book reviewer. He started it in 1930 and finished it in 1940. Since then, books on Joyce's life and every aspect of his work have proliferated. Richard Ellmann's *James Joyce* was published in 1959 and revised in 1982. This virtually definitive biography has become the major source of reference for all Joyceans. Ellmann also edited three volumes of Joyce's letters (London, 1966–75), so there is now almost no entry to the Joyce *oeuvre* without passing through the Ellmann gate. Once through the gate, however, there any number of shorter and less weighty works by a long list of distinguished writers, most recently Gordon Bowker, Peter Costello, John Gross, Anthony Burgess, Edna O'Brien, Declan Kiberd, and others too numerous to record or read. I am indebted to two books in particular: Brenda Maddox's fine biography *Nora* (London, 1988), still the only book that deals with Joyce's wife separately, and John McCourt's excellent *The Years of Bloom: Joyce in Trieste 1904 – 1920* (Dublin, 2000), which covers that period when Bloom blossomed.

As for Svevo, after the great success of *The Confessions of Zeno* in the late 1920s and '30s in France, Italy and the U.K., Svevo's other work was slow to come to international attention. His three major and three shorter novels were all eventually published in many languages. In the English translations of *La coscienza di Zeno*, Svevo was well served by Beryl de Zoete (London, 1930) and William Weaver (New York, 2001). In Italy, his complete works, novels, plays, essays and journalism were published in 6 volumes (Milan, 1966-78). I am indebted to the two fine biographies in English, P.N. Furbank's *Italo Svevo. The Man and the Writer* (London, 1966), and John Gatt-Rutter's *Italo Svevo: A Double Life* (Oxford, 1988). and the moving memoir by his wife, Livia Veneziani Svevo, *Memoir of my Husband* (Trieste, 1950; New York, 1990).

As for institutions, I would like to thank the friendly and cooperative staff of the Reading Room of the National Library of Ireland, likewise the Reading Room of the British Library, and the Museo Sveviano in Trieste and, in particular, its chief archivist, Dr. Riccardo Cepach and his colleague Barbara Furlan. Also, on several occasions, the Tyrone Guthrie Centre at Annaghmakerrig in County Monaghan, has provided me with the perfect setting for some creative thought.

I am enormously grateful to Ita Daly, Fiana Griffin, Tony Glavin and Peter Zentner for their support and enthusiasm in the early days of this project. Jonathan Williams has not only been a resilient agent, but a reader with a fine-toothed comb. Andrew and Jane Russell of Somerville Press have been sympathetic and painstaking, and Jane Stark's fine design for the cover and book are much appreciated. Angela Young has been an enthusiastic and efficient indexer. Closer to home, I would like to thank Len Samaroo, my computer doctor, who has come out on many urgent house-calls. Even closer, my wife, Judy, has discreetly exercised her blue pencil and her patience, and Munro Price has read and advised on the wider view.

INTRODUCTION

JAMES JOYCE WAS VERY CONFIDENT about his reputation. He boasted that *Ulysses* alone would 'keep professors busy for two centuries arguing about what I meant'. For ninety-four years he has been right, but there are still another hundred and six years to go. It is not my intention to become involved in that argument. This book is not all about *Ulysses*, and only half of it about Joyce himself. The other half is about the Italian novelist Italo Svevo, who has always had a major reputation on the Continent, where he is mentioned in the same breath as Kafka, Proust and Joyce himself. It is an extraordinary literary coincidence that two of the four great modernist writers should have been living at the same time in the same small city, Trieste, on the fringe of the Austro-Hungarian Empire, and become close friends.

I have always been fascinated by the dramatic and touching story of their friendship, set against the violent political and cultural upheavals of the first quarter of the twentieth century. Naturally, their friendship is mentioned in many books about Joyce, but it has never been treated as a story in its own right. There is also a particular personal reason for my fascination with it. As a child, I spent several summers in a house that my grandparents rented in the shadow of the Joyce Tower at Sandycove, County Dublin. Aged about six, I learned that the tower was not named after a girl, but after a great Irish writer, who had stayed there briefly in 1904. I was told that the hero of his book *Ulysses* was Leopold Bloom, a Dublin Jew. Because my family were Dublin Jews, and Bloom was basically a good man and famous, they were very proud of him. There had been some speculation in that small Jewish community as to whose father or grandfather was the model for Bloom.

7

When I finally came to read the novel, I suspected that few, if any, of that generation of Irish Jews had actually read the entire book, even if they had managed to get hold of a copy. If they had really known what Bloom had got up to, they would perhaps not have been so proud. He had married out of the faith – to a Catholic, he adored pork kidneys, lusted after other women and had been to a brothel in Nighttown, though he did not actually avail himself of the facilities. Perhaps, worst of all, he was, by his own admission, not circumcised.

I discovered the genuine model for Bloom only many years later when I read Italo Svevo's *The Confessions of Zeno*, one of the twentieth century's great comic novels – and there are not too many. Like *Ulysses*, it was a book well ahead of its time, and published only after many setbacks. I learned more about its author, and discovered that Leopold Bloom was modelled – inspired is probably a better word – not by a Dublin Jew but by a Triestine one. In 1907, Italo Svevo had gone to the Berlitz School to arrange for English lessons. There he met Joyce, who was to be his English teacher for the next eight years. Stanislaus Joyce shared a flat in Trieste with his brother James for most of this time. Once, when James was ill, Stanislaus taught Svevo and reported that he had been asked: 'Tell me some secrets about Irishmen. You know your brother has been asking me so many questions about Jews that I want to get even with him.' In Zurich, where Joyce wrote the bulk of *Ulysses*, he did so with a portrait photograph of Svevo on his desk.

In their backgrounds, Joyce and Svevo could not have been more different – Joyce, a lapsed Catholic from Dublin, Svevo, a lapsed Jew born and bred in Trieste. There was a twenty-year age-gap between them. The contrast in their appearance was striking – Joyce, tall, gangly and bespectacled; Svevo, shorter, with the comfortable look of a prosperous bourgeois. There were major differences in their private lives too. Joyce was notoriously difficult, renowned for exploiting many of the relationships in his life and quick to take offence. Svevo was a genial family man, exceedingly generous and loyal to his friends. Their vices were also different, but equally damaging in the long run. Joyce was frequently a heavy drinker, Svevo always a heavy smoker.

They gradually discovered how much they had in common. There were striking parallels in their earlier lives, despite their different religious and family backgrounds. Both men were polymaths and spoke several languages. Svevo was fluent in German, Italian and French, and his English, with Joyce's help, would improve dramatically. Joyce could match Svevo in languages and had mastered the local Triestine dialect of Italian within months of his arrival in the city. Later, he taught himself Dano-Norwegian so he could read his hero, Ibsen, in the original.

Both men had wit: Joyce's sharp Irish, Svevo's ironic Jewish. Their most important similarity, however, was that both were dedicated writers, dealing with the pitfalls of the literary life in their own particular ways. Each had irksome day jobs. Literary success came to both of them late in life, a reward for perseverance as much as genius. They were of great help to each other. *Ulysses* was published in 1922, *The Confessions of Zeno* in Paris in 1926. In literary terms it was a happy ending, and their friendship lasted until Svevo's death three years later. European literature was to benefit enormously from that chance meeting in Trieste.

CHAPTER ONE

First Meeting

THE VIA SAN NICOLÒ IS IN THE centre of Trieste, a five-minute walk from the sea and the old port. No. 32 San Nicolò is a four-storey, mid-nineteenth-century grey stone house. On its impressive portico there are three plaques. The first reads (in translation): *James Joyce lived on the 3rd floor with his brother Stanislaus in 1907.* The second reads: *The Berlitz School started on the 1st floor in 1905 for the teaching of English Language.* The third reads: *The Berlitz School where Italo Svevo arranged his English lessons with James Joyce.* These form part of a series of plaques that mark the Joyce and Svevo *Itinerari* that today help guide scholars and tourists around Trieste.

When they first met in the spring of 1907 on that first floor, James Joyce was twenty-five and Italo Svevo forty-five. Joyce had been earning a scant living teaching English since he had arrived in Trieste two years before. Svevo was a successful businessman in the mercantile paint company belonging to his wife's family. His business took him on regular visits to England and he desperately wanted to improve his English. He had taken some lessons from an expatriate Englishman, but the lessons bored him. It was probably through friends in the prosperous business community that Svevo first heard of the young Irishman, bohemian and eccentric, a good, if unorthodox, English teacher. For his part, Joyce welcomed pupils like Svevo, because he was trying to recruit an affluent clientele for private lessons. Joyce quickly discovered that his new pupil had a wide-ranging knowledge of European literature in several languages, though English was his weakest. Svevo was equally surprised to find that, despite the age difference, Joyce's literary knowledge was almost equal to his own. Their lessons soon widened into discussions of comparative literature.

Initially the relationship was very formal and Mr. Joyce called his pupil Signor Schmitz. He would not have known anything about Italo Svevo, the pen name Ettore Schmitz had adopted. The reason for taking it, Svevo used to explain, was 'out of pity for the one vowel surrounded by six consonants in the name of Schmitz.'[1] The pseudonym, which translates as Italian Swabian, neatly summed up his hybrid background. He was Italian by language, Austrian by citizenship (Trieste did not become part of Italy until 1919), and by ancestry and education German. In Italian, Svevo derives from Swabian, which is synonymous with southern German. His paternal grandfather, however, was Hungarian. This became a significant fact later, when Leopold Bloom makes his entrance into *Ulysses*. Joyce never forgot any detail that might some day prove useful. He makes Leopold Bloom's father originally Hungarian. When he first comes to Dublin his name is Virag, which translates into English as Bloom, the name he then adopts.

At this early stage in their English lessons, neither Joyce nor Svevo had yet discovered that the other was a writer. In 1907 neither had much to boast about in terms of literary success. Joyce's published work was a slim volume of poetry, *Chamber Music*, and two short stories in a Dublin magazine. He had, however, nearly finished *Dubliners*, the collection of short stories that was eventually published in 1914. Svevo had written two novels which were published privately, one in 1893 the other in 1898; to his intense disappointment, the critics had largely ignored them. 'Write one must,' he said, 'What one needn't do is publish.'[2] Since then, he had limited himself to occasional newspaper articles on politics and art, several unproduced plays, and a collection of unpublished fables. He was, however, two published works ahead of Joyce at the time, and that didn't change for another seven years. Within a few weeks of their meeting, Joyce was going as often as three times a week to the Svevo home at Servola, on the sea just south of Trieste. The lessons there often included Svevo's wife, Livia, who was well-read and spoke Italian, French and moderate English. Svevo and

Livia lived in a spacious apartment on the first floor of her family's imposing early nineteenth-century villa. It was a far cry from Joyce's current cramped two-room apartment off the Piazza Vico, and it took him forty minutes and a change of trams to get there.

Despite the age-gap, the two men found that they had much in common, even before they discovered that they were both unsuccessful writers. After that, it was not too surprising that they became increasingly friendly – neither man knew anyone else in Trieste to whom they could talk seriously about their writing. What is more surprising is that they met in the first place and what eventually grew out of that meeting. The string of coincidences is what the Italian-speaking Triestines, with their strong operatic sense, would call *la forza del destino*.

To meet Joyce on that particular spring day in 1907, all Svevo had to do was take the tram to the centre of Trieste and walk a few blocks to the Via San Nicolò. For Joyce to meet Svevo had been a longer journey – 1,500 miles by boat and train across Europe, with several enforced detours. The journey had really started three years before, on 10 June 1904 in Dublin, when Joyce first saw and talked to Nora Barnacle on Nassau Street. Joyce biographers are in agreement about her appearance. Richard Ellmann writes, 'He caught sight of a tall, good-looking young woman, auburn-haired, walking with a proud stride. When he spoke to her she answered pertly enough to allow the conversation to continue.'[3] Because Joyce was wearing a sailing cap and had blue eyes, Nora at first thought he might be Swedish. A more recent biographer, Gordon Bowker, writes, 'His eye was caught by a shapely, proud and sauntering young woman with rich auburn tresses and an inviting air.'[4] Nora's biographer Brenda Maddox, writing about love at first sight, says, 'Not that Joyce could see very much. In 1904, although he had had trouble with his eyes all his life, he was not wearing glasses, for a doctor had advised him that going without might strengthen his sight. All he could have made out as he peered near-sightedly at the young woman was her figure, her hair and her stride.'[5] Clearly Joyce was attracted to her, however much of her he did see, and he introduced himself. She reciprocated. If her surname did not have an immediate romantic appeal for him, her first name did. Nora was the heroine of Ibsen's *The*

Doll's House. She was twenty years old and had left Galway earlier that year to work as a chambermaid in a Dublin hotel.

Six evenings later, after an exchange of notes, Joyce went out with Nora. They walked along the River Liffey, past the docks, and found some secluded spot at Ringsend. They more or less made love – in the sense of it being more satisfying for Joyce and less so for Nora. It seems she took the initiative and was clearly experienced enough to know about pleasing a boyfriend without becoming pregnant by him. Later, Joyce referred back to the experience at Ringsend as the night Nora 'made a man of me'. The letter that referred to this event, was written by Joyce five years later.[6] It was one of a series of pornographic letters that Joyce sent from Dublin to Nora in Trieste. In this one, he reminds Nora that she took the initiative at their first encounter. In retrospect, Joyce is plagued by the thought of what Nora's experiences might have been before she met him. Maybe she was too experienced. Jealousy became a stimulant for him and found its way into his work.

Joyce had fallen in love with Nora on Nassau Street and soon realised that she reciprocated his feelings. Famously, the entire action of *Ulysses* is crammed into that one day in Dublin, 16 June 1904, the day he and Nora first walked out together. It is a unique memorial to their relationship. It was a whirlwind courtship. Four months later, on 8 October, Joyce and Nora boarded the mail boat at Kingstown (Dun Laoghaire) for Holyhead. It was as though meeting and falling in love with Nora had finally given Joyce the courage to make the break with home and country. He was only to come back for three brief visits, none after 1912. Joyce was seen off at Kingstown by Stanislaus, his favourite aunt, Josephine, and his father, John Stanislaus. Joyce and Nora had boarded the boat separately because he had borrowed seven pounds from his father, but had not mentioned that he was travelling with a woman to whom he was not married, and, what's more, she was a chambermaid from Galway called Nora Barnacle. Joyce knew his father would disapprove morally and socially, and, even more importantly, he would want his money back. When John Stanislaus did finally hear the name of his son's travelling companion, he reputedly said, 'Well, she should certainly cling to him.'[7] At least he was right in that. They stayed together for the rest of Joyce's life, thirty-eight years, and were married for the last ten of them.

Joyce and Nora had borrowed enough money to get them to Paris, where Joyce had arranged, through a teaching agency, a job at the Berlitz School. They went via London, where he borrowed further money. From his father, Joyce had inherited a very powerful borrowing gene. When they arrived in Paris, Joyce found that no job had actually been arranged for him, but he was told there was one available in Zurich. This was to be no romantic, illicit honeymoon. So far, it had all been boats, trains and feeling exhausted in squalid hotel rooms. Joyce had made a couple of friends on a previous trip to Paris. He now borrowed money from them and, with a flagging Nora, took the train for Zurich. There at least they found a comfortable, small hotel and finally consummated their relationship. By one of those coincidences that punctuated Joyce's life, Zurich was also the city where he was to write most of *Ulysses*.

Within hours of the consummation, Joyce was writing about it to Stanislaus. '*Elle n'est encore vierge, elle est touchée.*'[8] He reverted to English for a bilingual pun, asking his brother 'to touch' all their mutual friends for enough shillings to make a few pounds and forward them to him. Here, in two sharp sentences, he managed to combine three of his primal interests – sex, puns and borrowing money. From the time he left Dublin to the time Stanislaus himself arrived in Trieste a year later, Joyce wrote to him constantly. He wrote about everything – his teaching, his writing, his literary and political opinions and, uninhibitedly, about his relationship with Nora, often quoting verbatim her very personal views of their life abroad. Nora was unaware that he wrote so much about her in his letters to 'Stanni'. Joyce was always writing, but Nora never knew what he was actually writing – the end of a short story, the start of a novel, or just another letter to his brother.

Joyce never pretended that Nora shared his intellectual or literary interests. She had left her convent school at fifteen. To Stanislaus he wrote that she did not care 'a rambling damn for art'.[9] Very early in their relationship he seems to have convinced her that one day he would be a famous writer, though she would have preferred him to be a famous singer. Initially this irritated him, but he came to accept it.

He saw other things in her, apart from the strong physical attraction. She had a quick tongue, a sharp natural wit and, most importantly, she represented a certain sort of Irish woman of her time and place. That place was Galway, and she expressed herself in its specific down-to-earth way. With his extraordinary memory in several languages, Joyce was a human tape-recorder, particularly as far as Nora was concerned. The finest example of his gift is Molly Bloom's final very long soliloquy in *Ulysses*, over forty pages long – depending on the edition – without a punctuation mark, except for the final full-stop. Living with Nora, Joyce never had to feel entirely cut off from his own country. He had taken a piece of it with him.

Their next day in Zurich, 12 October, was not so successful. There was no job at the Berlitz School there. Fortunately, a sympathetic director phoned the head office in Vienna and assured Joyce that there was definitely a vacancy in Trieste. Joyce and Nora got on another train and took the exact route, but in a reverse direction, which they would take eleven years later after the start of the Great War. Their arrival in Trieste was not auspicious – for Nora, particularly inauspicious. It had already become a habit that when they arrived in a city, Joyce would leave Nora on a bench in the park nearest to the railway station. She would look after their two suitcases while he went off to find accommodation or his supposed place of work. This time Nora sat and waited for hours. It was a portent for much of her life in Trieste – waiting for Joyce to come back from wherever he was. Now, sitting on the park bench, she had no money and even less Italian. What terrible tragedy had happened to her poor Jim? It turned out more farce than tragedy. Joyce had stopped for a quick drink to admire the sheer size of the Piazza Grande, still today the largest piazza in Italy. In the bar it was his linguistic skills that got him into trouble. He became involved as interpreter in an argument between several drunken English sailors and some prostitutes, soon joined by several Triestine policemen. Joyce was arrested with the sailors and taken to the police station. Eventually the British Consul was sent for (Joyce was to keep his British passport all his life) and he was eventually allowed to return to the by now distraught Nora.

It had taken them twelve days to travel from Dublin to Trieste and they scarcely had time to register its delights before they were involved in another Berlitz paperchase. The vacancy that Joyce was meant to fill was not in Trieste but in a branch office just opened at Pola, the Austrian naval base 150 miles to the south. Joyce was deeply disappointed. He had very much liked the little he had seen of Trieste, but a job was vital so he accepted the offer. At this point, Nora, not understanding the language or the currency, might have been much happier returning to Dublin, or even Galway, but, with no money and Joyce's determination to continue their journey into freedom, going home was not an option.

In Pola, Joyce's duties were to teach English to Austrian naval officers. His most distinguished pupil was Lieutenant-Commander Horthy, who was to become first an Admiral and then dictator of Hungary from 1920 to 1944. It was never recorded how good his English was, or whether he spoke it with a Dublin accent.

Joyce, and even more so Nora, led a very restricted life in Pola. They were friendly with one other couple, Alessandro and Clothilde Francini-Bruni, met through the Berlitz School. Since the two women did not have a common language, the couples' social intercourse was usually limited to singing and, particularly in Joyce's case, drinking. Fortunately for Joyce and Nora, after a five-month stay, a spy ring, reputedly led by Italians, was uncovered in the town, and all foreigners were expelled. To his great relief, Joyce was transferred back to Trieste and found a place on the staff of the Berlitz School at 32 Via San Nicolò. They rented a small one-room apartment above the school and soon moved to a larger one next door. It was the first of their nine changes of address, all now listed and commemorated for the Joycean tourist in the official Joyce *Itinerari*. Nora was by now five months pregnant. Their son, Giorgio, was born in July 1905; their daughter, Lucia, followed two years later, and Joyce and his family were to live in Trieste for the next ten years. Joyce's first favourable impression of the city was confirmed, and he and Nora came to regard it as home, even though they found it hard to find a suitable permanent apartment.

Whereas Pola was almost exclusively a naval base, Trieste was a large, commercial and passenger port, the only port of the Austro-Hungarian Empire. It had a vast hinterland that covered all the many national and ethnic areas that, apart from Russia, formed

Europe's greatest land mass. In its heyday, nearly half of the Empire's commercial output passed through Trieste, which was 300 miles from the imperial capital, Vienna, and 500 miles from Prague, the second city of Empire. With its population of 150,000, Trieste came third, but by the nature of its geographic position and maritime importance, it was the most cosmopolitan imperial city. Two-thirds of the population were Italian-speaking, just under a third Slav, with separate languages and political ambitions of their own, and a sizeable number of Germans and other expatriates of varied nationality.

Geographically and politically, the city had, for Joyce, many similarities with Dublin. It was on the sea and it was backed by mountains. Dublin was the second city of one Empire, Trieste the third city of another, but both were basically large provincial towns with predominantly Catholic populations. Politically, there was also a similarity between Trieste's Irredentist movement, which wanted freedom from the Habsburg Empire and union with its true motherland, Italy, and the Irish Nationalists wanting freedom from Britain for an independent Ireland. There was great interest in this parallel in Trieste, and Joyce wrote several articles about Irish Home Rule for *Il Piccolo della Sera* and *L'Indipendente*, the main Trieste newspapers published in Italian. Svevo wrote for the same papers on cultural and political matters under another pseudonym – E. Samigli.

In terms of climate, however, there was no similarity between the two cities. In Trieste the hot summers could be oppressive, with an incredibly fierce wind called the *bora*, which is one of those ill winds – like the *mistral* or the *sirocco* – that blows nobody any good. The *bora* was blamed for all of Trieste's ills – literally. It was held responsible for a sort of endemic hypochondria. When it blew, depression descended and the suicide rate soared. Since the mid-nineteenth century, a great many literary and artistic expatriates had lived in the city and most of them commented on the *bora*. In 1839, Henri Beyle (Stendhal) was in Trieste as French Consul. He was unimpressed with the town and wrote 'I am living among peasants here who have only one religion, that of money.' Later he added that the only original thing they had was the *bora*, and it left him 'with a feeling of rheumatism in his entrails'. The explorer and pornographer Sir Richard Burton translated his bestselling *The Arabian Nights* here, and served as British Consul from 1872 until his death in 1890. He had crossed the Arabian Desert twice, but when the *bora* blew in Trieste, Burton moved to the mountains outside, despite his consular duties.

Even the young Sigmund Freud was deeply depressed by the *bora*. He came to Trieste in 1876, on a research grant from Vienna University's Institute of Comparative Anatomy, to discover how eels copulated. As yet, no one had even been able to locate the eel's reproductive organs. Freud experienced the *bora* as he dissected four hundred eels – without solving the mystery. After three months, he returned to Vienna, depressed as well as frustrated. It was shortly after his insoluble problem with the eels that he made his decision to specialise in the more tangible mysteries of the human mind.

Joyce talked of 'the damned monotonous summer'. Neither he nor Svevo needed the *bora* when it came to hypochondria – they had a head start. In Svevo's *The Confessions of Zeno*, its author's alter ego, Zeno Cosini, says that a *maladie imaginaire* is worse than the real thing because it is incurable'.[10] Unfortunately, Joyce had 'the real thing' as well, with his already weak eyesight and troublesome teeth. Svevo merely had a mild heart condition. His friend the poet Umberto Saba wrote of 'the melancholy of Trieste – a place where one asks oneself "What am I here for? Where am I going?" '[11]

James Joyce would have had no problem answering that question. He was in Trieste because it had the only Berlitz School that had a position for him as an English teacher. His other answer, unquestionably, would have been that he was there to write. It was an answer that would have been true of any place where Joyce lived – provided it was outside Ireland. Joyce had chosen to escape what he considered to be 'the fetters' of the conventional Irish life. In *A Portrait of the Artist as a Young Man* Stephen Dedalus proclaims:

> I will not serve that in which I no longer believe, whether it calls itself
> my home, my fatherland, or my church: and I will try to express myself
> in some mode of life or art as freely as I can and as wholly as I can,
> using for my defence the only arms I will allow myself to use – silence,
> exile and cunning.[12]

These seem a strange trio of attributes for Joyce's artistic credo. 'Exile', yes, but 'silence' seems inappropriate for one of Ireland's most brilliant talkers, and, as a writer, he certainly didn't 'allow' himself silence. It was publishers refusing to bring out his work for many years which silenced him. As for his 'cunning', that seemed mainly to extend to borrowing, very openly, other people's money, unless the 'cunning' lay in the writing style of *Ulysses* and *Finnegans Wake*, perhaps purposely intended to keep the professors arguing 'for two centuries'.

The mixed European culture of Trieste offered Joyce a much greater choice of music, opera and drama than he would ever have found if he had stayed in Dublin. There were two opera houses, several sizeable theatres and many smaller ones, two large concert halls and twenty-one cinemas, whereas Dublin at the time had no cinemas. In Trieste, despite his constant shortage of funds, Joyce treated himself to tickets in 'the Gods' for operas and plays. He occasionally took Nora, sometimes Stanislaus, but most often he went alone. When a production of *La Bohème* came to the opera house, Joyce bought and read the score, then went eight times in the two weeks it was running. He saw Mahler conduct a Wagner concert, Eleonora Duse act in Ibsen's *Rosmersholm* and the Triestine premières of plays by Strindberg and Pirandello.

Of the numerous ethnic and religious communities in Trieste, the one that most interested Joyce was the smallest, but most influential. In the 1910 census the Jewish population numbered 5,500, just over 3 per cent of the town's 150,000 people. In contrast, Dublin had 4,000 in a population of 1.25 million, under 0.3 per cent. Joyce had always been interested in Jews, their culture and the parallels between Jewish and Irish history. Yet while he lived in Dublin, he did not mix with or get to know the city's Jewish community. His friend the writer Padraic Colum wrote in his memoir of Joyce in 1956, 'It is odd that the creator of the most outstanding Jew in modern literature did not at that time know any of the Jewish community in Dublin.'[13] What Joyce found out about the community and the names of some of its members was achieved by research after he had left Dublin, thanks to Aunt Josephine and the use of Thom's *Dublin Directory*. It was only in Trieste that he had an opportunity to meet and know Jews from the different strata of the local society. In her biography of her husband, published in 1893, Lady Isabel Burton wrote that she and her husband regarded 'the enlightened and hospitable Hebrews of Trieste as their best friends....It is the Jews who lead society here, the charities and the fashion. They are the life of the town.'[14] Stanislaus Joyce recorded in his diary in April 1906:

> Today until sundown was a Jewish holiday. Jim and I walked through some of the principal streets to see how many shops were shut. It was astonishing: a good third of the principal firms in the city are Jewish. Besides many names I knew to be Jewish, I found many, like Morpurgo and Bolaffio, I had never suspected before.

Jews held important positions in shipping and maritime insurance, as well as in journalism and the arts. Joyce was to know and write for Theodoro Mayer, the proprietor and editor of the two largest newspapers, *Il Piccolo* and *Il Piccolo della Sera*. There was also a separate Jewish newspaper, *Il Corriere Israelitico*. There was no situation comparable to this in Ireland's small Jewish community. However, one similarity between the two communities was the social divide between the long-established and the recently arrived families. There had been a sizeable and open Jewish community in Trieste since the thirteenth century, but in the 1680s a large, central ghetto was built, though more affluent Jews were allowed to live outside it. In 1785 the ghetto was opened by imperial decree and Jews were allowed to live and work freely anywhere in the city. A policy of toleration was followed which attempted civic integration. This became a considerable attraction to Jews in those parts of Central and Eastern Europe where anti-Semitism was prevalent. Trieste's Jewish establishment looked down on these latecomers. The same social process was to happen at the turn-of-the-century in Dublin. In 1881 there were only 360 Jews in the city, mostly English or German in origin. By 1901, as a result of the Russian pogroms in the 1880s, the Jewish population swelled to over 2,000, most of them from Russia and its territories.

There was a further similarity with Ireland: Trieste was divided on nationalistic and linguistic lines. Lady Burton wrote:

An Austrian would not give his hand to an Italian in a dance. An Italian would not sing in a concert where an Austrian sang. If an Austrian gave a ball an Italian threw a bomb into it, and the Imperial family were always received with a chorus of bombs – bombs on the railway, bombs in the gardens, bombs in the sausages. In fact it was not at such times pleasant.[15]

This corresponded to the basic Catholic-Protestant schism in Ireland. In divided societies, already preoccupied with long-standing animosities, there is usually less inclination and time to turn on the Jews. Most Irish Jews claimed, and would still claim today, that they found less anti-Semitism in Ireland than in the places from which they or their forebears had come. In Trieste, as well as the Italian Irredentists versus the pro-Austrians and Germans, there were the Slavs, who had their own separatist ambitions. In this nationalist melting-pot, anti-Semitism could be only a minor distraction.

When the Schmitz family, with their very mixed origins, first arrived in Trieste in the 1840s, they lived in extreme poverty. They had moved through several social strata of Triestine Jewry before Ettore Schmitz (eventually Italo Svevo) was born in 1861. His father, Francesco, had started out on his travels at sixteen. He peddled trinkets in Vienna, worked on the Hungarian railways and returned to Trieste at the age of twenty-two where he found a job in a glass factory. He worked his way upwards, married the boss's daughter, and by the time his second son, Ettore, was born, Francesco had started his own glassware company. There were to be two further sons and four daughters. The family were practising Jews, but not of a very orthodox kind. They belonged to a synagogue, where Francesco was respected as a successful and charitable businessman. The family observed the Sabbath and the main festivals but did not keep a kosher diet. All the children went to a Jewish primary school which, by imperial edict, also had to teach the main secular subjects. Francesco was determined that his sons should have a better education than he himself had. He regarded each of them as a blessing that would help extend his business empire, regardless of their own personal ambitions. He admired the German system and decided his boys should go to the Brussel Academy, an expensive boarding school, at Würzburg in Bavaria. Founded in 1838, it offered a combined academic-commercial curriculum. Since its pupils were predominantly Jewish, there was also religious teaching. This was to stand Ettore in good stead when Joyce, thinking about a Jewish Ulysses, started questioning him. By the time Ettore and his elder brother, Adolfo, aged respectively twelve and thirteen, arrived at the school in 1873, it had enlarged to 170 pupils with a more even mixture of Jewish and non-Jewish students and staff.

A year later the Schmitz brothers were joined by Elio, two years younger than Ettore. Elio and Ettore were both academically highly talented and had a very special relationship. Ettore was exceptionally well-read for his age and had already started writing essays and short plays. He gave everything he wrote to Elio to read and criticise, and Elio kept a journal principally devoted to his brother's achievements and his work in progress. Not as robust as his two older brothers, Elio hated the school, suffered acutely from homesickness, and left after a year. Ettore went on sending him his writing, and Elio continued to keep a journal. Later Elio wrote, 'Even Napoleon didn't have a chronicler who admired him as I admired Ettore.'[16] Napoleon may not have had, but James Joyce did. In Dublin, Stanislaus, three years younger than his brother, kept a journal of James's ideas and writings.

When Ettore left school at seventeen, he was regarded as a brilliant all-rounder. He spoke three languages fluently, had a firm knowledge of the classics, and his reading ranged from Goethe and Heine to Shakespeare in translation. He had also made two important decisions. The first was that, despite all his religious education, maybe because of it, he was an agnostic and was to remain one for the rest of his life. The second was that he would not go into the commercial world as his father wished. He was determined to continue studying literature and become a writer. Like Joyce, he was initially drawn to the theatre and decided that he would be a playwright. He persuaded his father to let him go to the nearest thing that Trieste had to a university, the Instituto Superiore Commerciale Revoltella. He registered for a literature course but, to appease his father, he also registered for medicine and then changed to law. He continued to write plays.

In February 1880, Elio, acting as a sort of creative conscience, recorded in his journal:

> From the tenth of this month Ettore has been working on a play in 'versi martelliani' – *Ariosto Governatore*. So far he has written twenty stanzas. But he is very lazy about everything and I don't know when he will ever have actually finished a work. So far he has never done so. This time, however, I have made him sign an agreement to finish the play by the 14th of March; otherwise for the next three months he is to pay me 10 soldi for every cigarette he smokes.[17]

Svevo's life-time smoking habit had begun early, as well as his perennial habit of trying to give it up. Another anxiety beset his creative life, which may account for his early preference for writing plays. Plays were predominantly dialogue and Svevo was not confident that he had a sufficient grasp of classic Tuscan Italian to attempt to write a novel. There was a great literary snobbery, based on a veneration of Dante, which bedevilled all writers who wrote in any regional dialect. Svevo remarked bitterly that Italians never wrote without a dictionary in their hands. It was particularly difficult for him, brought up to speak in Triestine dialect and educated in Germany. His political sympathies may have been with the Italian-speaking Irredentists, but culturally he was a European.

The news about *Ariosto Governatore* was not good. On 18 July 1880 Elio recorded: 'Ettore has begun a new play. The last one is not to be completed. "Le Roi est mort; vive le Roi!" But I don't suppose he will finish this one either.' In fact he didn't. He paid his fine to Elio and continued to smoke and write his new play. As for his higher education, it lasted for only a year. In 1880, disaster struck the Schmitz family fortunes. During a general slump in Trieste, profits at the glassware company dropped. Francesco had over-expanded the company and various debts were called in. He had been too lavish with dowries and trousseaux for three of his daughters, too generous to the poorer members of his extended family, and was now faced with crippling financial responsibilities. In addition, several much-loved older members of the family had recently died, and Francesco was suddenly surrounded by personal as well as financial losses. Elio was now working reluctantly for his father – he had wanted to be a musician – still kept his journal, chronicling his brother's literary progress, but now it was interspersed with entries about his father's slow disintegration under the strain of his business and domestic life. Other members of the family were called upon to contribute, including two resentful sons-in-law. The eldest son, Adolfo, was already working in a bank in Vienna and, through influence, found a job for Svevo as a correspondence clerk in the Trieste branch of the Viennese Unionbank. Svevo was to work there for the next eighteen years.

Despite the disappointment of his uncongenial career prospects, Svevo had no intention of giving up his further education or ambition to become a writer. He continued writing plays and having Elio read and criticise them. Nearly every day after work he went to the municipal library and spent two hours there reading. He discovered and admired the new naturalism of Zola and Flaubert which had influenced so many of the aspiring writers of his generation, including Joyce. After Svevo had been working for a year, he had one small literary triumph. He had written an article about *The Merchant of Venice* that had just opened at the Teatro Rosetti, and *L'Indipendente* published it. It was his first by-line; he was nineteen. (Joyce's first published piece was also a drama review. It appeared in a London magazine when he was eighteen.) Svevo went on writing short plays that were never produced, but he had more success in writing critical pieces for *L'Indipendente*. Meanwhile his father's health, financial and physical, continued to deteriorate. He was only fifty-five, but Elio, in his journal, was already noting symptoms that today would be classified as the early onset of dementia.

Now twenty, Elio himself began to exhibit the first signs of Bright's disease, a form of nephritis. No treatments seemed to help and, to avoid the winter, he was sent to stay with an uncle in Egypt. He took his diary with him and it was discovered in his belongings after his death. One of his last entries, just before he left Egypt, was worthy of Goethe's *Werther*:

Goodbye hopes! Goodbye illusions! Everything is gone now; there is almost nothing left for me to lose. If they rob me of certain illusions about my country's future, the love of my family and the thin thread of hope in the future that I imagine even the suicide has for a minute before killing himself, everything will be taken from me … and now you, who were my companion for many years, perhaps goodbye – or perhaps *au revoir*.[18]

Sadly, it was soon to be goodbye to his diary, not *au revoir*. Elio returned to Trieste the following spring, in 1884, and died a few months later. It was a huge blow to the family. If Svevo was regarded as the cleverest and most intellectual of the brothers, Elio certainly came next, and was always seen as the kindest and most sensitive of the sons. Svevo was devastated by the loss. Elio had been both his confidant and most discerning critic. They shared a room in the family's large but increasingly ramshackle apartment. In the final year of Elio's life, there were fewer entries about his brother's work in the journal. Svevo had continued to start but not finish plays, and Elio put this down to a certain laziness and lack of determination. Elio knew that he had no artistic future of his own, but feared that his brother's writing might not be destined for posterity. To make family matters worse, at least financially, Francesco decided to recoup his losses with some very ill-judged gambling on the Bourse.

Despite some promotion, Svevo felt ever more trapped by his job as a foreign correspondence clerk in the bank. It seemed at least a temporary relief when he was called up for National Service in 1885. Every male over twenty, if passed medically fit, had to serve for at least a year in the Imperial Army. Svevo trained and served with the 22nd Infantry Regiment, where he had to stretch himself physically for the first time since school. He also encountered anti-Semitism in the Army. Later, he gleefully told his friends how on a training manoeuvre he was crawling up a hill behind a minor aristocrat, Baron Gottwald. 'Don't come too close or you'll bite my bum,' the Baron said. Svevo replied, 'Don't you know we Jews don't eat pork.'[19] It sounds like a line Svevo might have dreamed up after the event, since he had a growing reputation for his *witze* (witticisms). Not exactly cut out for the military life, Svevo left the Imperial Army with the modest but respectable rank, for a conscript, of corporal. He returned to the bank, the library and, when he found the time, the life of a discontented young man about town.

He also embarked in 1887, with considerable misgivings, to write his first novel. It was very much a *roman à clef*, modelled on his own and Elio's first experiences of commercial employment. The main character, Alfonso Nitti, is a bank clerk, torn between the boredom of his work, his desire to write, and his pursuit of love. Like his creator, he also spends two hours a day reading in the library. His daydreams fluctuate between single-handedly saving the bank from ruin, achieving literary fame and seducing his boss's daughter. He manages to achieve only the last, but then, in a fit of contempt about his life and his work, he abandons her, gives away the little money he has and contemplates suicide:

> He was, he thought, very close to the ideal state he dreamed of in his reading, the state of renunciation and quiet. He no longer even felt enough agitation to work up the energy for more renunciation....[20]

Nitti's author was himself a great repudiator of things – smoking, drinking, playing the violin, women. Despite all discouragements, however, Svevo never repudiated writing. He chronicled Alfonso Nitti's life with a precision and psychological insight to be found only in Zola and Flaubert, certainly not in the current Italian literature. His novel graphically captures his own mood at the time. He was well into it when he wrote in his journal:

> Today I am 28. My dissatisfaction with myself and with other people couldn't be more complete. I note this impression down, in case some time in the future I am able to look back and either call myself a fool for writing in this way (things being even worse by then) or cheer myself up, finding I am not as bad as I was. The money questions gets worse and worse; I am not happy about my health, my work, or about the people around me....Two years ago exactly I began that novel which was to have been God knows what; and in fact it's a disgusting mess and will choke me in the end. My real strength always lay in hoping, and the worst of it is, I'm even losing my talent for that.[21]

Not too surprisingly, Alfonso Nitti does eventually take his own life. When the novel was finished, Svevo called it *L'inedito* (which translates as

The Unpublished One). He sent it to a publisher in Milan, who said that he would never publish a book with that title. Svevo eventually changed it to *Una Vita*. Given the story, this title has a typical Svevo irony. Even with the new title, no publisher showed any interest. Finally, in 1892, Svevo had the novel published privately in Trieste. His initial fears about the snobbery of the Italian literary establishment were to prove well-founded. Where the book did receive a mention, his Triestine style was disdained as 'inelegant'. One local review commented on its 'psychological insight', but the novel was ignored in the national reviews. Svevo commented, 'There is no unanimity like the unanimity of silence.'[22] Thirty years later when the book was republished, one critic called it 'a massive, Zolaesque case-history of maladjustment', and another hailed it as 'a bleak little masterpiece'. That was no help to Svevo's morale in 1892. He continued to write, but not novels – for the time being. He had two short stories published in *L'Indipendente* and, to show his intellectual versatility, he wrote articles on subjects as varied as Schiller and Heine, Zola and the naturalists, Wagner, Schopenhauer, of whom he had become a great admirer, and pieces on daydreaming and smoking.

L'Indipendente had always had strong Irredentist sympathies, but in 1889, during an outbreak of street protest against the government in Vienna, the paper's editorial went too far. The entire staff were arrested and briefly imprisoned. For two weeks volunteers brought out the paper. Svevo was one of them, probably the oldest. He came into the newspaper's office every morning at 6.30, wrote a column on foreign politics culled from his reading of the French and German newspapers, and left promptly to be at his desk in the Unionbank by nine o'clock. One of the other volunteers was the seventeen-year-old Silvio Benco, a Renaissance young man, soon to become the paper's art critic, and subsequently one of Trieste's leading intellectual and literary figures. Not many details of Svevo's life in the late 1880s and early 1890s are known, and Benco is the only contemporary source who later wrote about him in this period. Because of the twelve-year age difference between them, they were not initially close friends, but Benco observed Svevo closely, and later, when Svevo was better known, wrote of their time together as volunteer journalists:

He was a conscientious worker, precise and quick. From time to time, as if in boredom, he would raise his head from the sheets and, with his fine, deep, drawling voice, deliver himself of some witticism about the day's events. Then he would again pick up his cigarette and his pen and return to work with a patient smile…. We were two or three lads, or little more than lads, running *L'Indipendente*. A man of thirty, Ettore Schmitz represented among us the other face of life, maturity. He did not make us feel this. His courtesy – a combination of nature and breeding – would not allow him to let boys like us feel they were any different from him, even in experience. He could not converse with a human being without putting him on the same level … he talked a lot and enjoyed having an audience. Humour was for him the natural tone of conciliation. He found it to be a seemly and pleasant mask behind which to hide his embarrassment as an onlooker and a thinker, secretly plagued by painful love-affairs and by his failure to win recognition as an artist, but surrounded by more casual and practical men.[23]

Svevo was at this time still living at home with his mother, a younger brother and two sisters, one separated, the other single. It was assumed that, like many men in his situation, he had settled for short-lived mercenary affairs, but it is Benco who remembers the telling detail of Svevo suffering a 'smarting disappointment'. He was courting the tall, good-looking and elegant Giulia Babersi, a Catholic. Her father heard that Ettore was a Jew and forbade his daughter to see him.

The most crucial affair for Svevo, however, took place several years after this 'disappointment'. It is Benco again who has the facts. He writes of meeting Svevo at the opera house in the interval before Act Three of *Carmen*, the act in which Carmen betrays her lover, Don José. Svevo says, 'Now I am going to suffer,' and tells him about an anguished affair, recently ended, with a working-class *femme fatale*, a well-known beauty. Her name was Giuseppina Zergol, and he told Benco of:

The winter nights he spent out in the frost and *bora*, jealously watching the front door of a humble dwelling where there may or may not have been the faithless creature who was not worth the torment she caused him.[24]

Since this was written some time after the meeting, Benco's words scarcely capture Svevo's normally wry and ironic tone. In the end, however, Giuseppina made Svevo's torment worthwhile by becoming the inspiration for his second novel, *Senilità*.

During this period between 1889 and 1893, while Svevo was having this affair and starting to write about it, his closest friend was the painter Umberto Veruda. They first met in 1890 when Svevo was twenty-nine and Veruda twenty-two. After studying at several prestigious art schools, Veruda already had a reputation as a fine painter and an uncompromising bohemian. He seemed happy to *épater les bourgeois*, while still being commissioned to paint their portraits. For Svevo, frustrated in his home and work life, and able to write only in his spare time, Veruda appeared the ideal of the free, independent artist, everything to which Svevo aspired. Benco knew them both and later gave Veruda the credit for being the first person to understand Svevo completely and instil in him a painter's sensibility that would influence his writing style. He wrote:

> They were always to be seen together, passing remarks on women in the streets, or frequenting fashionable drawing-rooms (which they were both fond of); Svevo always very correct and bourgeois, with a look of a clerk à la mode; Veruda immensely tall and spectacular, wearing fantastic clothes with imperturbable gravity.[25]

Veruda was also to make an appearance in *Senilità*, thinly disguised as the sculptor Balli. The friendship between him and the novel's protagonist, Emilio, has many aspects of the author's own friendship with Veruda. Svevo's admiration for the courage and confidence of a younger artist, and his almost paternal protectiveness, was to be repeated in his relationship with Joyce over a decade later.

Svevo's father, Francesco, had been suffering from dementia for several years before he died in 1892, aged sixty-four. The illness had made it impossible for Svevo to have any reasonable relationship with him. Afterwards he suffered considerable guilt that, ever since leaving school, he had disappointed his father. He had not become the dynamic, young businessman who would restore the family fortunes.

He had not married at all, let alone well. In his father's eyes, he was wasting his time with his pointless writing and philosophic interests. In the blackest of black comedy scenes, Svevo later dramatised his own guilt in 'The Death of My Father', the third chapter of *The Confessions of Zeno*. Zeno, basically Svevo's alter ego, is sitting beside his father's deathbed. He is told by the doctor to keep his agitated father calm and not to let him leave the bed. That is exactly what the father tries to do, the minute the doctor leaves. Zeno struggles with him to keep him in bed, but his father shakes him off.

> With a supreme effort he struggled to his feet, raised his arm high above his head, and brought it down with the whole weight of his falling body on my cheek. Then he slipped from the bed on to the floor and lay there – dead! I did not realise he was dead, but my heart contracted with grief at the thought of the punishment that the dying man had tried to administer to me.[26]

There is no factual account of the death of his father and no doubt Svevo used a degree of dramatic licence, but his three major novels were all profoundly autobiographical. The symbolic guilt and punishment of Zeno would be an accurate reflection of Svevo's own remembered feelings.

Since his older brother, Adolfo, lived and worked in Vienna, Svevo was now, in practical terms, the head of the family. He was thirty-one, living at home and helping support his mother, two sisters and a younger brother. In 1893, the year following his father's death, he had *Una Vita* published privately and encountered that 'unanimity of silence'.[27] Despite this, he had enough confidence to continue the novel he had begun about his unhappy love affair. It was to be published five years later, by which time Svevo was married and Giuseppina Zergol had become a successful circus equestrienne.

CHAPTER TWO

Parallel Lives

THE SCHMITZ AND JOYCE FAMILIES had several things in common, the principal one being the size of their respective families. In Trieste, Francesco and Allegra Schmitz had eight children; there were also eight miscarriages. In Dublin, John Stanislaus and Mary Joyce had ten children, with only three miscarriages. Fecundity was no blessing when it came to accommodation. Both men had dysfunctional fathers in common. Francesco Schmitz was impulsive, overbearing and over-generous when he had the money. John Stanislaus Joyce had similar traits, but, whereas Schmitz suffered the early onset of dementia, Joyce had the early onset of heavy drinking. As a result, both Ettore Schmitz and James Joyce grew up in families that were rapidly sliding down the social and economic ladder. This was an experience they shared with two other great writers, Shakespeare and Dickens – an experience that clearly sharpens literary sensibilities. James was born in Rathgar, a respectable district of Dublin, in 1882, the first of the ten Joyce children, and always his father's favourite. His father was from a prosperous Cork family which owned several local properties and, as an only son, John Stanislaus came into a sizeable inheritance. He had already squandered a large part of it by the time he got married at the age of thirty-one. His wife, Mary Murray, ten years younger, could do little to curb either his extravagance or his drinking. A friend described him as 'a man who would not let a few debts get him down'. One of John Stanislaus's ways of supporting his ever-growing family was to keep taking out mortgages on the properties he had inherited. Then, when he had overspent again and there was not enough left to cover current

rent and expenses, the family would move house, always keeping one step ahead of the rent-collector. They moved from Dublin out to Bray, back to Dublin, out to Blackrock and then round increasingly less salubrious Dublin suburbs. When James was twelve, his father took him for company on a trip to Cork, where he sold off the last of the family properties.

When it came to earning a living, John Stanislaus changed his job almost as quickly as he changed his accommodation. In *A Portrait of the Artist as a Young Man*, Stephen Dedalus is asked by his college friend Cranly what his father was:

> Stephen began to enumerate glibly his father's attributes.
> – A medical student, an oarsman, a tenor, an amateur actor, a shouting politician, a small landlord, a small investor, a drinker, a good fellow, a storyteller, somebody's secretary, something in a distillery, a tax-gatherer, a bankrupt and at present a praiser of his own past.
> Cranly laughed, tightening his grip on Stephen's arm, and said:
> – The distillery is damn good.[1]

It was an accurate description of John Stanislaus's career and habits. However, one of John Stanislaus Joyce's saving graces was that very early on he appreciated his eldest son's gifts. Along with drink, buying books for James was a priority. Because he had a good education himself, although failing to pass his medical finals at Queen's College, Cork, he was determined that James would have the best education money could buy, even if it was other people's money. In 1888, at the age of six-and-a-half, James was packed off to Clongowes Wood, an expensive boarding school in County Kildare. He immediately shone both academically and at all the school sports. After four successful years, in which Joyce always won the form prize, his father could no longer pay the school fees and Joyce was withdrawn from the school. He returned to live with his still-growing family at yet another Dublin address. He joined two of his brothers as a day-boy at the more plebeian Christian Brothers School on North Richmond Street in north Dublin. He left there after only a year because his father had a fortuitous meeting in Mountjoy Square with a Jesuit priest he happened to know. Father John Conmee had been the rector of Clongowes Wood and had recently moved to Belvedere College. He remembered the young Joyce's abilities, and, rather in the role of scholastic talent agent, arranged for James, as well as his brother Stanislaus, to attend the school on full scholarships. Father Conmee went on to become head of the Jesuit Order in Ireland. Joyce was to become Belvedere's most famous alumnus.

Belvedere, reputedly then the best school in Ireland, was a day school and the two brothers had to return daily to a home-life where their father's unreliability with money and drink created continual crises. There were two younger brothers and six sisters. James referred to them as 'his twenty-three sisters'. Their mother was a devout woman who wanted to raise a good Catholic family. Stanislaus, as he later wrote, grew up 'with a double detestation of drunkenness and religion'.[2] James showed no such intolerance of either. Stanislaus wrote about being interrogated repeatedly by his father about his homework, 'It would seem incredible to people who are not familiar with the imbecility of drunkenness, that malodorous mixture of partial paralysis and semi-insanity.'[3] The two brothers took very different views of their father. James, aware of being the favourite, reacted to his father with a general air of tolerance and amusement. Perhaps it was an early sign of the novelist in him that enabled him to take an objective view and see his father as a 'great character'. He was to appear in various guises in Joyce's work, including as Stephen Dedalus's father, Simon, in both *A Portrait of the Artist as a Young Man* and *Ulysses*. His well-worn jokes and catch phrases crop up frequently there and elsewhere. The genetic streak linking father and son was too strong for James not to accept it in his life, as well as benefit from it in his work. On the other hand, Stanislaus, the less favoured son, despised his father and thought of him as an impecunious drunk who was dragging down the whole family. James was frequently to accuse Stanislaus of being 'a puritan, too blunt and dour'. They were opposite types, both in physique and personality. James was taller and slighter than Stanislaus, giving the impression of being quicker and more agile. Later in life, when he had – to use the euphemism – drink taken, he would perform what onlookers described as his 'spider dance'.

Published in 1958, Stanislaus's posthumous, unfinished memoir, *My Brother's Keeper*, covers the first twenty-two years of James Joyce's life and gives the best insight there is into his family, particularly the relationship between the two eldest brothers and of each with their father. Stanislaus had kept a diary for ten years from the age of ten. Like Elio Schmitz's diary in Trieste, it has many long entries devoted to his older brother, his ideas and works. Whereas Elio criticises Ettore for occasional weaknesses, such as his frequent inability to finish a project, he has none of the strong fluctuations of feeling that Stanislaus records about his brother. Stanislaus veers from greatly admiring his brother's intellect to frequently deploring his character:

> It is terrible to have a cleverer older brother. I get small credit for originality. I follow Jim in nearly all matters of opinion, but not all. Jim, I think, has even taken a few opinions from me. In some things, however, I have never followed him. In drinking, for instance, in whoring, in speaking broadly, in being frank without reserve with others…. I perceive that he regards me as quite commonplace and uninteresting – he makes no attempt at disguise – and though I follow him fully in this matter of opinion I cannot be expected to like it. It is beyond the power of either us to help…. Jim is a genius of a character. When I say 'genius' I say just the least little bit in the world more than I believe; yet remembering his youth and that I sleep with him, I say it.[4]

Given their ever-changing accommodation, Stanislaus may have had to sleep with more than one of his brothers. The sisters always slept more in dormitory conditions than actual bedrooms. James often looked at Stanislaus's diary and was not above plagiarising from it. On one occasion, irritated by what he had read, he burned it. Undeterred, Stanislaus started another diary. Despite the great contrasts in their characters and temperaments, and the three-year age difference, there was an extraordinary bond between them. James respected Stanislaus's taste and analytic powers enough to confide his ideas and show his early essays and poems to him. He admitted that Stanislaus was 'his whetstone', and Stanislaus, despite the continuous slights and humiliations, could still write of his brother:

> He has extraordinary moral courage – courage so great that I have hoped that he will one day become the Rousseau of Ireland…. His great passion is a fierce scorn of what he calls the 'rabblement' – a tiger-like, insatiable hatred.[5]

Stanislaus's own 'fierce scorn' was reserved for all religions, but for Roman Catholicism in particular. What his brother particularly anathematised was 'the sexual morality, which that confederacy of morbid bachelors the Church hierarchy, has striven rather unsuccessfully for ages to impose on reluctant males'.[6] Both brothers were exposed to an identical Jesuit religious education at Belvedere, but, whereas Stanislaus almost instantly turned against it and remained an atheist for the rest of his life, James was initially attracted by the drama and ritual of the Church. When he was fourteen, in a Dublin back street, he accepted a prostitute's invitation and subsequently suffered the agony of guilt and fear, so graphically recaptured in *A Portrait of the Artist as a Young Man*. He went to confession, prayed, mortified himself and contemplated studying for the priesthood. The authorities at Belvedere would have welcomed that decision as a great coup. Later that year, however, Joyce won a first prize of £3 in an All-Ireland essay competition for his age-group. His gift for writing and languages quickly triumphed over his religious calling. He chose sin over celibacy, a life devoted to art rather than prayer. Yet he did not turn his back entirely on the Church as Stanislaus did. He lapsed gradually while he was at university but, in later life, he was still drawn to the Church's rituals and music.

Joyce was sixteen-and-half when he won a scholarship and was admitted to University College Dublin to study Italian, French and English literature. A remarkably fast and retentive reader, Joyce skimmed over the curriculum, attended few lectures and concentrated on his own reading list, devoted to aesthetics, philosophy and contemporary European fiction and drama. He quickly built up a reputation as a leading undergraduate intellectual, certainly the best-read one. He told Stanislaus that he was probably the cleverest man of his year. He made friends, and several observed that 'he is the most remarkable man any of us have met'. Inevitably he also made enemies, who thought him pretentious and his ideas mad. Joyce became accustomed to this sort of reaction. He wrote numerous essays and delivered papers, mostly about art and drama. The most provocative was delivered to the Literary and Historical Society, championing Ibsen and the new European drama at the expense of the classical and the traditional. He ignored the Irish theatre as it then was.

The classicists and the nationalists both turned on him, but his paper did what it was intended to do – it made him much talked about.

During his second year, his great coup was to have a piece published in the influential *Fortnightly Review* in London. He had originally suggested an article on Ibsen, which the editor turned down, but said that he might be interested in a review of Ibsen's latest play, *When We Dead Awaken.* There was no possibility of Joyce seeing the play, but he obtained and read a French translation and wrote a review. He received an acceptance letter on 3 February 1900, the day after his eighteenth birthday. Joyce was always superstitious, particularly about his birthday. Having certain things happen on his birthday was a good omen. (Twenty-two years later, he went to enormous lengths to have *Ulysses* first published in Paris on his fortieth birthday.) Joyce received a cheque for twelve guineas and the piece was published two months later. Most gratifying of all was to receive a letter from William Archer, Ibsen's English translator, saying:

> I think it will interest you to know that in a letter I had from Henrik Ibsen a day or two ago he says 'I have read or rather spelt out, a review by Mr. James Joyce in the *Fortnightly Review* which is very benevolent and for which I would greatly thank the author if only I had sufficient knowledge of the language.'

For Joyce, no greater blessing could have been bestowed at the start of his writing career. He was elated and a few days later replied to William Archer:

> Dear Sir,
> I wish to thank you for your kindness in writing to me. I am a young Irishman, eighteen years old, and the words of Ibsen I shall keep in my heart all my life.
> Faithfully yours,
> Jas A. Joyce[7]

On the proceeds of the article, Joyce treated his father to a trip to London and while there he tried to further his own contacts, managing to arrange meetings with both William Archer and the editor of the

Fortnightly Review. Already confident of his talent, he had no shyness when it came to promoting himself. Joyce returned to Dublin and immediately wrote a play which he sent to William Archer, who read it and wrote back saying that he felt it was impossible to produce, but he still managed to sound encouraging. Archer was to be a source of good advice to Joyce for the next few years. Meanwhile Joyce's literary and intellectual reputation continued to grow at the expense of his academic one. His poor final exam results in 1902 reflected the fact that he had continued to follow his own personal reading list.

During this period, life at home degenerated further for the family. John Stanislaus was drinking more heavily and had yet another change of job, which meant one more change of address for the family. Stanislaus had left Belvedere and would have liked to follow in his brother's footsteps and go to university. Without a major scholarship or family money, there was no possibility of this. He also had ambitions to become a writer, but for years his gift was limited to his journal. He was found a job as a clerk in Apothecaries Hall in Mary Street, Dublin. Like James, Stanislaus contrived to spend as little time as possible at home, often staying out in the company of his brother and his friends. He wrote:

> For my part, I stayed on the borders of these friendships, dubiously accepted by the students as my brother's rather taciturn henchman. My father, Thersites-like, called me my brother's jackal, and when his tongue tired of that, he would explain to me scientifically that I gave no light of my own, but that I shone with borrowed light like the moon. On this simile he harped lovingly, until I retorted that, instead of worrying about the moon, he had better do something about his nose, which was beginning to shine with its own light. He was still strangely vain and vulnerable to remarks on his personal appearance[8].

Stanislaus clearly did not take lying down all the slights and humiliations offered by his father and brother, and he also had his diary as a safety valve. He used what survived of it as a first draft of *My Brother's Keeper*. Remarkably, he never lost his admiration for one aspect of his unpredictable brother:

It seems to me little short of a miracle that anyone should have striven to cultivate poetry or cared to get in touch with the current of European thought while living in a household such as ours, typical as it was of the squalor of a drunken generation. Some inner purpose transfigured him.[9]

Tragedy was never far from the Joyce family, however, and in early 1902, the youngest brother, George, aged fifteen, contracted cholera. He was the member of the family of whom everyone, especially Stanislaus, was most fond. In March he died of peritonitis. Joyce wrote about this illness and death in *Stephen Hero*, the novel he started shortly afterwards and never finished. Possibly George's illness and death played some part in influencing James's unexpected career choice after graduation. He followed in his father's footsteps by going to medical school, and with an equal lack of success. He quickly discovered that the courses and lectures were very dull. However, he found the drinking habits of his fellow medical students more congenial, and indulged in some spectacular binges. His attendance at the medical school lasted for only a few months.

In this postgraduate period, Joyce was writing poetry and using whatever connections he possessed to mix in Dublin literary circles. He was very aware of the Irish Literary Revival and had meetings with its leading figures, Yeats, George Moore and Lady Gregory. An even greater achievement was that he managed to borrow money from all of them, and became known among the *literati* as 'the genius with bad manners'. There are varied reports of his meeting with Yeats in a Sackville Street restaurant. Joyce read him his own poetry and discussed and apparently criticised some of Yeats's work. Despite this, Yeats was clearly impressed by the young man's talent as much as by his effrontery. He asked him to write a play for the Literary Theatre, which was soon to move into the Abbey. Joyce promised to write it within five years. His parting remark to the most respected contemporary Irish poet was, reportedly, 'We have met too late. You are too old for me to have any effect on you.' Yeats himself left a brief account of the meeting. His version ended:

Presently he got up to go, and, as he was going out, he said, 'I am twenty. How old are you?' I told him, but I am afraid I said I was a year younger than I am. He said with a sigh, 'I thought as much. I have met you too late. You are too old.'[10]

Yeats was only thirty-seven at the time. At the end of his account, Yeats wrote: 'The younger generation is knocking at the door.' Nevertheless, he loaned Joyce money and gave him useful introductions in London and Paris for his forthcoming trip. Joyce also exchanged letters with Lady Gregory, announcing that he 'had broken off his medical studies here' but intended to pursue them in Paris, and also continue to write. He ended his letter to her: 'And though I seem to have been driven out of my country here as a misbeliever, I have found no man yet with a faith like mine.' They later met for dinner and Lady Gregory subsequently lent him money and used her influence with the editor of the *Dublin Daily Express* so that Joyce could review books for the newspaper from Paris. At Lady Gregory's urging, Yeats met Joyce at Victoria Station as he was passing through London, gave Joyce breakfast at his flat and introduced him to another literary editor.

From an early age, there had never been any doubt in Joyce's mind that he was a genius. It was a self-belief no doubt nourished by his father's special treatment and encouragement, his brother Stanislaus's admiration, and the intellectual respect of his school-teachers and university lecturers. Joyce also had the additional gift of being able to convince others that he was a genius. Now, at just the point when he was beginning to make a small reputation, he turned his back on it. After the years of Belvedere, University College Dublin and his stressful, overcrowded home life, he seemed determined to achieve genuine independence. Yeats may have seen him as one of the 'younger generation…knocking at the door', but Joyce knew that he must write something worthy of himself for the door to open. In Paris he would start his life as a dedicated artist. In the last two grandiose paragraphs of *A Portrait of the Artist as a Young Man*, Stephen Dedalus, his hero and alter ego, writes in his diary:

26 April: Mother is putting my new second-hand clothes in order. She prays now, she says, that I may learn in my own life and away from

home and friends what the heart is and what it feels. Amen. So be it. Welcome, O life! I go to encounter for the millionth time the reality of experience and to forge in the smithy of my soul the uncreated conscience of my race.

27 April: Old father, old artificer, stand me now and ever in good stead.[11]

The old father-artificer addressed was certainly not John Stanislaus Joyce. It is the mythical Dedalus, maker of wings. Stephen is about to take flight. His clothes neatly packed by his mother, he is off to Paris for *la vie de bohème.*

John Stanislaus had scraped together enough money to cover part of the cost of his son's intended medical course. Perhaps because he himself had tried and failed, he wanted his son to succeed in a reputable and secure profession. Joyce himself was still interested, reckoning that being a part-time doctor would give him the time to write. After all, many great writers – Goldsmith, Schiller, Chekhov – had been doctors first. Despite his very weak qualifications, Joyce managed to gain admission to a Paris medical school. He had scant scientific knowledge in English let alone in French, and since he was bored by the courses in Dublin, there was little reason to think they would be any less tedious in Paris. He had not even enquired whether a French medical degree was acceptable in Britain. The question became irrelevant as he survived being a French medical student for only two months. It was the last time he ever considered finding a secure job. Now, by giving English lessons and writing occasional book reviews, he tried to earn enough to eat and drink. With his discovery of cheap French wine, it was the eating that had to be sacrificed. There was certainly no money left over for women and song.

Joyce was occasionally bought a meal by another expatriate Irish writer – John Millington Synge. Synge was eleven years older than Joyce and had already had some literary success in Ireland and showed Joyce his new play *Riders to the Sea*, which was to be produced in Dublin the following year. Joyce was not impressed with it, but the two men remained in friendly disagreement for the rest of Joyce's stay. During this period, Joyce suffered from intermittent toothache, but could not afford to go to a dentist. Meanwhile, Joyce's mother had become concerned about his health and well-being and persuaded his father to raise the money to bring him home for Christmas.

After the copious but temporary food and drink of the festive season, Joyce returned to the straitened reality of his Parisian life. He wrote some reviews, took the first tentative steps on what he intended as an autobiographical novel, *Stephen Hero*, and spent a lot of time reading in libraries. The book that influenced him most was one he bought at a kiosk in the Gare du Nord. It was a briefly popular avant-garde novel called *Les Lauriers sont coupés* by Edouard Dujardin, written largely in *monologue intérieur*. It was the first time Joyce had come in contact with this free associative style and the seed stayed in his mind and grew steadily through *A Portrait of the Artist as a Young Man* into *Ulysses* and, ultimately, into *Finnegans Wake*.

Whatever Parisian routine he had managed to establish was interrupted on 10 April 1903 by a telegram reading 'MOTHER DYING COME HOME FATHER'. Joyce borrowed the fare home from one of his French students. The family had been concerned about Mary Joyce's health for some time, but attributed it to problems with her eyes and teeth. When Joyce arrived back in Dublin on 12 May, he was informed that his mother was suffering from cirrhosis of the liver. It was a terrible irony that she, who hardly drank alcohol, was the one to get cirrhosis. While she was ill, John Stanislaus tried to curtail his drinking habits. James also tried, but with even more difficulty. Stanislaus found his brother changed since his stay in Paris.

He had learned in Paris that the world was not waiting for him, at least not just yet. He experienced it in the most unfavourable conditions, as the only life for him. Above all he had learned that extreme hunger and physical suffering and anxiety are less inimical to the growth of the soul than the invisible pressure of religion and nationalism. As a by-product of that sojourn in Bohème there must be noted an attitude towards money that to me, with my middle-class ideas on the subject, was like a hair-shirt during all our life together.[12]

Meanwhile Joyce strode round Dublin wearing his Bohemian outfit:

a broad-brimmed hat, black cloak, flowing hair and an ashplant stick. It was the outward show of his Parisian experience. He spent time beside his mother's sickbed and read some of his pieces and poems to her. Briefly, his presence seemed to cheer her up, and she tried to persuade him to make confession and take communion. Her son could not be persuaded. Mary Joyce became progressively weaker and died on 13 August 1903 with her family around her bed. Her devout brother, John Murray, knelt by the bed and led the prayers. Everyone knelt, except James and Stanislaus. Their uncle motioned them to kneel, but they refused. It was a gesture that was to haunt only one of the brothers – James. Stanislaus wrote:

> Religion, either as consolation or remorse, was so completely eliminated from my system that the refusal to pray had no part in the confused pain of loss.... I saw that my mother's life had been made unhappy for the last fifteen years or so by circumstances that were far from inevitable. She ought to have rebelled. And I saw clearly against whom, near and far, and against what she ought to have rebelled. But in the hateful country and hateful times in which she lived it would have required very considerable strength of character, which she did not possess.[13]

Mary Joyce's nine children were in the house, the three boys aged from sixteen to twenty-one, the six girls aged from ten to nineteen. The one most obviously affected by the death was the ten-year-old Mabel. She sat on the stairs, sobbing, and Stanislaus remembers James putting his arm round her shoulder and comforting her: 'You must not cry like that because there is no reason to cry. Mother is in heaven....You can pray for her if you wish. Mother would like that. But don't cry any more.'

A few days later, the brothers found a packet of letters that had been written by their father to their mother before they were married. James immediately sat down to read them, as Stanislaus observed, 'with as little compunction as a doctor or a lawyer, who wants to get at the truth.' When he had finished, Stanislaus asked 'Well?' James merely replied 'Nothing.' Stanislaus wrote:

'Nothing' for the young poet with a mission, who applied the acid test inexorably to the written word; but evidently something for the woman who had kept them for all those years of squalor and neglect. I burnt them unread.

A month later in his diary, Stanislaus, still trying to come to terms with James's contradictory nature, wrote:

…not that he is not gentle at times, for he can be kind and one is not surprised to find gentleness in him…. But few people will love him. I think, in spite of his graces and his genius, whosoever exchanges kindnesses with him is likely to get the worse of the bargain.[14]

Joyce did not deal with his mother's death either in his abortive novel *Stephen Hero* or in *A Portrait of the Artist as a Young Man*. The death scene was to surface twelve years later in the opening of *Ulysses* at the top of the Martello Tower in Sandycove. Stephen Dedalus has just spent the night there, staying with Buck Mulligan, and in the morning Mulligan teases him:

–The aunt thinks you killed your mother, he said. That's why she won't let me have anything to do with you.
   –Someone killed her, Stephen said gloomily.
   –You could have knelt down, damn it, Kinch, when your dying mother asked you, Buck Mulligan said. I'm hyperborean as much as you. But to think of your mother begging you with her last breath to kneel down and pray for her. And you refused. There is something sinister in you….[15]

A little later Mulligan returns to the subject:

…you have the cursed Jesuit strain in you, only it's injected the wrong way. To me it's all a mockery and beastly.[16]

'Stately, plump Buck Mulligan' was a very thin disguise for Oliver St. John Gogarty, a recent friend. He was four years older than Joyce, in his final year of medicine at Trinity, and eventually became a distinguished ear-nose-and-throat surgeon. He was already known as a poet, wit and man-about-town, and when it came to words, whether poetry, puns or bawdy limericks, he and Joyce were highly competitive, and frequently quoted by others. Gogarty had rented the Martello Tower from the local council and, to help the impoverished Joyce, offered to put him up for a while. After five nights, another of Gogarty's drunken friends, who was staying, opened fire on Joyce with a pistol. Joyce quickly moved out, just as Stephen Dedalus does.

Because of their literary competitiveness, neither man completely trusted the other, but they drank a lot together in the company of another medical student, Vincent Cosgrave, who was to become a Judas figure in Joyce's life. Joyce was again drinking heavily and, when he could afford it, resumed his trips into Nighttown with the inevitable medical results. In March 1904, he needed Gogarty's help because he was the most senior medical student he knew. Gogarty was currently at Oxford, and Joyce wrote him there. Gogarty replied:

> Congratulations that our holy mother has judged you worthy of the stigmata. It would be absurd and pernicious for me to prescribe for a penis in a poke so to speak. I enclose a letter for you to hand to my friend Dr. Walsh, one of the best…. If I would venture an opinion – you have got a slight gleet from a recurrence of original sin. But you'll be all right.[17]

After seeing Dr. Walsh, and being treated for gonorrhoea, Joyce was indeed all right, but, in his diary, Stanislaus wondered how his 'reckless brother' had avoided the greater danger of syphilis. Meanwhile Stanislaus was continuing to chronicle the increasing dilapidation of his family life. Two of the girls were sent off to a convent school, while four tried to run the home on the pittance they could get out of their father, and occasional help from Aunt Josephine, their mother's sister-in-law. As for the menfolk:

> The youngest surviving brother, Charlie, the one who had been in a seminary, began to drink rather heavily for a youth of his age, so that I had to cope with three drunken men at the same time. Another, perhaps, might have been able to distil low comedy out of a situation in which a

drunken father rails at two drunken sons for being drunk, but I fancy that to do so, one must know the situation only at second-hand.[18]

Joyce, who had been doing some teaching in a small private school in Dalkey, decided on a change of career and accommodation. It was the general opinion that he, like his father, had a fine tenor voice and he had often toyed with a singing career. Now he borrowed money from Gogarty to take lessons from one of Dublin's best singing teachers. He also had the good fortune to find a room with a low rent in Shelbourne Road, large enough for a grand piano, so he could accompany himself while he practised. Within a few months Joyce had sung in several recitals. At one, the great John McCormack was on the same bill, but was regarded at this point, like Joyce, as only 'very promising'. In his rented room, apart from singing, Joyce was writing. He was far enough into his novel to show it to Stanislaus, who was very impressed, and suggested the title *Stephen Hero*. He also sold two short stories to the magazine *Irish Homestead*. They would later be included in *Dubliners*. Drunk or sober, broke or living on loans, Joyce was never to be short of energy, physical or mental.

One week in June 1904 contained two momentous events for Joyce. On 16 June he went out with Nora for the first time – the memorable trip to Ringsend. Four days later he had another less successful evening out. There is some disagreement between biographers as to whether the incident happened in Nighttown or St. Stephen's Green. If Joyce was at all chastened by his encounter with gonorrhoea, the event is more likely to have happened in St. Stephen's Green than in Nighttown. There is agreement that Joyce was accompanied by Vincent Cosgrave, that they had both been drinking heavily and that Joyce accosted a woman. Perhaps he was again not wearing his glasses, but he failed to notice that the woman, whatever her status, was accompanied by a British soldier. The soldier punched Joyce in the face and set about roughing him up. Joyce sustained 'a black eye, sprained wrist and ankle, a cut chin and hand'. Biographers agree that Cosgrave did not come to his rescue, but a passer-by did. Apparently his name was Alfred H. Hunter and he helped Joyce to get up, brushed him down and took him home, where his wife provided some restorative tea or drink. Her name was Marion – Molly for short.

Subsequently Joyce heard a rumour that Hunter was a Jew and a cuckold. The rumour was never substantiated, but these two facts stuck in Joyce's mind. There were at the time just over a thousand Jews living in Dublin and some of them might well have been cuckolds. Alfred H. Hunter may have been a cuckold too, but there is no record of anyone of that name in the Jewish community. It was this scene, however, between an Englishman, an Irishman and a 'Jew' that inspired Joyce to create his most famous character. Eighteen years later, Leopold Bloom and Stephen Dedalus re-enact the scene in *Ulysses,* and Bloom 'handed Stephen the hat and ashplant and bucked him up generally in orthodox Samaritan fashion'.[19]

That this actual scene occurred on 20 June, only four days after Joyce's first outing with Nora, implies that he was not yet committed to her. Possibly it was those two events, getting infected and being beaten up, which played some part in making Joyce realise that there had to be a less painful way of achieving sexual satisfaction. Nora walked down Nassau Street at just the right moment. She was twenty years old, a striking-looking woman, whom Joyce had found willing and uninhibited. There was no way that they could have lived together openly in Dublin. If they had, life would have been even more impossible for Nora than for him. In any case, the scandal they would create by going away together would be infinitely more dramatic and romantic. Marriage never seems to have been discussed. Anyway, he was going abroad to be an artist. So, at Kingstown on 12 October 1904, the couple embarked on the journey that would take them to Trieste.

CHAPTER THREE

At the Admiralty

JAMES JOYCE STARTED HIS LIFE WITH Nora fourteen months after his mother died in 1903. Svevo married Livia Veneziani eight months after his mother died in 1895. Whatever psychological factors were involved, neither man married an obvious mother figure. Joyce was two years older than Nora. Svevo, at thirty-five, was thirteen years older than Livia. She was his second cousin, and they had seen each other at family gatherings while she was growing up, and before she went away to finish her education in France. It was an incident at his mother's death-bed that brought them together again. Most of the family were present, but it was Livia who noticed Svevo's distress at his mother's suffering, and brought him a glass of Marsala. He was touched by this gesture, and realised that Livia had grown into a very attractive young woman. She was fair-skinned, with green eyes and magnificent blonde hair. Joyce was later to use her hair symbolically to represent the River Liffey, and also borrowed her name for the heroine of *Finnegans Wake* – Anna Livia Plurabelle. Years later, Joyce told an Italian journalist, 'They say I have immortalised Svevo, but I've also immortalised the tresses of Signora Svevo. These were long and reddish-blonde.'[1] Joyce and Svevo both chose young partners whose most striking feature was their fine heads of hair.

Both men also had in common certain superstitions about birth and death. Joyce had his about events happening on his birthday. Svevo gave particular significance to the moment of his mother's death – 4.07 p.m. on 4 October. He juggled with these figures to make a propitious time for any important decision or occasion – like stopping smoking, or getting married. A month or so later, no doubt around 4.07 p.m., Svevo decided it was time to give up being a confirmed bachelor. He felt he was genuinely in love with Livia, and he made several visits to the grand Veneziani villa – visits that were complicated by the presence of three other second cousins, Livia's sisters, all of marriageable age. Svevo used this situation, twenty years later, in *The Confessions of Zeno*, in a chapter called 'The Story of My Marriage', a classic comedy of indecision and mistaken identity. He was sure Livia returned his feelings and, with a favourable date in mind, he made a formal proposal of marriage through her parents. Her mother, the formidable Olga Veneziani (née Moravia), would not hear of it and forbade Svevo to speak of it to Livia. Her stated objection was that Svevo was too old for her daughter. Because they were only second cousins, being related was acceptable, but, unfortunately, the Schmitz were poor relations. Naturally, this was never said out loud.

The Venezianis were a rich family and Olga had four daughters to marry off. Livia was her favourite, but they all had to be protected from potential gold-diggers. A further, also unspoken, objection was that Svevo was Jewish. Olga herself had a Jewish grandparent on each side, as did her husband Gioachino, something else not spoken about, since both Jewish grandparents had converted to Catholicism. A member of each family, a Moravia and a Veneziani, had come together in a paint business, and it was Gioachino Veneziani, a talented chemist, who had invented the Moravia Anti-Fouling Composition, a marine paint that preserved the hulls of ships from corrosion, seaweed and barnacles. This improved the ship's speed and cut down the need for frequent overhauls. The company's logo was an ocean liner with large wings sprouting from its sides. The formula of the composition was a closely guarded secret, known only to certain members of the family. Since this was the period of huge naval rearmament by the Great Powers, the paint was soon much in demand. It was mixed and distributed exclusively from the Veneziani factory at Servola, just outside Trieste. The Veneziani villa and its extensive gardens lay just a few hundred metres from the factory.

When Livia heard, via her sisters, what her mother had done, she was furious. She had much of her mother's will-power, and she confronted her parents and managed to change their minds. Svevo was accepted into the family and the couple were officially betrothed just before Christmas 1895. The marriage was arranged for July 1896. Inevitably, during this waiting period, Svevo's anxieties surfaced. He was used to these attacks and called them his *ranocchi* (frogs). Now they began to croak loudly. Instead of using his numbers combination to find the exact moment to give up smoking, he smoked even more. He started keeping a Betrothal Diary and would read extracts to Livia, desperate that she should understand him and marry him with her eyes open:

> My indifference towards life is still there: even when I'm by your side enjoying myself, there is something inside me that isn't sharing my enjoyment and that says to me: 'Watch out, it's not as you think it is, it's all a comedy, the curtain will come down at the end.'[2]

This *Betrothal Diary* was published posthumously. By nature a self-questioner, Svevo was quietly conducting his self-analysis in Trieste at much the same time that Freud was psychoanalysing his first patients in Vienna. When he discovered Freud's early published work, Svevo was fascinated and became an admirer. *The Confessions of Zeno* was largely inspired by the idea of psychoanalysis, but Svevo developed it in his own unique and whimsical way. In the spring of 1896, however, he had more immediate and practical matters on his mind – such as how and where to get married. Since he had no religious beliefs, Svevo was determined, despite Livia's and her family's wishes, neither to convert to Catholicism nor to be married in a church. They were married at the public register office in Trieste on 30 July, as near to 4.07 p.m. as could be arranged, and moved into a large second-floor apartment in the Veneziani villa.

For their honeymoon, they went on a train journey around Switzerland and southern Germany. The most extraordinary aspect of the honeymoon was that Svevo read Livia extracts from the manuscript of *Senilità*, his still unfinished second novel. The only person to whom he had ever read parts of it before was his mistress, Giuseppina Zergol, the book's protagonist, Angiolina. He read it to her more or less as he was writing it.

He hoped it would make Giuseppina more conscious of her behaviour and of his reactions to it – a bizarre form of literary psychoanalysis. There was a strong Pygmalion element to that whole procedure. Now, in reading it to the well-educated Livia, who already knew about the affair, Svevo showed his own need for confession and absolution. That he also had Pygmalion-like intentions towards Livia is clear from the semi-comic family chronicle that he wrote covering the first year of the marriage:

> I, created for rebellion, indifference, corruption, always entranced by what might be and never acquiescent towards what is, married with the conviction that this was a highly novel experiment in sociology, the union of two equals..., a union which imposed no alteration on either party for, after all, in order to stay together people do not need to be alike! I married feeling certain that if either of us had to change it certainly wouldn't be me! Rather I wanted to change my wife slightly in the sense of giving her more freedom and teaching her to know herself. I bought some books by Schopenhauer, Marx and Babel, intending not to impose them but to insinuate them little by little. Instead, literature, at least of the sort I particularly had in mind, vanished entirely from our relationship....After all, good *bourgeoise* that she is, what matters to her is to live in peace and harmony, keeping one's own ideas inside one's own head protected by all that hair. She is not concerned with convincing others. Whilst we are all apostles of some ideas or of nothingness! [3]

'We', of course, meant men, intellectuals like himself. Svevo was never far from irony and a sense of his own ridiculousness. After all, this was no secret diary – more like a joke that he shared with his wife. Livia had had a reasonable education for a girl of her class, some of it in France, where her parents had worked for a couple of years. She spoke French, good German and passable English. As a Veneziani, living so close to the company offices and factory, she had developed a sound business sense, which later would be of great help to her husband. Livia was always aware of her husband's high-flown ideals. She was impressed by, without sharing, his intellectual and literary pursuits, and tolerated his impractical nature. All she really disliked about him was his constant smoking and she pressed him to give it up, which he frequently did. Svevo always had a fear of turning into the successful bourgeois that, because of his business and home life, would inevitably happen. He never blamed Livia for this, or ever underrated the happiness and affection in their marriage. This was demonstrated in the almost daily letters he wrote her when he was away on business. At one point in the family chronicle he admits to an argument with Livia about the cost of buying some domestic gas heaters, which, surprisingly, he wins:

> So you see I am a genuine *paterfamilias*. In short, my wife, my parents-in-law, my cousins, male and female, all say I am a good husband, and the worst of it is that when they tell me this I don't get angry.[4]

Though he had married into a rich, bourgeois family and lived at a very nominal rent in the Veneziani villa, Svevo and Livia were not well-off. Livia had not come with a dowry, and Svevo was determined to remain independent and continued to work at the Unionbank and, part-time, at *L'Indipendente*.

In early 1897, Livia became pregnant, which led to a recurrence of their pre-marital religious differences. She knew that, because of their civil marriage ceremony, they were not considered to be married in the eyes of the church. She became anxious to the point of becoming ill. Svevo decided that the health of his wife and unborn child was more important than his agnostic principles. There are varied accounts of the details, but Svevo is reported to have said to Livia, 'You accepted the idea of having a Jewish husband. Well then, I'll make you a present in return. I'll get baptised.'[5] Livia recovered almost immediately from the fever she had developed. Svevo said, 'I have never troubled to decide whether it was the Jewish God or the Christian who performed the miracle.'[6] On 25 August he was baptised and married Livia as a Catholic in the parish church at Servola. Their daughter, Letizia, was born a month later. He had kept his word, but never relinquished his agnosticism.

In the midst of all this domestic and work activity, Svevo still managed to put the finishing touches to *Senilità*. It had taken him nearly four years to write and it finally emerged as a sort of a sado-masochistic *Pygmalion*. With ironic detachment, but in minute detail, Svevo records the ebb and flow of his protagonist Emilio's passion. Emilio becomes obsessed with Angiolina's suspected infidelities. The woman he has wanted to possess and educate comes to possess him. His friend and confidant throughout is the sculptor Balli, who struggles to keep up with Emilio's changes of mood. In the end Emilio confronts Angiolina, calls her a whore and, in a fit of childish vindictiveness, throws handfuls of pebbles after her as she walks away up the street.

Since Livia knew all about Svevo's affair with Giuseppina Zergol, there was now no reason not to have *Senilità* published. It first appeared in instalments in *L'Indipendente* in June 1898 and then Svevo had it published at his own expense by Ettore Vram, the publisher who had brought out *Una Vita*. *Senilità* had a similar lack of acclaim. The few local reviews expressed moral distaste at the too explicit nature of the subject matter. Even his young friend at *L'Indipendente*, Silvio Benco, now twenty-three, damned him with faint praise, criticising his 'naïve literary style', but at least acknowledging the author's psychological insights.

Fifteen years after his death, Livia Veneziani Svevo wrote a memoir of her husband. She wrote it in hiding from the Fascists at the end of World War II, having managed to save many of her husband's papers. Recalling the time after the publication of *Senilità*, she wrote:

Shaken by the public silence and indifference, Ettore wrote: 'I don't understand this incomprehension. It means that people don't understand. Write one must; what one needn't do is publish.'…So, sadly and reluctantly, Ettore moved away from literature, hiding his bitter regret and only occasionally allowing it to show. He no longer spoke of plays or novels but slaked his thirst for them at night by reading…. His repressed literary longing sometimes returned to him and he would then write at any hour, in any place, on scraps of paper. At intervals he would make notes on thoughts and impressions, as if to peer more deeply into himself, and analyse his inner life more accurately…. If

Senilità [*As a Man Grows Older*] had brought him success, I am sure he would have carried on writing, even though the demands of the family prevented him from giving up his job. He would fully have accepted a double life, and smilingly hidden the strain it cost from all of us.[7]

Here, Livia has not yet reached the point in her memoir where her husband finally achieves his great success with *The Confessions of Zeno*. The gap between the publications of the two novels was twenty-five years. It became known as 'the longest sulk in literary history'.

Meanwhile, Svevo was finding the running of even a small family a strain on his finances. His income from the bank and even some part-time teaching of a commercial course at the Revoltella Institute were inadequate. He gambled on the stock exchange, not as extravagantly as his father, but enough to get into debt. He kept this to himself, but Livia probably guessed and talked to her father about their financial problems. Svevo had always been on good terms with his father-in-law, Gioachino, but trod carefully with the dominating Olga, whom he privately called 'the monster'. The business was expanding and needed more responsible hands, especially on the accounting side, where Svevo's banking experience would be useful. For the sake of Svevo's pride, the matter had to be handled tactfully. It was, and the son-in-law was offered a reasonable, if not generous, salary for a position that entailed considerable business responsibility. He was told the formula of the anti-fouling composition and sworn to secrecy. By now, the Venezianis had another factory on the small island of Murano, near Venice, and Svevo was soon dividing his time between the two factories. He found he preferred supervising the workforce than doing the accounts, which reminded him too much of his years in the bank. The Moravia Anti-Fouling Composition was now hugely in demand. By 1903 the Veneziani Company brochure lists its contracts with the navies of Britain, Austria, France, Japan, Italy, Spain and Greece, as well as numerous large international shipping companies.

Svevo may have renounced the idea of having another novel published, but he stuck to the first half of his statement – 'write one must'. He continued to write occasional pieces for both *L'Indipendente* and *Il Piccolo* and the former published one of his long fables. Among the papers that Livia saved, there is even Svevo's timeless *credo* for writers:

> I believe, I sincerely believe, that there is no better way to become a serious writer than to scribble every day. You have to try and bring to the surface, every day, from the depths of your being, a sound, an accent, the fossil or vegetable remains of something that may or may not exactly be thought, that you may or may not be feeling, but a whim, a regret, a sorrow, something genuine, pinned down in its completeness. Otherwise, on the day you think yourself authorised to pick up a pen, you will fall into cliché, and the object will escape you. In other words, apart from the pen there's no salvation.[8]

There can be no doubt that Svevo was a serious writer who did 'scribble every day'. His use of the word 'authorised' before 'to pick up your pen' would have given great pleasure even to that fanatic for precise word-play, James Joyce.

Svevo was travelling increasingly for the Veneziani Company and when abroad he 'scribbled' every day in the form of letters to Livia. She read them several times over and marvelled at their descriptions and their length. He replied, 'See what it is to send a novelist on a journey.' One very satisfied customer of the Veneziani Company was the 4th Baron Muskerry. Holder of an Irish peerage, he sat in the House of Lords, was extremely wealthy, owned a great deal of property in County Cork, and two large yachts. He had heard good things about the Moravia Anti-Fouling Composition and, in 1899, arranged to have it applied to the hull of one of his yachts while it was moored in Malta. He subsequently spread the word of its efficacy around his friends at the British naval base. There, it must have reached the ears of the Commander-in-Chief of the Mediterranean Fleet, Admiral Sir John Fisher. Within a few years Fisher became First Sea Lord, and it was his decision to paint the entire British Fleet grey which was considered the best form of camouflage at sea in case of naval warfare.

In May 1901, when Svevo was on a business trip in the south of France supervising contracts in Marseilles and Toulon, he received a telegram from Olga informing him of the British navy's interest in the company's paint, and telling him to go immediately to the dockyards at Chatham. Clearly the Venezianis considered his English good enough for him to be able to cope in England. Svevo felt their confidence misguided, but an order from Olga was an order and he left for England. He was amazed by what he found there. In his first letter to Livia, he wrote:

> This England is so different from what we imagine that it's impossible for me to give you any idea…. You've never seen such a difference between two neighbouring peoples as the French and the English. I'm talking about outward appearances, that's all I know. For a start, the emblematic hat which is taken off only on the rarest occasions! The pomposity of pretending you can't see people you haven't been introduced to![9]

Svevo soon had little time for such leisurely observations. He was plunged into a whirl of business activity. The British Navy was enthusiastic about the Moravia Composition and Svevo was summoned to a meeting at the Admiralty. Twenty-five years later, when he was finally a full-time literary man, Svevo reminisced with his old Triestine friend, the poet Umberto Saba, about his business triumphs. The one he was proudest of, as Saba tells it in his memoir, was at the Admiralty:

> Svevo climbed the steps of the Admiralty with his heart pounding. He was expected and was immediately taken into a small, cheerless and bare room that was more the size of a closet than an office. After a few minutes a young man appeared and offered him the only chair. The official himself sat on the table, which, together with the chair, made up the room's only furnishings. He offered a cigarette and lit one for his guest and himself. He showed himself to be informed on the matter, asked two or three questions, then announced that everything seemed all right and that the deal was essentially concluded. Italo Svevo thought that he was dreaming. He had anticipated a long string of documents and a series of interminable discussions. And here it took only five minutes for his cherished underwater paint to be adopted by the most powerful navy in the whole world. In Italy or even France, he said, it would have taken five years. When he left the Admiralty (although the deal was completely

honest and, as all really good deals are, advantageous to both parties), he fell prey to a vague sense of guilt. Yet, at the same time, it seemed to him that his feet had grown wings.[10]

An enormous order for the Moravia paint was soon placed. The Admiralty had decided that if all warships were being painted grey, it would be a good idea, at the same time, to add a coat of Moravia Anti-Fouling Composition to their hulls. Svevo was immediately in touch with his in-laws about the urgent necessity of setting up a factory near the London docks. Within eighteen months, a Veneziani factory was fully operational close to the Thames at Charlton in south London. A house was rented nearby for Svevo and other members of the family coming over to do business. Meanwhile, Svevo had to make all the initial arrangements. Missing Livia and trying to speak English were his two main problems. He wrote her long letters as frequently as he could and in one he explains a particular embarrassment:

> If you did but know of my agitation over all the other divergences in character between myself and the English. It seems that in this country I am quite ridiculous on account of my mode of gesticulation. I observed that when I once – just once—spoke *my* English at the Admiralty, the Sea-Lords stared at my hands which seemed to dance about the room. My halting speech made me gesticulate even more than usual. Stick your hands in your pockets and then alone will you be able to speak English.[11]

He was also concerned about Livia's health. After the birth of Letizia, Livia had gynaecological problems and went for treatment to several clinics in the mountains near Trieste. None was successful, and there were to be no more children. In early July 1901, after arguments with Olga about his wife's travelling expenses, Svevo welcomed Livia to London. First, he showed off his knowledge of the city, and then he took her on a business trip, combined with a holiday. They sailed to Ireland where Lord Muskerry wanted Svevo to supervise the coating of his other yacht with the anti-fouling composition. The yacht was moored at Queenstown (now Cobh), and afterwards Svevo and Livia toured County Kerry and were 'enchanted by the wild beauty of the countryside'. At that time Joyce would have been in his second year at University College Dublin and the English lessons Svevo so badly needed were still six years away. Meanwhile he took some lessons in Trieste from an English expatriate which he did not much enjoy.

Supplying their paint to the British Navy soon became the most lucrative contract the Veneziani Company had, and Svevo found himself committed to frequent trips to Charlton. He became increasingly fascinated by English manners and mores, and his letters to Livia reflect this. He also became interested in British politics, and later wrote essays on the subject which were published in the Trieste press. Socially, he never managed to feel comfortable with the British Establishment, with whom he had some entrée through naval circles. Because of his egalitarian views, he felt more comfortable with ordinary, working-class English people. He was no longer upset when, on visits to dockyards, they laughed at his English. He became a great supporter of the local football team, Charlton Athletic, and always tried to go to their home matches. He even claimed to find his new life among the English rejuvenating:

> Those 50,000 other inhabitants of my district, of whom, as far as I know, not one was nursing dreams of literary fame, or if he was, was managing to conceal it, gave me back my peace of mind. I was living in a place where, if I admitted out loud the ideas I had once had about myself, I would have been put in an asylum. Among such neighbours resignation came easily. True, I got to know the star footballer of the district, and he introduced me to a national Rugby hero; but in their case there wasn't the same thirst for glory. One enters the football field primarily for the good of one's health and appetite. Glory is only an afterthought. Whereas with us writers the lust for glory is something morbid. A beaten footballer still has his self-respect; a failed writer is merely ridiculous.[12]

Svevo was being hard on himself. Looking at the more positive side, how many maritime paint-salesmen from Trieste had the opportunity to mix with the sporting celebrities of Charlton S.E.7?

Svevo was to continue these trips to London, often with Livia, until almost the start of the Great War. Other members of the family also came and stayed in the Charlton house and shared in the running of this important branch of the business. On the company's letterhead, Charlton now vied with Murano and Trieste.

One casualty of Svevo's new life, however, was his relationship with his old friend Umberto Veruda. Their relations had cooled ever since Svevo's marriage. Livia and Veruda did not get on and were jealous of each other. When Svevo joined the Veneziani business, Veruda clearly thought his friend had abandoned art and surrendered to bourgeois capitalism. He wrote Svevo a caustic letter on the subject. At the time, Veruda was also travelling frequently, holding exhibitions and accepting commissions in Vienna and Venice. He travelled as far afield as Blenheim Palace to paint portraits of the Churchills. The two men did still meet and discuss art and literature, but Veruda was an unreliable time-keeper, which irritated Svevo. Veruda was becoming increasingly depressed and neurotic about being just a fashionable portrait painter at a time when fashions in art were changing so drastically. He temporarily gave up painting, and Svevo invited him to come and rest at Murano. There, Veruda established better relations with Livia and started painting again. Two of the pictures he painted were accepted for the 1905 Venice Biennale, but Veruda was never to see them there. His mother, to whom he was devoted, suddenly became ill with a high fever. He rushed to be at her bedside. The doctor instructed him not to let his mother drink any water. When she asked for water, Veruda refused to give her any. She cursed him as a cruel and ungrateful son, hit out at him and died shortly afterwards. Svevo heard this story and filed it away in his mind. It reappears, twenty years later, in *The Confessions of Zeno*, amalgamated with the story of the death of Zeno's father. For good or ill, death-beds play a major role in the work of Svevo and Joyce.

After his mother's death, Veruda became increasingly obsessed with her dying curse. He stopped painting again and convinced himself that the curse was killing him. He had an attack of appendicitis, refused treatment, and died from peritonitis. He was thirty-six. When Svevo heard the news, Livia wrote in her *Memoir*: 'I saw him that day, for the first time, lying on his bed, crying like a child.' He had lost his closest friend, the one he most associated with a precious part of his life.'[13]

It was another two years before Svevo met James Joyce. Their friendship was never quite as close as the one Svevo had with Veruda, although it had many of the same qualities. Svevo admired them both for their independence and their uncompromising attitude to their art, and he shared their wide-ranging cultural interests. The principal difference between the two friendships was the wider age-gap. Whereas Svevo had been seven years older than Veruda, he was twenty-one years older than Joyce. If Veruda had been the wayward younger brother, Joyce became the very prodigal son. In the Svevo-Joyce relationship there remained always a slight student-teacher formality, but in terms of their writing, they treated each other as equals. Eventually, there was a more tangible connection between Joyce, Svevo and Veruda. In 1927, Svevo sent Veruda's portrait of Livia to Joyce. He sent it in gratitude for all the help Joyce had given him in Paris, but also as a reminder of the 'reddish-blonde' tresses that Joyce had asked Lucia's permission to incorporate into *Finnegans Wake*. The portrait was to hang on Joyce's wall in the many places he lived in Paris.

CHAPTER FOUR

Roman Interlude

EARLY IN THEIR CREATIVE LIVES BOTH Joyce and Svevo became used to having a resident literary critic. Svevo had replaced his brother Elio with Veruda. Joyce had always had Stanislaus, but when he went to Trieste, he was without him for the first time, except for his seven-month stay in Paris. From Trieste he sent most of his writing back to Stanislaus in Dublin and received prompt replies, but Joyce wanted a more resident service. He also missed his brother's intellectual companionship. Although Nora had many virtues and strengths, providing intellectual companionship was not one of them. In the summer of 1905, when Joyce heard that there would be a teaching post coming up at the Berlitz, he immediately notified Stanislaus. The job would pay a one-way fare, and Joyce offered to scrape together some travelling expenses for him. He gave no consideration to the fact that his brother had never been out of Ireland, never taught before, and spoke no Italian. The most relevant facts for Joyce were that he needed his brother's company and part of Stanislaus's salary would relieve Joyce and Nora's continuing financial problems.

In Dublin, Stanislaus had become deeply bored with his clerkship at Apothecaries Hall. He had no desire to qualify as an accountant. After eighteen months of clerking, he gave it up, and survived on odd jobs. His writing ambitions were confined to his scrupulously kept diary and to criticising, usually constructively, his brother's work. He felt he had no prospects in Dublin, except the dreaded one of continuing to live at home with his impecunious, drunken father and his six sisters. His brother's offer represented a tangible opportunity for escape, although his conscience was troubled by the thought of leaving his sisters to cope with their father. In the end his feeling for his brother and his own need for freedom triumphed over his conscience. In September 1905, two months before his twenty-first birthday, Stanislaus set off for Trieste. He was never to return to Ireland, or to see his father again.

Stanislaus did not jump blindly from the frying pan into the fire. He knew, more or less, what he was getting into, although with Nora and Giorgio added to the equation, the relationship might be differently balanced. Nearly three years younger than his brother, Stanislaus looked and seemed several years older. He was shorter and more stockily built, a physique ideally suited to pulling his brother out of bars and carrying him home. Since this became a frequent duty, it must have often seemed to Stanislaus that he had merely exchanged one drunk for another, but at least his brother was one he admired rather than despised. By nature, Stanislaus was mostly sober and always responsible, two characteristics scorned by Joyce. Over the years, the serious Stanislaus was to receive little gratitude for all his fraternal assistance, physical, intellectual and financial. As Richard Ellmann, who got to know him in his later years in Trieste, saw it, 'Stanislaus was bound to James by affection and respect, but also by indignity and pain.'[1] Less elegantly put, it was a long-running love-hate relationship.

The brothers' reunion did not augur well. Joyce met Stanislaus at the railway station and almost the first thing he asked was if he had any money left over from his travel expenses, because he and Nora were down to their last centesimo. Later, Stanislaus complained that he had been asked precious little else about himself. Within two days of his arrival, Stanislaus was teaching at the Berlitz. He was paid forty crowns in advance, and usually handed half of it over to Joyce for board and lodgings. To begin with, he had a small room in an adjacent apartment. Then a series of the moves began that characterised the Joyces' life in Trieste. Stanislaus usually ate his evening meal with them, whether he was actually staying in their apartment or not. As Brenda Maddox pointed out in her biography of Nora, two brothers and one wife living together was a quite common rural family pattern, especially in Ireland. Unfortunately, Stanislaus had arrived at a period of turbulence in the Joyce marriage. Joyce wrote to Aunt Josephine:

> I have hesitated before telling you that I imagine the present relations between Nora and myself are about to suffer some alteration. I do so now because you are a person who is not likely to discuss the matter with others. It is possible that I am partly to blame if such a change as I foresee takes place, but it will hardly take place through my fault alone. I daresay I am a difficult person for any woman to put up with, but on the other hand I have no intention of changing.... I am not a very domestic animal, after all I suppose I am an artist – and sometimes when I think of the free and happy life which I have every talent to live, I am in a fit of despair.[2]

He goes on to complain about Nora's frequent 'indifference to him' and her 'sharp tongue'. Aunt Josephine Murray, then in her sixties, was his mother's sister-in-law, a highly intelligent, well-read woman who had encouraged her nephew to write, in the firm belief that one day he would be a great writer. After Stanislaus left, she was the only person in Dublin to whom Joyce wrote regular letters and, in them, he often tried out many of his literary ideas. She also acted as a sort of unpaid researcher when Joyce required information about Dublin or certain of its citizens. She took a sympathetic interest in Stanislaus and, aware of his being overshadowed by James, always tried to bolster his self-esteem. Now, with him in Trieste, she had a spy in residence. Because both brothers confided in her, Aunt Josephine was able to see both sides of any situation and attempt, by remote control, to keep the peace between them. After Joyce's letter to her about Nora, Aunt Josephine wrote back to Stanislaus:

> But honestly, Stannie, I can't understand Nora. Surely it is a monstrous thing to expect Jim to cook or mind the baby when he is doing his utmost to support both of them....I wonder does she realise what it is to be a person with a scurrilous tongue from which you are never safe. There is some excuse for Jim drinking. It is the old story of finding forgetfulness.[3]

Aunt Josephine had never been happy about her nephew's elopement with Nora. She thought her an unsuitable partner for her brilliant nephew 'Jim', apart from the fact that they were not married – although she was slightly more broad-minded about that than the rest of the family. Yet, 'scurrilous tongue' or not, she was not being exactly fair to Nora, who was having a very difficult time. Joyce was hardly 'doing his utmost' to support a family. His income from the Berlitz was meagre, and he was still spending a fair proportion of it on drink, as well as outings to the theatre and opera. Nora was never able to stop him drinking, nor was Stanislaus, even though he sometimes resorted to force. Joyce was not a noisy, aggressive drunk, but a floppy, garrulous one. He had never told Nora that he would earn money by finding a better day-job. The most he had ever promised was that one day – through his books – they would be rich and famous. And Joyce did write prodigiously, whatever the adverse conditions. In their numerous apartments, Joyce nearly always had to write in the bedroom, sitting on the bed and using an open suitcase as a desk-top. Most frequently he had to write at night, in poor light, and his sight was already beginning to cause him problems. He took to wearing a white jacket while writing, since he thought it reflected more light onto the page. In that early period in Trieste he had already finished most of the stories in *Dubliners* and was several hundred pages into his autobiographical novel *Stephen Hero*. Stanislaus read several chapters of the latter and wrote in his diary:

> The chapters are exceptionally well-written in a style which seems to me altogether original. It is a lying autobiography and a raking satire. He is putting nearly all his acquaintances in it, and the Catholic Church comes in for a bad quarter of an hour.[4]

Stephen Hero was the first of Joyce's alter egos, an early version of Stephen Dedalus. Joyce's uninhibited command of language was indeed striking and 'altogether original', but the book's style was also discursive, polemical and frequently pretentious, not surprising given that the author was only twenty-three. Its admiring critic was himself only twenty, and no doubt influenced by finding in the novel a sympathetic brother character called Maurice, even though he too receives a share of that 'raking satire'.

Meanwhile, Stanislaus was living in the middle of a battlefield. Nora, usually exhausted from the day's chores, would fight with Joyce, eager to escape to the two things he enjoyed most – writing and drinking. When they were tired of fighting each other, they turned on Stanislaus. Viewed in dramatic terms, the situation was closer to Strindberg than Joyce's other Scandinavian hero, Ibsen. Joyce was fascinated by triangular relationships, a subject that was later the theme of his one produced play, *Exiles*. The arguments between Joyce and Nora came and went, but their basic attraction and need for each other remained. Stanislaus was also attracted to Nora, but his feelings were definitely not reciprocated. He was no threat to the marriage. In his role of punch bag, he may even have been a help.

Both Joyces had full teaching schedules at the school. Stanislaus, conscientious and feeling his way as a teacher, used straightforward methods. Joyce, quickly bored with grammar and pronunciation, would launch himself into extempore performances on a wide range of subjects. A fellow teacher, Francini Bruni, with whom the Joyces had become friendly in Pola, kept notes of some of these improvisations and collected reports from his students, as though he suspected that one day it would make good copy. Early in their stay in Trieste, Joyce and Nora had moved in with the Francini Brunis. It was not a successful cohabitation, but it gave Bruni another opportunity to collect Joyce material. He cleverly used this in a public lecture he gave in 1922, the year when *Ulysses* was published. The lecture was later published as a pamphlet entitled *Joyce: Intimo Spogliato in Piazza* (*Joyce: Stripped Naked in the Piazza*). It was good Joycean polemic, interesting as a preview of some of the ideas that were later developed in *Ulysses*:

> Ireland is a great country. It is called the Emerald Isle. The metropolitan government, after centuries of strangling it, has laid it waste. It's now an untilled field. The government sowed hunger, syphilis, superstition, and alcoholism there; puritans, Jesuits and bigots have sprung up.... And in spite of everything, Ireland remained the brain of the United Kingdom. The English, judiciously practical and ponderous, furnish the over-stuffed stomach of humanity with a perfect gadget – the

water closet. The Irish, condemned to express themselves in a language not their own, have stamped on it the mark of their own genius and compete for glory with the civilised nations. This is then called English literature....

Bruni may not have captured Joyce's words exactly, but they have the genuine Joycean rhythm and ring, and Bruni's humour was on the same wavelength. His description of Joyce shows his own linguistic versatility:

He was inconceivable and absurd, a composite of incompatibilities with the unchanging laws of the elements, which, however, by a miracle of molecular aggregation, formed a whole. He was constitutionally fragile and hysterical, suspended by natural gravitation between the mud in which he wallows and a refined intellectualism that touches the limits of asceticism. He accepts unquestioningly the existence of the rabbit and the eagle, sun and mudheap.[5]

In February 1906, Joyce received the exhilarating news that Grant Richards, a London publisher, had signed a contract to publish *Dubliners*. The exhilaration was short-lived. Two months later, Richards informed Joyce that the printers were refusing to set some of the stories on the grounds of obscenity, as well as insults to the monarchy and the church. Joyce was outraged, refused to cut the stories as requested, and began the first of his many battles with publishers over what he considered to be their censorship. *Dubliners* became a shuttlecock between publishers, and was not published for another seven years. Joyce now had only one literary iron left in the fire. He had sent *Chamber Music*, a collection of thirty-six poems to Elkin Mathews, another London publisher, but placed no great hopes on finally seeing it in print.

These setbacks and the stress of finding time to work on his novel, made him think about leaving Trieste. There was an incentive when he heard that the Berlitz School was having financial problems and it might soon be able to afford the salary of only one Joyce. Depressed and restless, Joyce persuaded Nora that they both needed physical change. He answered an advertisement for a job as a multilingual correspondence clerk at a bank in Rome. It was better paid than his teaching job, and he thought it would allow him more time to write. After gathering some impressive references from Dublin and Trieste, he applied. He was very quickly offered the position. Ironically, it was the same sort of job that Svevo had done and hated in Trieste. Once in Rome, it would not take Joyce long to hate his new job too.

Joyce had persuaded Stanislaus to come to Trieste so he could enjoy his intellectual company. Now, after only seven months, Stanislaus was left to his own company looking after the Joyces' apartment, paying all the rent, and trying to hold Joyce's creditors at bay. Joyce's regular letters to Stanislaus are the main source of information about how he felt about Rome, his work and his literary progress. On all these scores the news was not good. As usual, the Joyces had trouble finding affordable accommodation and there were several moves. Nor were they greatly impressed by the city's ancient monuments. Joyce wrote, 'Rome reminds me of a man who lives by exhibiting his grandmother's corpse.' He regretted not knowing more Latin and more Roman history, but decided 'it's not worthwhile beginning now. Let the ruins rot.'[6] His working hours, from 8.30 a.m. to 7.30 p.m., were far longer than those at Berlitz, and he was dealing with up to two hundred letters a day. His view of his fellow-clerks and their conversation was not flattering: 'When I enter the bank in the morning I wait for someone to announce something about his *cazzo*, his *culo* or his *coglioni*' (his penis, his anus or his testicles). His opinion of other Roman men was not much higher. He informed Stanislaus that their chief pastime and subject for jokes was 'breaking wind, which is an expletive that I am reserving for the day when I leave the eternal city as my farewell and adieu'.[7] After two months, Joyce managed to escape the boredom of the bank's correspondence by moving to the reception desk, but he had to write to Stanislaus for money to buy some suitable clothes. On most days, Nora and the two-year-old Giorgio would meet Joyce for a frugal lunch at a nearby café. Joyce would give them money, if he had any, so they could go to a cinema to pass the long hours until he finished work.

Some evenings he was very late, because he gave an English lesson on the way home to earn extra money and, inevitably, some of this went on 'a drink' en route. He and Nora made few friends in Rome. Both were lonely, and increasingly homesick, not for Dublin, but for Trieste.

Joyce read and wrote at a phenomenal speed, but was finding Rome more conducive to reading than writing. He managed on very little sleep, got up early, and went to a café to read for an hour before the bank opened. He had decided to tackle contemporary British novelists. He wanted to know what the opposition was like before he took it on. He read Hardy, Kipling and Gissing, and wrote to Stanislaus about them. He asked rhetorically: 'Why are these English writers so boring?' In his next letter, he answered his own question, 'What is wrong with these writers is that they always keep beating about the bush.'[8] His own novel, *Stephen Hero*, was bogged down at chapter twenty-five, and he realised that he too had indulged in too much 'beating about the bush'.[9] It was not developing into the novel he intended, the one that would take the literary world by storm and be the start of a totally new style of fiction. The story of Stephen Hero's religious education, abandonment of faith and conversion to a life devoted to Art, had somehow lost its way in those twenty-five chapters. Sitting at his café in Rome, Joyce decided to abandon it – at least for the time being. His feelings at the time were amazingly similar to those of Svevo, confided to his journal at much the same age, in a similar job, twenty years before.

Yet Rome was not entirely a creative desert for Joyce, even though at the time he thought it was. He did, however, have an idea. Now a wanderer himself, he had started thinking about the classical journey of Ulysses. Initially he saw it as a long short story about a contemporary Ulysses. He wrote to Stanislaus about it on 30 September 1906, mentioning the title for the first time. He also asked Stanislaus to try and find out more information about Alfred H. Hunter, the Dubliner who had rescued him from that beating by the British soldier on St. Stephen's Green. Stanislaus forwarded the request to Aunt Josephine, but there was no information other than the original rumour that Hunter was thought to be a Jew and a cuckold. Joyce was already toying with the idea of making his Ulysses a Wandering Jew, an Everyman figure. He had always been fascinated by how many attributes Jewish and Irish history had in common. He characterised them in *Ulysses* as 'dispersal, persecution, survival and renewal'. He saw the Irish and the Jews as two peoples with their own languages but forced to speak another's. Joyce now felt he had a particular personal connection. The Jews were exiles, and he was an exile too, albeit a lapsed Catholic, self-imposed one. However on 6 February 1907 he wrote to Stanislaus, 'Ulysses never got any forrader than the title.'[10] His version of Ulysses, the man who would be Bloom, was to remain in Joyce's very capacious mind for several more years.

Meanwhile another idea for a short story took over. He started writing 'The Dead' in Rome. It became the last and longest story in *Dubliners*, and eventually the most admired. In January 1907, much to Joyce's surprise, he was offered a contract by Elkin Mathews for *Chamber Music*. There was to be no advance; he would be paid only out of royalties. In the first year it would sell only one hundred and seven of the five hundred copies printed, but at least Joyce would be a published author, though as a poet and not as a novelist.

That same month Nora discovered a more pressing family matter – she was pregnant again. Nora was a slightly less lapsed Catholic than Joyce – she had wanted Giorgio baptised – but, despite the proximity of the Holy Father, the thought of giving birth in Rome deeply depressed her. Joyce was already feeling low and hated Rome and his work there. They decided they would escape and he would teach in France. They chose Marseilles and Joyce wrote off to a language school there. He wrote to Stanislaus about their decision, and complained that in Rome 'his mouth was full of decayed teeth and my soul of decayed ambitions'.[11] Stanislaus replied trying to discourage them from moving again. Acting as if he were an older brother, he advised Joyce to stay and try to make a secure living in Rome. Stanislaus clearly had a premonition that otherwise he might well have the wandering Joyces on his back again. He had already ascertained from Artifoni, the director of the Berlitz School in Trieste, that there would be no work for his brother there. Joyce, however, had already handed in his notice to the bank. On the final day, he drew his last month's salary of 250 lira. He did not, however, leave Rome with that defiant, farewell fart. It was Rome that had the last gesture. Joyce went on one final binge, this time with a full wallet. In a bar he bought drinks for two of the locals. Less drunk than Joyce, they helped him out into the street, knocked him down and relieved him of his wallet. Appropriately, this all happened in a thunderstorm. Joyce arrived home wet, broke, and still drunk. Fortunately, Nora had managed to keep a little money hidden in their apartment. It paid for their tickets next day, not to Marseilles – there had been no reply from the school there – but to Trieste. They telegraphed Stanislaus to say they would be arriving that evening. Stanislaus met them at the station in a reverse replay of his arrival the previous year. This was not a happy family reunion either. Joyce told Stanislaus that his stay in Rome had been a total *coglionera* (balls-up).

Back in Trieste, Joyce's luck finally changed. When Artifoni heard that he was actually back, he changed his mind, and offered him his old job. He was concerned that some of his more distinguished pupils, who had previously enjoyed Joyce's teaching, might now be poached by him. Joyce accepted happily. Then, one of those pupils, Roberto Prezioso, the editor of *Il Piccolo della Sera*, commissioned his teacher to write three pieces for the paper about the evils of British rule in Ireland. Prezioso realised that the parallels with Austrian rule in Trieste would be very clear. On the strength of his first article, Joyce was asked to give a public lecture at the Università del Popolo. The lecture, 'Ireland: island of saints and sages', was a great success. Even though he was living in cramped squalor with the pregnant Nora, Giorgio and the sullen Stanislaus, Joyce could pride himself on having made the right decision in returning to Trieste.

The plaque on 32 Via San Nicolò reads, in English: *The Berlitz School where Italo Svevo arranged his English lessons with James Joyce*. The Italian word used is *concordo*; the nearest translation is 'arranged'. That raises the question of whether Svevo just met Joyce there to arrange lessons in his own home, or actually arranged one-to-one lessons in the school. The most likely answer is that initially he had some lessons in Via San Nicolò. Later, discovering he liked Joyce and his eccentric teaching methods, Svevo arranged for him to come to his home. However, no date is put on their their meeting and there is no record of it. It would most probably have been after Joyce's article had appeared in *Il Piccolo della Sera* and he had given his lecture in late April 1907. Svevo would have read the article and may have been at the lecture. He would also have known several of the people to whom Joyce gave, or had given, private lessons. Svevo wanted more English lessons, and Joyce sounded like an interesting man to have as a teacher. Svevo's lessons, however, were interrupted in mid-July, when Joyce fell ill with rheumatic fever and was rushed into hospital. A few days later Stanislaus had to escort Nora into the same hospital and she gave birth to Lucia in what was known as 'the paupers' ward'. She came out days later with a twenty crowns charity gift. Joyce stayed in the hospital for another two weeks.

He came home to recuperate in their small apartment, now crowded with Nora nursing the new baby, the lively Giorgio, nearly three, and Stanislaus effectively supporting the entire family. Although debilitated both in hospital and afterwards, Joyce went on working. Too weak to write, he worked out various projects in his head – how *Stephen Hero* could be turned into *A Portrait of the Artist* ..., and how to finish 'The Dead'.

In early September, frustrated at still not being able to write properly, he dictated the last few pages of 'The Dead' to Stanislaus. There is something very touching in the image of the two brothers sitting together, a thousand miles from Dublin, finishing the last story in *Dubliners*, an ending considered by many to be one of the finest in modern literature.

CHAPTER FIVE

An Encouraging Word

WHEN JOYCE WAS FIT TO GO BACK to teaching, he decided he would work only for himself. He was desperate to get on with the writing of *A Portrait of the Artist as a Young Man*. He gave up his job at Berlitz and took the gamble of becoming an itinerant language teacher. He would teach in other people's homes and sometimes even in his own flat, tidied up for the occasion. He believed that in this way he could earn more money in less time. He estimated that his small core of wealthy Triestine pupils would guarantee him a basic living wage. How basic would, of course, depend on how much of his earnings he drank. Svevo figured prominently in these financial plans. Joyce returned to his thrice weekly visits to the Svevo second-floor apartment in the Veneziani villa. He taught in a room whose windows overlooked well-stocked gardens and, just beyond them, the family's factory where the marine paint was mixed to its secret formula.

At this period, the business was growing and prospering. Svevo, despite his original reluctance to join the firm, had become increasingly involved in its activities in Murano and Charlton. He travelled frequently and, regretfully, had to miss his English lessons. Aware of Joyce's financial straits, however, he paid him monthly and in advance. The ever-impecunious Joyce also took occasional loans from his pupil. It is an extraordinary serendipity that a man who made his money from selling a paint that repelled barnacles was lending it to someone who lived with a woman called Barnacle. Their sessions together, often attended by Livia, were usually turned into wide-ranging discussions of

European culture rather than language lessons. Within a few months the two men were friendly enough for Joyce to ask his pupil to write an essay, in English, describing his teacher:

> *Mr. James Joyce described by his faithful pupil, Ettore Schmitz*
>
> When I see him walking on the streets I always think that he is enjoying leisure, a full leisure. Nobody is awaiting him and he does not want to reach an aim or to meet anybody. No! He walks in order to be left to himself. He does also not walk for health. He walks because he is not stopped by anything. I imagine that if he would find his way barred by a high and big wall he would not be shocked in the least. He would change direction and if the new direction would also prove not to be clear he would change it again and walk on, his legs moving without any effort to lengthen or to fasten his step. No! His step is really his and of nobody else and cannot be lengthened or made faster.... He wears glasses and really uses them without interruption from the early(?) morning until late in the night when he wakes up. Perhaps he may see less than it is to suppose from his appearance but he looks like a being who moves in order to see. Surely he cannot fight and does not want to. He is going through life hoping not to meet bad men. I wish him heartily not to meet them.[1]

The English may not be perfect, but it is still a wonderfully imaginative and whimsical piece of writing, a style Svevo went on to perfect in his later books and fables. If one substitutes the word 'write' for 'walk' in his description of Joyce's body language, it could equally well apply to the attitude Joyce took to his writing. Svevo had somehow sensed Joyce's determination to find his own way both in his life and his work. For his part, Joyce realised that someone who could write like this, even in a foreign language, was no simple marine paint manufacturer trying to improve his English.

In early November 1907, at the end of a lesson, Joyce read 'The Dead' to Svevo and Livia. Apart from Stanislaus, they were the first people ever to hear this story. It says much for their taste, as well as their English, that they were both deeply moved by it. Livia went into the garden, picked some flowers, made a bouquet, and presented it to Joyce. Later, after he had told his brother about the incident, Stanislaus wrote in his journal: 'It was the first genuine and spontaneous sign of pleasure in the literary work of that outcast artist that I can recollect.'[2]

Shortly after this, Svevo was emboldened to admit to Joyce that he too was a writer and he produced the blue-bound volumes of his two novels, *Una Vita* and *Senilità*. (The latter was eventually published in English under the title *As a Man Grows Older*, a title Joyce suggested.) Joyce was a very fast reader, with a remarkable memory. A week later, at their next lesson, Joyce had read both novels and told Svevo that his books had been unjustly neglected. Stanislaus, who knew Svevo well, wrote in his diary:

> My brother has never praised or disparaged half-heartedly. He told Svevo that there were passages in *Senilità* on which even the great French master, Anatole France, could not have improved. He already knew these passages by heart, and quoted them with huge satisfaction. He expressed his opinions roundly, as was his wont, of the obtuseness of critics.

Svevo was amazed to hear his two novels commended in such unambiguous terms. Stanislaus's account of his brother's enthusiasm and Svevo's reaction is borne out in Livia's memoir of her husband:

> These unexpected words were a balm to Ettore's heart. Never had he thought to hear such praise of his forgotten novels. That day he could not leave Joyce. He accompanied him all the way back to his home in Piazza Vico, telling him about his literary disappointments. It was the first time he had opened his heart to anyone and showed his profound bitterness....From then on, during their lessons, they spoke constantly of literary plans and problems. Svevo confided to Joyce that he was planning to write a story about an old man and a girl – later written under the title *La Novella del Buon Vecchio e della Bella Fanciulla* (*The Story of the Nice Old Man and the Pretty Girl*) – and Joyce discussed with him in detail the concept of Bloom which he later developed in *Ulysses*.[3]

Stanislaus confirms these facts in an introduction he wrote to *As a Man Grows Older* in 1932. Joyce had originally been asked to write it, but was too preoccupied with his own work and passed the commission to his brother, who wrote:

What my brother found in Italo Svevo was a mentality akin to his own, an analytic method which was congenial. There was so much in common between them that my brother, who then had the idea of Bloom in his head, discussed it with Svevo from all angles.

With considerable insight to the core of the relationship, Stanislaus continued:

> Svevo seemed almost to have come to regard his two early novels as juvenile errors. In my brother instead, the fighting instinct is strong, and perhaps more than his sincere admiration for Svevo's work, the example of my brother's overweening confidence was useful to Svevo.[4]

Joyce and Svevo began to spend time together outside their lessons. Because Svevo was only a very moderate drinker and devoted to his wife, this time together did not include visits to bars and brothels. Mainly they went on long walks. A mutual friend, Ettore Settanni, recalled seeing them 'clinging to the ropes fixed along the steep side-streets under the *bora*'s blast, as if they were climbers roped together, and talking incessantly.'[5]

Joyce sang the praises of Svevo's two novels to his Triestine friends and pupils in an attempt to boost his literary reputation and his sales. It was to no avail. Joyce's enthusiasm was met by the same snobbery that had been used by the critics – Svevo did not write good Italian. After Svevo's death, Settanni remembers Joyce saying of him:

> He was a great man before being a great writer, because he learnt to bear the weight of his *coscienza* in solitude. We travelled a long way together and Svevo is to my mind the first Italian novelist to introduce the technique of the interior monologue.[6]

Joyce presumably specified 'Italian writer', because he had already acknowledged the French writer Eduard Dujardin as the first exponent of interior monologue in *Les Lauriers sont coupés*, published in 1888, the novel Joyce had bought at a Paris railway station. Joyce certainly claimed to be the first novelist writing in English to use that technique. When it came to free-association, Joyce, unlike Svevo, was always very anxious to distance himself from the influence of Freud.

There is, of course, no record of what Joyce and Svevo talked about 'so incessantly'. There is perhaps a clue in the 'Eumaeus' episode of *Ulysses*, when Stephen Dedalus and Leopold Bloom finally meet and talk, over three-quarters of the way into the novel:

> Of what did the duumvirate deliberate during their itinerary?
>
> Music, literature, Ireland, Dublin, Paris, friendship, woman, prostitution, diet, the influence of gaslight or the light of arc and glowlamps on the growth of adjoining paraheliotropic trees, exposed Corporation emergency dustbuckets, the Roman Catholic Church, ecclesiastical celibacy, the Irish nation, Jesuit education, careers, the study of medicine, the past day, the maleficent influence of the pre-Sabbath, Stephen's collapse.[7]

In other words 'the duumvirate' of Joyce and Svevo deliberated during their itineraries about nearly everything.

Joyce, now a published poet, read Svevo and Livia some of his poems from *Chamber Music*. They were very appreciative, though Svevo had some secret reservations about poetry, which he was to reveal only to his daughter Letizia, who also became a pupil of Joyce. He appears to have given her intermittent lessons, usually when her father was away on business trips. These would have been more straightforward language lessons, for Joyce's poems would have been too much for her English, though Letizia was also an aspiring poet. A poem she sent her father in Murano elicited one of his most charming letters, and one that shows some of his talents. His letter survives, her poem doesn't.

10 April 1908

Dearest Letizia,

I have received your dear letter and I thank you very much for it. I can see the signs of such excellent feelings in your rhymes (which are not bad at all for a ten-year-old) that I am really delighted with them. Just for this once I should like to tell you something that may be hard for you to understand. You are the only poet I enjoy; I dislike the rest of them. So far all will be clear to you; but now I must try to explain why I dislike them, and if possible make you agree when I shout 'Down with all poets.'

I once knew two carpenters. One was a cheerful, smiling, silent man; he made the most beautiful wardrobes, much admired by everybody, and he worked the whole day long. The other made a living too, for he had found a new profession. Instead of making wardrobes, which was a too tedious business for him, he had set up as a describer of wardrobes, and everyone listened and paid him for it. Indeed he deserved it, as he could describe things excellently....He could describe the different shapes and lines very well, the scrolls and bosses, and curlicues and other ornaments. And so they went on, year after year, the one making wardrobes and the other describing them.

Svevo's gift for fantasy creates a climax in which the wardrobe describer is confounded by a customer who wants 'a living wardrobe'. The moral of the story comes at the end of the letter to Letizia:

I am sure you can see what a stupid creature that describer of live wardrobes was. But it wasn't really his fault, you know. If you go on describing, day in and day out, and all the time you're making nothing, day in and day out, you are bound to end up describing all wrong.[8]

From this, Svevo could be seen, in allegoric form, to be criticising the business of being a writer, as opposed to being a practical person. Or, it could be a self-justification to show that by manufacturing and selling marine paint as well as writing, he was getting the best of both worlds. Or, finally, as a great renouncer of things, did he mean that writing was something he personally should give up, like his other 'juvenile errors' – smoking and playing the violin? Later that year, on the subject of poetry, Svevo wrote to Cyril Ducker, a young man who had befriended him in Charlton and who had asked for advice about becoming a writer: 'Stick to prose, please. It is so very extravagant to use only partly the piece of paper for which you were obliged to pay in full.'[9]

By the end of 1907, Joyce had become very much a part of the Svevo family. Yet it was essentially a relationship between the two men. The two families did not mix. Joyce and Nora were never invited to the house socially, and Joyce came only in his role as a teacher. In the class structure of Trieste, an itinerant language teacher was certainly a cut above a servant, but certainly not an acceptable member of the respectable middle-class. When Joyce and Nora's finances were at a particularly low ebb, Nora took in washing and ironing from Livia. The latter saw the interior of the Joyces' flat and was appalled that they could live in this state. Nora later claimed that Livia once did not acknowledge her in the street. Three years later when Joyce's sister Eileen came to stay in Trieste, Livia employed her as a governess for Letizia; she considered Eileen so much more couth and educated than Nora. Svevo paid very little heed to his wife's social pretensions, but would not cross her. He valued a peaceful home life and, after all, he was working in the family business. He was perfectly happy talking with Joyce about the higher things of life and ignoring the social niceties. He was also fascinated by the Joyce-Nora relationship, with its echoes of the relationship of Emilio and Angiolina in *Senilità,* the highly cultured man and his working-class, under-educated mistress. In Trieste, Joyce and Nora did not broadcast the fact that they were not married, but Svevo and Livia knew. A couple of years later, the Joyces hit a slightly more prosperous patch, and moved to a larger, better apartment for which Svevo had contributed generously towards the deposit. The Joyces could now afford to employ a live-in maid, a young, country girl called Maria Kirn. They were visited here by Svevo, sometimes even accompanied by Livia, who presumably thought the place would now be cleaner and more hygienic. Maria Kirn lived to a ripe old age and, in several interviews, remembered opening the front door to Svevo, coming for late night conversations with Joyce, and leaving in the early hours.

When Livia, in her memoir, referred to Joyce and her husband discussing 'the concept of Bloom', it is the word 'concept' that is significant. Not surprisingly, a loving wife, especially a highly respectable, Italian Catholic, one like Livia, would scarcely want to admit that her husband was anything like Leopold Bloom in either appearance or character, although there were some superficial similarities. The two men, the imaginary and the real, were much the same age, and the age difference between Svevo and Joyce was the same as between Bloom and Stephen Dedalus. Both Svevo and Bloom were married to attractive women to whom they were devoted. Both couples had only one child, a daughter, and each wife had a subsequent miscarriage. Both Svevo and Bloom were nominally Catholic, agnostic by conviction, but accepted that they were originally Jewish, although Bloom, having a Catholic mother, would not be considered in Jewish law to be a Jew since it decides identity on a matrilineal basis. Certainly neither went to church, nor belonged to a synagogue.

Svevo was hostile to all organised religions. He had no regard for Christianity and his view of his own Jewishness was highly ambivalent. He never spoke in public about his Jewish origins, though in private, among friends, he was perfectly open and joked about it. His friend Sergio Solmi writes about a conversation they had, late in Svevo's life, walking in the gardens of Miramare, just outside Trieste:

> We were talking about races and nationalities, a subject he was particularly fond of, and, among other things, about that under-note of Jewish scepticism and despair which some critics think they can trace in his *La coscienza di Zeno*. 'It isn't race that which makes a Jew,' said Svevo sadly, 'it's life!'[10]

Svevo would not have forgotten his early encounters with anti-Semitism, although Trieste, unlike Vienna, had no reputation for this. Yet just after leaving college, Svevo discovered he had been turned down for a good job because he was Jewish. He met this discrimination again during his Army service. Then there was Giulia Babersi, his first serious love, whose father had forbidden her to see Svevo because he was Jewish. Svevo's 'It's life!' illustrates the idea that Jewish identity is often defined, not by personal choice or heredity, but by the anti-Semitism of others. It becomes the club that one cannot leave.

This may account for a particular aspect of his three novels on which some later critics have commented. None of the three principal characters, Nitti, Emilio or Zeno, very much Svevo alter egos, are ever described as Jewish. In fact the word 'Jew' is only mentioned twice in *The Confessions of Zeno*. It comes in a scene when, in a psychoanalytic session, Zeno is recalling his much-loved nanny, Catina, getting angry with him for demanding some of his brother's sugar in exchange for the loan of his spoon. She reprimands him, saying, 'For shame, you little Jew.' It continues:

Fright and shame brought me back with a start to the present. I should like to have argued with Catina, but she, my brother, and I – that tiny, innocent little Jew – plunged together into the abyss and disappeared.[11]

That is from the translation by Beryl de Zoete in 1930, now in the Penguin Modern Classics edition. A new translation in 2001 by the American translator William Weaver (the Everyman's Library edition) now has Catina reprimand Zeno with 'Shame on you! Little shark'. It continues:

Fright and shame plunged me again into the present. I would have liked to have argued with Catina, but she, my brother, and I – as I as then, small, innocent and a usurer – disappeared, sinking into the abyss.[12]

In fact, the word Svevo used in Italian was *strozzino*, which does mean 'little shark', but, in the vernacular, also means loan shark, and is sometimes used pejoratively for Jews.

Jews or little sharks, Svevo certainly did not identify any of his characters as Jewish, or himself as an Italian Jewish writer. On this score, one of his staunchest admirers, the Italian critic Giacomo Debenedetti, was critical of him. In a posthumous appreciation of Svevo's work, Debenedetti, himself Jewish, regretted that Svevo had not in his novels explored more 'the mystery of his own origins'. He felt that many of Svevo's characters were really undeclared Jews, and therefore had the problems of a split identity. In Svevo's defence, it could be argued that his choices were influenced by time and place. He had enough difficulty in being accepted even as an Italian writer because he wrote in the Triestine dialect. Svevo lived in a city already divided by multiple nationalities without adding the further subdivision of a minority religion. He never denied his origins, but he held no Jewish beliefs and played no part in the life of that community. In the Veneziani family that he had married into and worked for, there was never any discussion of their quarter Jewish roots on both sides. The cruel irony of this was to become apparent only twenty years later in Mussolini's Fascist state.

Because race and nationality were subjects of which Svevo was 'particularly fond', he would have had no inhibition discussing these questions with Joyce, who was equally fascinated by them. In the 'Cyclops' episode in *Ulysses* he throws Bloom into the middle of the farcical argument with the anti-Semitic citizen and others in Barney Kiernan's pub:

–But do you know what a nation means? says John Wyse….
–A nation? says Bloom. A nation is the same people living in the same place.
–By God, then, says Ned, laughing, if that's so I'm a nation for I'm living in the same place for the past five years….
–Or also living in different places….
–What is your nation if I may ask, says the citizen.
–Ireland, says Bloom. I was born here. Ireland.
The citizen said nothing, only cleared the spit out of his gullet and, gob, he spat a Red Bank oyster out of him right in the corner.

And after a long, Joycean digression about a 'much treasured and intricately embroidered ancient Irish facecloth', Bloom continues the argument:

–And I belong to a race too, says Bloom, that is hated and persecuted. Also now. This very moment. This very instant.
Gob, he near burnt his fingers with the butt of his old cigar.
–Robbed, says he. Plundered. Insulted. Persecuted. Taking what belongs to us by right. At this very moment, says he, putting up his fist, sold by auction in Morocco like slaves or cattle.
Are you talking about the new Jerusalem? says the Citizen.
I'm talking about injustice, says Bloom.[13]

And the scene ends with Bloom finally reminding the citizen:

….Mendelssohn was a jew and Karl Marx and Mercadante and Spinoza….Your God was a jew. Christ was a jew like me….
–By Jesus, says he, I'll brain that bloody jewman for using the holy name. By Jesus, I'll crucify him so I will. Give us that biscuit box here.[14]

And the citizen hurls the biscuit box after the departing Bloom – and misses.

One of the odder aspects of this racist high comedy, however, is Bloom's choice of Jews. His creator perhaps meant to illustrate the wide range of secular Jews there were. Mendelssohn was baptised a Protestant, Karl Marx rejected all religion and was frequently anti-Semitic, associating Jews with capitalism. Spinoza was one of the few Jews ever to be excommunicated by his community, in Amsterdam, for his heretical views. Mercadante was the strangest, most esoteric choice, an early nineteenth-century Italian operatic composer, known to Joyce, but hardly anybody else, and he was not a Jew. Joyce was not above private jokes. Perhaps Saverio Mercadante, a contemporary of Bellini and Donizetti, was one of those items Joyce dropped in to keep professors busy arguing about what he meant. And what does the citizen mean by 'the new Jerusalem'? Was he well-informed about early Zionism?

The Leopold Bloom confronting the citizen in Barney Kiernan's pub is a fighting Irish-Jewish Bloom, one more side of the multi-faceted character that Joyce had developed from his genesis in Alfred H. Hunter, the supposedly cuckolded Dublin Jew. His birth was in Rome, but it was in Trieste that Bloom's complex character blossomed in Joyce's imagination. His friendship with Svevo helped it grow. This was Joyce's first close encounter with a particular sort of European Jew, secular, intellectual and culturally very integrated. Joyce met others as he visited their homes in his role as English teacher, and he was to meet more in his years in Zurich when he was writing *Ulysses*. They were people who fascinated him, and he would have been hard-pressed to find one in Dublin on 16 June 1904. On that auspicious day, the great majority of Ireland's two thousand Jews would have been first-generation immigrants from Russian Lithuania, who had fled the pogroms in the 1880s and '90s. They were nearly all orthodox rather than secular. A very small minority, who had lived in Ireland for longer, were either originally German or from England and much anglicised. Bloom himself would have not been at home in any of these communities, though he did know some Jews, their names taken by his creator from Thom's *Dublin Directory* – Moisel, Citron and Mastiansky are mentioned. Some of their descendants still live in Dublin. In Zurich, when the Swiss critic Jacques Mercanton asked Joyce why Bloom had to be Jewish, he replied, 'Only a foreigner would do. The Jews were foreigners at that time in Dublin. There was no hostility towards them, but contempt, yes, the contempt that people always show towards the unknown.'[15]

Ulysses is full of biblical and Jewish references, even some Yiddish as well as Hebrew letters and words spelt phonetically in English. Most of these ingredients Joyce collected in Trieste with its flourishing Jewish community. When Joyce first arrived in the city there were four synagogues, and Joyce visited two of them. During his stay, a new one, a mixture of Romanesque and Byzantine in design, was being built to replace the others. When it was finished in 1912, it was one of the largest synagogues in Europe. Joyce attended part of a service there, and was surprised to recognise several of his students in the congregation. However, the chief provider of Joyce's detailed Jewish knowledge was Svevo, with his fine memory for his early upbringing and later education at the Brussel School in Würzburg. Svevo had his brains thoroughly picked by Joyce on their long walks and in their late night conversations.

Another aspect of Triestine Jewish life that Joyce became familiar with was Zionism. On this subject, Joyce gained most of his knowledge from another pupil, Moses Dlugacz, who came to him for lessons between 1912 and 1915. Dlugacz was a couple of years younger than Joyce, then thirty. The son and grandson of Ukrainian rabbis, he became a rabbi himself at an early age. He was also mathematically precocious, went into business, and in 1912 was appointed chief cashier in the Cunard Line office in Trieste. This was his reason for needing English lessons. Rather as had happened with Svevo, Joyce discovered common interests with Dlugacz – literature and etymology, music and philosophy. At one point, Dlugacz even gave Joyce Hebrew lessons. He was an ardent Zionist and very active in the movement in Trieste, which concentrated largely on recruiting young people. Ships from Trieste sailed regularly to Haifa and Jaffa, the ports of the Ottoman Empire. Many young Zionists sailed on those ships to become pioneers in Palestine, on land bought from the Turkish government by Jewish public subscription and individual philanthropists like the Rothschilds and the Montefiores. Working for Cunard, Dlugacz helped arrange their passages, as well as trying to obtain cheaper fares for those East European Jews who, having fled the earlier pogroms, were trying to continue their journeys to America, via Trieste.

Knowing Joyce to be a philo-Semite, Dlugacz was keen to turn him into a Zionist as well. Joyce was not really a joiner of anything, and distrusted 'all enthusiasms'. He was, however, fascinated by the ideas that Dlugacz propounded, and made frequent reference to them in *Ulysses*. In their etymological discussions they focused on the links between the Gaelic and the Semitic languages. For Joyce, the most powerful factor that connected the Jews with the Irish was that they were both people fighting to recover their homelands from the occupiers. Joyce stored away a vast amount of the information and knowledge that he had gained from Dlugacz. In exchange, Dlugacz is given an early appearance in *Ulysses*, transformed, cruelly for an observant Jew, into a 'ferret-eyed pork butcher'. Bloom goes into his shop on Dorset Street to buy the succulent pork kidney for which he yearns. Dlugacz wraps it in a page from one of the Zionist news-sheets that were piled on the counter. On the way home, Bloom reads on the wrapping paper an advertisement for buying plots of land in Palestine that can be made quickly fertile and produce exotic fruit. Bloom's reaction to this Zionist aim was 'Nothing doing. Still, an idea behind it.' Then, as a cloud passes over the sun, he goes gloomy and thinks of modern Palestine: 'A barren land, bare waste....Sodom, Gomorrah, Edom. All dead names. A dead sea in a dead land, grey and old.'[16] Bloom then compares it unflatteringly with an old woman's body. Nothing fruitful would come from these Zionist dreams.

Later, in the 'Ithaca' episode, when Bloom has taken the slowly sobering Stephen Dedalus back to his house – as Hunter did with Joyce – Joyce used something else he had learned from Dlugacz. Bloom chants to Stephen: '*Kolod balejwaw pnimah/ Nefesch jehudi homijah.*' These were the opening lines of the *Hatikvah*, the Zionist anthem. Stephen responds by singing 'Little Harry Hughes', an anti-Semitic song that contains the blood libel. In Paris in 1921, A.J. Leventhal, a young academic from

Trinity College, with whom Joyce had become friendly on one of his earlier trips to Dublin, visited him in his flat. Leventhal knew Hebrew and Joyce showed him some of the words he was using in *Ulysses*. After that, Joyce sat down at the piano and played and sang the *Hatikvah*.[17] Twenty-seven years later it became the national anthem of the state of Israel.

CHAPTER SIX

The Cinema Business

JOYCE NOW PUT BLOOM AND *Ulysses* to the back of his mind, although, with Joyce, the back of his mind was never very far from the front. He did not settle down to writing *Ulysses* properly until 1914. Meanwhile he was having problems with his attempt to turn *Stephen Hero* into *A Portrait of the Artist as a Young Man*, a title suggested by Stanislaus. He had rewritten the first two chapters to cover Stephen's early life, schooldays and experience with a prostitute. By April 1908, he had completed the third chapter, which covered his guilt, repentance and the three long hellfire sermons. He then made little progress for the rest of the year. His normally admiring critic, Stanislaus, read the chapters and was less than enthusiastic. As a convinced atheist, he clearly had little sympathy with the protagonist's spiritual struggles and fear of fire and brimstone. He was also obviously hurt that in the rewrite the character of the sympathetic younger brother, Maurice, was now reduced to a walk-on part. Joyce later wrote in *Ulysses*: 'One can forget a brother as easily as an old umbrella.'[1] Although the line appears in a different context, it is an accurate comment on how Joyce was in the habit of treating his brother.

In creative frustration, Joyce's answer was always to turn to drink, or rather increased amounts of it. This caused inevitable disruption in the crowded household. Stanislaus had to drag him out of bars more frequently and sometimes violently. He warned Joyce that, with his already bad eyesight, he would soon make himself blind. Nora also turned on him. As recorded by Stanislaus, she shouted, 'So now go and get drunk. That's all you're good for. Cosgrave always told me you were mad.'[2] Joyce's nemesis, Cosgrave, his rival for Nora, the man who had stood by while Joyce was beaten up by the British soldier, was to reappear, very unhelpfully, within the year. Nora swore she would leave with the children and, as a final threat, said she would have them baptised.

Joyce agreed to stop drinking. Equally radically, he decided to stop writing novels and concentrate once more on a singing career. He would use part of the income from his English lessons to finance his lessons with a leading singing coach. It was Joyce's sudden fecklessness about writing, as well as his ever-mounting debts, that finally made Stanislaus lose all patience. The brothers had a furious argument and Stanislaus gathered his few belongings and moved out. A few days later he confided in his *Triestine Diary*:

> I take little interest in the budding *tenorino* that has failed as a poet in Paris, as a journalist in Dublin, as a lover and novelist in Trieste, as a bank-clerk in Rome, and again in Trieste as a Sinn-Feiner, teacher and university professor.[3]

The worm had certainly turned. There was a four-month stand-off between them and then reconciliation. Stanislaus resumed eating his supper with them, but kept his separate small flat. The rift that began to grow between the brothers can be traced to this period in their relationship. It took a long time for Stanislaus to shake off the role of martyr, but the process had started.

Although Joyce could get no fraternal assistance in restarting *A Portrait of the Artist as a Young Man*, help was on the way from another direction. In January 1909, Joyce had given his three chapters to Svevo to read and criticise as his English homework. At this period in their lives, Joyce and Svevo were both novelists not currently writing novels. For Svevo, this condition was to last for a lot longer than it did for Joyce, and his method of dealing with it was very different. He had taken an oath of abstinence, not against drink, but against novel-writing itself. Instead, he immersed himself in his business life and, like the Ulysses figure into which he would one day be fictionally transformed, he travelled a great deal. This enabled him at least to keep his hand in as a writer. His almost daily letter to Livia from London was part love-letter, part travel book, as well as an exercise in social and political observation, and which were faithfully preserved by Livia. To further ease his artistic frustrations, Svevo turned to music. Whereas Joyce's dedication to singing was short-lived, Svevo's to playing the violin was long-lasting, even though he started learning late in life and constantly denigrated his ability. He wrote: 'If you learn the violin before you are forty, the bow becomes an extension of your arm, but with me it was always just something attached to it.' Nonetheless he joined a local string quartet as a second violin. With his gift for turning any experience into fable and fantasy, Svevo wrote a piece which he circulated to his three fellow musicians and other interested parties:

> Remember, I beg you, that for various reasons the three instruments are always on a level: the viola and the cello because of their tone, and the first violin because the limelight is always on him; meanwhile the second violin works away to support the others and no-one is aware of him unless he makes unpleasant noises. He is like a man's collar and tie; no one notices them unless they're untidy. There he is working away peacefully in the dark like an owl or a mole. But during every quartet there comes a certain moment when the poor mole, for a bar or two, has to come into the limelight and lead the others. He is all alone. The whole performance is in his hands. The bright light dazzles and frightens him. Not surprisingly, just when the greatest effort is demanded of him, he fails miserably.[4]

As with his parable about the two wardrobe-makers, a simile for the practical man and the poet, here Svevo clearly associates 'playing second fiddle' badly with his failure as a writer. His English biographer, P.N. Furbank, has the interesting idea that Svevo gives 'the impression that he deliberately allowed his playing to be tenth-rate, so that there should be no doubt in his mind that it was a second-best, a cure, not a substitute, for writing. It was like life itself: one was always learning, and never got any better. And, like smoking, it provided an excellent pretext for day-dreaming.'[5] Joyce and Svevo found consolation for their frustrations in very different sorts of bars.

Joyce had confronted Svevo with a daunting task, to judge him not as a teacher, but as a writer. Svevo admired what he had already heard of Joyce's work, but now he had to understand a very complicated piece of prose and criticise it in a language in which he was by no means fluent. Even its beginning came as a shock:

> Once upon a time and a very good time it was there was a moocow coming down along the road and this moocow that was coming down along the road met a nicens little boy named baby tuckoo....
>
> His father told him that story: his father looked at him through a glass: he had a hairy face.
>
> He was baby tuckoo. The moocow came down the road where Betty Byrne lived: she sold lemon platt.
> *O, the wild rose blossoms*
> *On the little green place.*
> He sang that song. That was his song.[6]

It took another page for Svevo to discover that this was not a children's book, but a recollection by Stephen Dedalus of his earliest childhood. With that behind him, he could go on to follow the journey of Joyce's alter ego through his secular and religious life until he left both his school and his faith. It also gave Svevo an introduction to Joyce's use – sparingly in this novel – of interior monologue. Svevo now faced writing his criticism. He tried to take confidence from the fact that Joyce had respected his writing enough to ask him to judge his. He began formally and diffidently:

> Dear Mr. Joyce,
> Really I do not believe of being authorised to tell you the author a resolute opinion about the novel of which I could only know partially. I do not allude to my want of competence but especially to the fact that when you stopped writing you were faced with a very important development of Stephen's mind....I like very much your second and third chapters and think you made a great mistake doubting whether you would find a reader who could take pleasure at the sermons of the third chapter. I have read them with a very strong feeling and I know in my little town a lot of people who would certainly be struck by the same feeling....[7]

Joyce was hugely relieved by Svevo's verdict on chapters two and three. The latter was the one that had worried him most. The three sermons included in it are extraordinary pieces of dramatic writing, describing purgatory and hell as one vast, horrendous concentration camp. It is forty-odd pages of sustained horror, coincidentally, or maybe significantly, as long as Molly Bloom's soliloquy at the end of *Ulysses*. The sermons describe the eternal punishment of the sinful flesh, Molly's soliloquy celebrates the earthly pleasures of a defiant flesh. Although an agnostic, Svevo appears comfortable with Joyce's extravagant diatribe. Many future critics would be less tolerant of the length and strength of its content. A possible reason for Svevo's positive reaction is perhaps best understood in the light of his remark 'in my little town a lot of people' would share these feelings. Trieste was, after all, a majority Catholic and Italian-speaking town, part of a culture whose greatest poet was Dante, his most read work *The Divine Comedy*, the first part of which was *L'Inferno*. The flaming circles of hell would still be shocking, but not unfamiliar, to 'a lot of people' in Svevo's 'small town'.

For Svevo, the problem was the first chapter, and he kept his criticism of that until last:

> I object against the first chapter. I did so when I had read only it, but I do so still more decidedly after having known the two others.... I think it deals with events deprived of importance, and your rigid method of observation and description does not allow you to enrich a fact which is not rich of itself. You are obliged to write only of strong things. In your skilled hands they may become still stronger. I do not believe you can give the appearance of strength to things that are of themselves feeble, not important.[8]

Svevo's criticism was a great relief and encouragement to Joyce. It also emphasised the different levels of their relationship. Ostensibly it was a teacher setting his student an exercise. The student wanted good marks. With this exercise, though, the student was simultaneously marking the teacher, who also wanted good marks. That the student was just old enough to be the teacher's father was also a factor in this equation. Joyce had always lacked a reliable father figure, and, to some extent, Svevo took on this role. Joyce now had a paternal approval for his work. He was particularly relieved by Svevo's good opinion of chapter three. Joyce had thought of cutting this almost entirely. Now he adjusted the first chapter minimally and left the rest alone. Some subsequent critics would not have agreed with Svevo, especially about chapter one. What they would praise in Joyce was exactly his ability to give strength to things that were not ostensibly 'important', that gift for language that 'made the ordinary extraordinary'. Some of those critics also found the sermons repetitious and overwritten. Yet whether critics would agree or disagree with Svevo, his criticism had the best possible effect on Joyce – it sent him back to start on chapter four, although he did not complete the novel until 1914.

Stanislaus may have been happy to see his brother writing again, regardless of who had inspired him, but peace was not restored for long in the Joyce household. The brothers had received a disturbing letter from their oldest sister, Margaret (Poppie). She wanted Stanislaus, since he was still single and obviously more responsible than James, to come home and help them cope with their increasingly abusive father. The resident younger brother, Charlie, already himself a heavy drinker, had got a girl pregnant. He was about to marry her and emigrate to America. Joyce thought it would be a good idea for Stanislaus to go and be accompanied by Giorgio, now seven, the family's first grandchild. He felt this gesture, plus a small financial contribution from the Trieste branch, would create some sort of family *rapprochement*. It did not quite happen that way. For a start, Stanislaus did not go. The departure was arranged for July 1909, but, in June, a pupil paid Joyce for a year's lessons in advance, and he decided that he, not Stanislaus, would take Giorgio to meet his grandfather. Also, after receiving more rejections for *Dubliners*, Joyce's frustrations had reached a peak. He was now desperate to pursue a contract with Maunsel and Co., a potentially sympathetic Dublin publisher, and he thought a face-to-face meeting might help. Stanislaus did not take kindly to this change of plan, particularly because he still had to pay for it. Nor did it help their relationship when Stanislaus learned that when Joyce and Giorgio arrived in Dublin, the whole family had asked 'Where's Stanni?' Stanislaus said later, 'That was a question I often asked myself.'⁹

Joyce arrived at Kingstown with Giorgio on 29 July 1909. It was almost five years since he had left. He was successful in at least one of the immediate aims of his homecoming. His father was delighted to see him and very impressed by his clever grandson. John Joyce finally seemed to accept his son's elopement and choice of partner. Father and son went to a pub and John Joyce played the piano and sang an operatic aria that his son identified. Harmony seemed re-established. Aunt Josephine thought her nephew had 'lost all boyishness'; his sister Eileen thought he was 'very foreign-looking' and all agreed he was too thin, but were pleased to see him. The meetings Joyce had with some old friends were not so successful. He had often referred to Dublin as a treacherous city, full of enemies. His problem now was that he was not coming home as the conquering hero, a successful expatriate returning to patronise old friends. He had written about that situation in the story 'A Little Cloud' that was to be in *Dubliners*. He was in exactly the reverse position. All he had to show for his literary ambitions was his one slim volume of poetry. The situation made him highly prickly, as his letters to Stanislaus illustrate. He bumped into his old rival Gogarty, who he thought had grown fat and turned into a self-satisfied medical consultant with a rich wife. They had a very unsatisfactory drink together in Gogarty's town-house. Joyce's meetings with Vincent Cosgrave had more disastrous consequences. At least Joyce had fared better than Cosgrave, who seemed to have merely idled away his time in Dublin. He had always been jealous of Joyce, a feeling now sharpened by the thought of Joyce's independent, bohemian life abroad with Nora. Cosgrave had lusted after Nora, but Joyce had carried off the prize. Now Cosgrave played Iago. He reminded Joyce of Nora saying she could go out with him only on alternate nights because of her duties in the hotel. Cosgrave claimed that this was not the truth. In fact, she had been seeing him after work. He added, with its obvious implication, that they had gone walking down beside the river Liffey. Ever prone to jealousy, which both appalled him but gave him a *frisson*, Joyce thought back to his own walk with Nora, and his suspicions about her previous sexual experience. His imagination ran riot and he went into an instant panic. He wrote Nora a frantic and accusatory letter. He even demanded to know if Giorgio was his child. Nora did not respond, and maintained her silence for two weeks. Fortunately, in his despair, Joyce sought out John Byrne, a more loyal old friend, who calmed him, assuring him there was no truth in Cosgrave's insinuations. He was merely a vindictive liar out to upset Joyce, and his old rival Oliver St John Gogarty had probably played some part in it.

Never one to waste material, out of this Joyce fashioned both the Molly Bloom–Blazes Boylan adultery theme in *Ulysses*, as well as his play *Exiles*. After seeing the play in London in 1926, Svevo questioned Joyce about the significance of the title and the theme: 'Exiles? Surely not people who can return to their own country?' Joyce replied, 'But don't you remember how the prodigal son was received by his brother in his father's house? It is dangerous to leave one's country, but still more dangerous to go back to it, for then your fellow-countrymen, if they can, will drive a knife into your heart.'[10] Joyce had a very long and accurate memory and, on some subjects, it was close to paranoia.

After a fortnight, Joyce received a letter from Nora. It was a hurt but dignified reply. Joyce sent an abject apology. Peace was restored to their correspondence, but something else entered into it. It was the first time Joyce had been separated from Nora for five years and his letters now expressed his desire for her. They were masochistic and scatological, their vocabulary highly explicit, and Joyce urged Nora to reply in kind. She obliged, and her letters were every bit as obscene and erotic as Joyce's. He was delighted to see written down what he shared with Nora. He wrote back: 'Are you too, then, like me, one moment high as the stars, the next lower than the lowest wretches?'[11] This was a sentiment echoed in Bruni's later description of Joyce, accepting 'unquestioningly the rabbit and the eagle, sun and mudheap'.[12] Joyce's pornographic letters survived, Nora's didn't, but biographers have pieced their contents together from Joyce's replies. (There was considerable outrage from the Joyce Estate and others when Richard Ellmann published his *Selected Letters of James Joyce* in 1975, and these letters were among the selection.)

In her biography of Nora, Brenda Maddox maintains that she may not have shared all, or even any, of Joyce's sexual preferences and fetishes. Her motives, in replying in kind to his letters, were twofold. One was that 'it gave her a hold on him that in some way compensated for his power over her'.[13] The other was a far more practical reason. She knew that Joyce had gone to prostitutes in the past and had contracted venereal disease. In his frustration he might well do so again. Nora's letters were masturbatory fancies, intended to keep him from straying in that direction again. From Nora's point of view, the letters were a necessary health and safety precaution, and, judging by his replies, they worked. Ten years later, in *Ulysses*, Joyce remembered their content and vocabulary well enough to use them in Molly Bloom's soliloquy.

Joyce was successful with George Roberts of Maunsel, and a contract was drawn up and signed for the publication of *Dubliners*. He was given an advance of £3, a minimal amount even in those days. Joyce was temporarily satisfied with his business trip. He now busied himself on the domestic front. He used most of his advance to pay for a tonsillectomy for Eva, his fourth sister, and arranged for her to return to Trieste with him. He felt it would relieve the Dublin Joyces of a mouth to feed, and Eva would be a help to Nora with the children and the housekeeping. Since the eldest sister, Poppie, was about to enter a convent in New Zealand, it meant that there would soon be only five Joyces in Dublin but six in Trieste, counting Nora as a Joyce. The only problem was that Joyce did not have the fare for Eva, Giorgio and himself. He cabled Stanislaus to send the money. Stanislaus took unkindly to the idea that his brother was bringing back a sister to put more stress on their finances, mainly his. He had been promoted to assistant director of the Berlitz School, and was working a great deal harder for very little more money, but again he found it impossible to refuse his brother. He was forced to borrow the money from Artifoni, the director, who kept him waiting for it. Rather than kick his heels in Dublin, Joyce took Giorgio, as he had promised Nora, off to Galway to meet his maternal grandmother. Joyce met his mother-in-law and her family for the first time. He got on well with them. His singing voice impressed them, and once more Giorgio made a good impression on a grandparent, this time on a grandmother, because Nora's father, an alcoholic baker, had long since been estranged from his wife. Both Joyce and Nora had much in common in their backgrounds. Both had been brought up by alcoholic fathers who had fathered too many daughters, six in each family. Because of constant financial problems both families frequently had to move house. Joyce, of course, would have known all this before he arrived. In Galway he found none of the things he hated about Dublin. On his return to Dublin, he found the money from Stanislaus had arrived. He pocketed his contract for *Dubliners*, gathered up Eva and Giorgio and set off for Trieste.

Joyce was delighted to see Nora again. Eva was welcomed. Only Stanislaus was not happy with the homecoming. He received no thanks from his brother for sending the fares. He listened to Joyce's news about Dublin and then enquired if anybody had asked about him. 'Oh yes, everybody,' Joyce replied. 'I got a whole lot of messages for you, but I've forgotten them.'[14]

Though Stanislaus now lived in his own flat and only ate with them, the Joyces' flat was crowded. For Eva the accommodation would have been little different from her home in Dublin, but Nora found her helpful, and was grateful to have someone around all day to whom she could speak English. Eva was immediately homesick for Dublin and not especially charmed by Trieste. One aspect of the city, however, did impress her – the number of cinemas. She mentioned to Joyce that Dublin, a far bigger city, did not have a single cinema. Her remark lit an instant fire in Joyce's imagination. Introducing the cinema to Dublin could make their fortune. The idea put Joyce into a familiar position – he needed money, but no longer just a small personal loan. This needed big money. He had intended to throw himself wholeheartedly into the rest of *A Portrait*, but now decided that finding backers for his scheme would come first. Joyce always had the feeling that he had the ability to be a successful businessman. In the past he had toyed with the idea of importing Irish whiskey into Trieste, and then, more seriously, introducing Irish tweed into the smart clothing stores of Vienna. With these projects he had never gone beyond the first tentative steps. Now he had the bit between his teeth. He was bored with the daily grind of being an itinerant language-teacher and he knew, despite having found a publisher for *Dubliners*, it would be years before he would earn a reasonable living from his writing. Trieste was a bustling business city, and all around him were the signs of its prosperity. He had an *entrée* into the homes of many rich people through his language lessons, but he was always like the boy with his face pressed against the shop-window. Didn't his abilities entitle him to a slice of the cake? His friend Svevo was the obvious person to talk to about his idea, but he stopped short of asking him to become an investor. An instinct may have warned Joyce against mixing friendship with business – at least big business. Svevo was already a source of useful, smaller loans in an emergency, and matters were probably better kept that way. He also knew that in business Svevo was a very cautious man. Manufacturing anti-corrosive paint at a time of international naval rearmament was a better business proposition than investing in the first cinema in distant Dublin. However, they did discuss the idea, and Svevo pointed him towards potential investors.

Very early in his search, Joyce was fortunate to find an unlikely syndicate of four small businessmen, Antonio Machnich, an upholsterer, Giuseppe Caris, a draper, Giovanni Rebez, a leather merchant, and Francesco Novak, the owner of a bicycle shop. Their syndicate had been very successful in backing two of Trieste's main theatres and financing, by happy coincidence, a cinema – in Bucharest. At a meeting, Joyce's first words to them were: 'I know a city of 500,000 inhabitants where there is not a single cinema.' He caught their immediate attention and curiosity. They instantly wanted to know which city. He kept them briefly in suspense before announcing that it was Dublin. They were very interested. Dublin was, after all, the second city of the British Empire. It was no more strange or remote to them than Bucharest. Joyce produced a map of Ireland and told them there could be further possibilities in Belfast and Cork. Joyce turned out to be a convincing salesman. The Irish 'gift of the gab' obviously worked equally well in Joyce's fluent Triestine. The syndicate was enthusiastic, and agreed to invest £1,600 in the project. Joyce would go to Dublin as soon as possible to find a suitable premises and make the initial arrangements. They would then come over and join him. A contract was drawn up so that Joyce received a per diem rate, and, even though he had made no investment, he would become a 10 per cent partner in the enterprise.

When Nora heard that Joyce planned to go back to Dublin after less than a month at home, she was furious. Stanislaus also dreaded that this would be another of his brother's hare-brained schemes, and he would be left, quite literally, holding the baby and paying all the bills. Nora was not mollified by Joyce's promises of the fortune that would soon be coming their way. He may have convinced four gullible Triestine businessmen, but a sensible woman from Galway could not believe that a man who had found it hard to support a small family for the past five years had, overnight, turned into a brilliant businessman. When Joyce departed on 18 October 1909, Nora's last word to him was 'imbecile'. The 'imbecile' was to be away for ten weeks.

Back in Dublin in his new role, Joyce had a surge of practical energy. Within two weeks he had found suitable premises in Mary Street, off Sackville Street (now O'Connell Street), an excellent position for the passing trade. He ascertained from the theatre inspector that it would be eligible for a licence, and went about applying for one, and getting electricity installed in the building. He then summoned the members of the syndicate to come and inspect his arrangements. Two of them, Machnich and Rebez, arrived shortly afterwards. Never one to miss an irony, Joyce now booked his two Triestine backers into Finn's Hotel in South Leinster Street, where Nora had worked as a chambermaid. He had already made a pilgrimage there, and asked the manageress to show him Nora's old bedroom. He had lunch in the dining-room, where he wept and wrote Nora a lachrymose letter. He was already missing her and prepared to forgive her for her farewell word. It did not take him long, however, to turn against his compatriots. He had been in Dublin only two weeks before he wrote to Nora: 'I see nothing on either side of me but the image of the adulterous priest and his servants and of sly deceitful women. It is not good for me to come here or to be here. Perhaps if you were with me I would not suffer so much.' He then goes on to reproach her for making no effort to understand his interests or his work. Subsequent letters become more lustful again. In one the endearment 'My dear little fuckbird'[15] is dropped in among the scatology and the promises of all the beautiful clothes and furs she would soon be able to buy. Inevitably, Nora found Joyce's quick changes of mood hard to cope with, on top of his long absence and the financial problems he had left her with. The landlord was threatening to throw them out of their flat unless the back rent was paid, and Stanislaus was nearly broke himself.

Joyce's position in Dublin now was very different from what it had been on his first trip home a month before. Now he was not just an unsuccessful, expatriate literary figure, but an enterprising businessman with rich backers behind him. His two backers had now summoned the third partner, Novak, the owner of the bicycle shop, to come to Dublin to give technical advice. Joyce was often to be seen walking around the city with these three strange, exotic figures looking as though they had stepped out of a foreign film. Dublin was a small city and word of Joyce's new status spread very quickly. When he met old friends or acquaintances, several now tried to borrow money from him. Others were old creditors trying to get their money back. The final irony was Stanislaus's cable asking him for money to stop the landlord from turning his family out in the street. Joyce had already spent any spare money helping his Dublin family from being thrown out into their street. His father was currently out-of-work and in hospital with iritis, an inflammation of the iris of the eye, the same complaint from which Joyce had already begun to suffer. In the end, Joyce borrowed money from Machnich, the upholsterer, and cabled it to Stanislaus.

Joyce was working incredibly hard to prepare the cinema for its opening. He arranged and supervised the decoration of the building and the provision of seating. The projection equipment had been ordered from London and arrived on time, although an experienced projectionist was not easy to find. In the course of all this, Joyce accompanied Machnich and Rebez to Cork to investigate the prospects for a cinema there. They had already gone on their own to Belfast and decided against it. Cork seemed a better possibility, but they postponed a decision until they saw the reaction in Dublin.

Joyce had probably never worked harder in his life and was earning very little for his pains, but he found the time to meet with the Dublin Woollen Company and become their agent in Trieste. The only outcome of this was that he sold a few lengths of Donegal tweed to some of his Triestine pupils. There was little time to worry about his literary life, but he was increasingly irritated by how long George Roberts of Maunsel was taking to send him the promised proofs of *Dubliners*. He hoped that seeing them in print would encourage him to finish *A Portrait* when he got home. It was to prove a forlorn hope.

The Volta Picture Theatre opened on 20 December 1909. A full house saw a double bill of a French and an Italian film, and the Press response was favourable. Subsequently, however, there was a church-inspired boycott campaign aimed at the cinema's supposedly evil influence on the minds of the faithful. This may not have proved an effective deterrent in the long run, but there were more immediate problems. Machnich and Rebez, uncomfortable with the language and the climate, went home for Christmas and did not return. Novak was left behind as the technical supervisor, but he had no administrative skills, and Joyce refused to stay beyond the New Year. He was desperate to get home to Nora and his children. He had briefly seen himself as a writer who dabbled successfully in business, but now he had dabbled enough. He had not made a sufficient profit from any of his Dublin ventures to buy Nora the elegant clothes and furs he had promised her as homecoming presents. The promise he kept was nothing to do with Nora. It concerned his second oldest sister, the 20-year-old Eileen, whom he had promised to take back with him to Trieste. She had a fine voice, and Joyce, with his passion for encouraging talent, felt he could find her a good teacher there. It would also ease his conscience about the state of his family in Dublin, who would have one less mouth to feed. He had written to announce the idea to Stanislaus, who had immediately replied that having one sister in the house was enough.

Joyce, undeterred, left Dublin with Eileen on 2 January 1910. Now there would be six Joyces in Trieste and only five in Dublin. The Volta Picture Theatre flourished initially because of the novelty of moving pictures, but soon the audiences diminished. Its main problem, apart from absentee backers, was the poor supply of English-language films. In late June, when its losses reached £1,600, the amount of the initial investment, the syndicate sold it to a London company for £1,000.

Once again Joyce returned home rather less than a conquering hero and with none of the grand presents he had promised Nora and the children. Joyce had had all his expenses paid and, despite the syndicate's losses, had been assured that he would receive £40 for his troubles. He was never paid. At his next English lesson, Joyce told Svevo about his Dublin experiences and the failure of the syndicate in Trieste to pay him the £40. Svevo no doubt listened sympathetically. He was about to leave for London to supervise the installation of new machinery in the Charlton factory. As Svevo's business was expanding, Joyce's had disappeared. From Charlton, Svevo wrote him a letter, dated 15 June 1910:

My dear Mr. Joyce,
I am sorry indeed that I could not take leave of you in a proper manner. On Saturday I did not know yet that I had to start so soon. Be so kind as to excuse me.

You were so excited about the cynematograph [*sic*] affair that during my whole travel I remembered your face so startled by such wickedness. And I must add to the remarks I already have done that your surprise at being cheated proves that you are a pure literary man. To be cheated proves not yet enough. But to be cheated and to reveal a great surprise over that and not to consider it as a matter of course is really literary. I hope you are now correcting your proofs and not frightened to be cheated by your publisher. Otherwise the book could not be a good one.

We are here in good health. I am smoking and my wife is enjoying the suave surroundings. By and by she will be caught by her anglomania and you will have a hard time to speak to her against your oppressors.

Please remember me most kindly to your brother.
I am, dear Mr. Joyce,
Yours very truly
Ettore Schmitz[16]

There was always a charming air of formality in Svevo's communications with Joyce. Often Joyce would respond in Triestine, or when writing in English address Svevo as 'Dear Hector'. Sadly though, Joyce was not correcting the proofs of *Dubliners*, and was beginning to be 'frightened to be cheated' by his publisher. George Roberts had sent him only the proof of one story, 'Ivy Day in the Committee Room', which takes place at a ward committee meeting during a municipal council election. The members are discussing the forthcoming arrival in Ireland of Edward VII in very colloquial Dublin dialogue, and Roberts was very unhappy with it:

–But look here, John, said Mr. O'Connor. Why should we welcome the King of England? Didn't Parnell himself…

–Parnell, said Mr. Henchy, is dead. Now, here's the way I look at it. Here's this chap come to the throne after his bloody old bitch of a mother keeping him out of it till the man was grey. He's a jolly fine decent fellow, if you ask me, and no damn nonsense about him. He just says to himself – *The old one never went to see these wild Irish. By Christ, I'll go myself and see what they're like*…And are we going to insult the man when he comes over here on a friendly visit? Eh? Isn't that right, Crofton?

Mr. Crofton nodded his head.

–But after all now, said Mr. Lyons argumentatively, King Edward's life, you know, is not the very….

–Let bygones be bygones, said Mr. Henchy. I admire the man personally. He's just an ordinary knockabout like you and me. He's fond of his glass of grog and he's a bit of a rake, perhaps, and he's a good sportsman, Damn it, can't we Irish play fair? [17]

This was one of several passages in the stories that had begun to worry Roberts, who wanted to avoid any scandal. He thought this one was too disrespectful to the monarchy, and wanted Joyce to cut and rework it. Joyce made one alteration – he changed 'bloody old bitch of a mother' to 'old mother'. He contested everything else and entered into an acrimonious correspondence which further delayed the book's publication. Once again Joyce was back to suffering the travails 'of a pure literary man'.

CHAPTER SEVEN

Anti-fouling and Freud

AFTER JOYCE RETURNED TO TRIESTE from Dublin in 1910, Svevo's English lessons with him became more intermittent. Svevo's business abroad, particularly in London, was taking up more and more of his time. There was an unprecedented period of shipbuilding in the decade before the Great War. Apart from many of the main commercial shipping lines, the Veneziani Company was supplying its Moravia Anti-Fouling Composition to the navies of nearly all the major powers. It became an enormously profitable enterprise, and, since the formula for their paint remained a well-kept secret, there was no competition. Svevo himself did not make a fortune. It was a close family business, and with several members actively involved, Svevo had to wait several years before he was offered a 10 per cent shareholding. The company was run very directly and firmly by his parents-in-law, Gioachino and Olga Veneziani, with the latter the dominant partner. Svevo and Livia, with only one child to bring up, were still able to live and travel comfortably. However, they were not so well off that Svevo did not complain bitterly, in several surviving letters, about the expense of Livia's wardrobe for her visits to various spas, still attempting to resolve her gynaecological problems.

The other conflict between Svevo and Livia, in an otherwise happy marriage, was the education of Letizia. As an observant Catholic, Livia wanted her daughter to go to a Catholic school. As a non-observant Jew, Svevo objected. An awkward compromise was reached. Initially, Letizia went to a secular school, but had religious instruction privately. She then moved to a convent school for the year before her confirmation, and returned to a secular school after that. Nonetheless she was to be an observant Catholic for the rest of her life. There were similar religious difficulties in the Joyce household. Nora did not go to Mass regularly, and, when she went, she knew better than to ask Joyce to accompany her. She still clung to her Catholicism, but Giorgio and Lucia's schooling was dictated by where the family was living rather than by religion. On the several occasions when Nora threatened to leave Joyce, her final threat was always that she would take the children with her and have them baptised.

Despite their very different backgrounds, Joyce and Svevo were broadly in agreement about religion and politics. Svevo was a strong supporter of Triestine irredentism and voted for the left-leaning Liberal party. Joyce basically saw himself as a socialist, despite his distrust of all politicians. Both men were pacifists, although in Svevo's case this posed a problem since he was doing business with navies that were busy rearming themselves. He comforted his conscience with the thought that he was not actively contributing to future warfare. The Veneziani product, as the brochure proclaimed, simply kept 'the ship's bottom clean and free from rust and barnacles' – a positively life-enhancing process. The Great War looms so large in the history of the twentieth century that the numerous other wars up to 1914 are usually overlooked. Living in Trieste during this period would have made one particularly conscious of the cost and folly of war. Apart from watching from afar the Boer War, a land war, and the Russo-Japanese War, a naval one, there were, closer at hand, a Turko-Italian War in 1911, and, practically on the doorstep, two Balkan Wars in which the countries that had recently become independent of the Ottoman Empire – Serbia, Bulgaria, Montenegro, parts of Greece, and Bosnia and Herzogovina, both annexed by Austria in 1908 – fought each other over their territorial and ethnic boundaries until the eve of the Great War.

The naval build-up in this period was an integral part of the Great Powers' drive to expand their colonial empires. Italy, united as a nation for only forty years, went to war with Turkey in 1911 with the aim of starting her own colonies on the other side of the Mediterranean. After her victories in North Africa, she took control of Libya and Cyrenaica. The largest Empire inevitably needed the largest navy, and, thanks to

Svevo's fortunate visit to the Admiralty in 1901, the Venezianis' most lucrative contract was with the British. Svevo's business experiences made him very aware of the dangers inherent in this Great Power rivalry, as a complicated series of defensive alliances were being formed. In the face of the growing ambitions of Germany, Britain and France had formed the *Entente Cordiale* in 1904. Three years later the *Entente* was joined by Russia. They were confronted by the central European powers of Germany and Austro-Hungary, soon joined by Italy in an opposing Triple Alliance.

As an avid newspaper reader, Joyce was aware of both the international and the local situation. In their early conversations, Svevo and Joyce had found common ground in the similar positions of Trieste *vis-à-vis* Austria, and of Dublin *vis-à-vis* Britain. Both men had written articles on this subject for *Il Piccolo della Sera*. Svevo, born and bred in Trieste, was inevitably more involved in local politics than Joyce, who, with the luxury of being an expatriate, could remain above the nationalist divisions. Both of them abhorred colonialism, whether it was Austrian, British, or Italian, but neither felt violence was justified to overthrow it. Although Joyce deplored the British political and cultural hegemony in Ireland, he was no great supporter of what an insular Irish nationalism wanted to put in its place. He was certainly never as passionate about politics as his brother. After Stanislaus had tried to discuss the subject with him, Joyce wrote, 'I'm not interested in politics. I'm only interested in style,'[1] a reply that may have just been a defence against another of Stanislaus's lectures on socialism. Joyce, despite his sympathy for irredentism and socialism, was not active in either movement, as his brother was. As events turned out, this was fortunate for him. In his self-imposed exile, Joyce was still living in the world of the Irish politics in which he been brought up. His father had been a great supporter of Parnell, the leader of the Irish Party in Parliament, and had been horrified by what he considered to be his betrayal by his own political followers. Joyce inherited these views, and became obsessive on the subject of betrayal, both in public and in private life.

Joyce had very little reason to suspect betrayal in his private life. Yet he got some perverse *frisson* from indulging his jealousies about Nora, as he had done after Cosgrave's malicious insinuations on his trip to

Dublin in 1909. Two years later in Trieste, his suspicions about Nora were again aroused. She certainly had an admirer in Roberto Prezioso, an ex-pupil of Joyce, who had become a friend of the couple. Prezioso also happened to be the editor of *Il Piccolo della Sera*, the paper for which Joyce occasionally wrote. He had also arranged for Joyce to give two lectures on Ireland at the Università del Popolo. Nora was quite open about a couple of visits from Prezioso for tea when Joyce was not there. She denied any other contact. This did not allay Joyce's suspicions, but how was he to confront such an influential benefactor? His jealousy soon became insufferable, and he met and confronted Prezioso in the Piazza Goldoni. Their meeting was observed by Tullio Silvestri, a friend of Joyce's, an impoverished portrait painter, whose main claim to fame was that he was the only man to have borrowed money from the great borrower himself.[2] He reported that he saw Joyce in full verbal flow and Prezioso appeared to be weeping.

It was after this domestic crisis that Joyce returned to his first love, the theatre. He began making notes for *Exiles*, the play he was to finish in Zurich. It is a complicated story about an Irish academic, an expatriate, who returns with his wife to live and work in Dublin. The characters are very close to Joyce and Nora. Its subject is betrayal, with the husband colluding in his wife's affair. Joyce never actually saw the play performed. It had its premiere in Munich in August 1918, but received bad notices and closed immediately. Joyce was not in time to catch it. There was a production in London in 1926, but Joyce was in Paris, and after two serious eye operations he was unable to travel. At the time, Svevo happened to be passing through Paris on his way to London on business. Joyce arranged for him to have two tickets to the play and asked him to write and send his review of the production. It was another coincidental twist in their story that it was Svevo who saw the play and not its author, also an echo of the situation eighteen years earlier, when Joyce set his pupil to write a description of his teacher for homework.[3]

While Joyce was making his notes for *Exiles*, Svevo also returned to his first love. He began writing a play, *L'Avventura di Maria*, also about betrayal, but artistic, not sexual. The play is largely autobiographical. Its principal character gives up art for a successful, bourgeois life, a predicament that continued to obsess its author. His mistress is also an artist but she stays faithful to her art, and gives up her lover. Svevo's play was never produced. Only one of his plays ever was in his lifetime, *Terzetto Spezzato* (Broken Trio) a farce that ran for a week in Rome in 1927, the year before he died. Joyce's theatrical record was little better. *Exiles* has been produced intermittently in several countries, but has never had a successful run.

Although both writers held similar views on many subjects, there was one on which Joyce and Svevo disagreed heartily – psychoanalysis. Svevo had first discovered Freud's work around 1908, when he read *The Interpretation of Dreams*, published in 1900, and *On Dreams*, published a year later. The mystery and meaning of dreams have always held a universal fascination. Both Svevo and Joyce had periods of noting down their dreams, and Joyce had even persuaded Nora to tell him hers and contrived to interpret them. Freud's attempt to explain and systematise his interpretation, based largely on sexual causation, inevitably led to controversy. Since it took some years for Freud to be translated into other languages, the interest was initially limited to German-speakers. Freud and his first colleagues were nearly all Viennese, most of them Jewish – an irony, because at this time Vienna had a reputation for its anti-Semitism.

Trieste was only a half-day's train journey from Vienna, and Freud's reputation travelled quickly. Svevo's reading moved on from dreams to *The Psychopathology of Everyday Life* and *Jokes and their Relation to the Unconscious*. The latter was obviously of great interest to a man renowned for his *witze*. Explaining the why and wherefore of a joke is a certain way of killing it, but Svevo was stimulated by Freud's theory that a joke was an 'impotent man's compensation and defence' against harm and embarrassment. It certainly did not discourage Svevo from either telling or writing his *witze*. A good illustration of this is the occasion when Svevo told Joyce an off-colour joke. Svevo records that Joyce responded by saying 'I never say that sort of thing, though I write it.' Svevo later wrote 'It appears then that his works are not ones that could be read in his own presence.'[4]

In 1908, around the time that Joyce and Svevo were talking about Freud in Trieste, the first international congress for psychoanalysis, organised by Freud, was meeting, not far away, in Salzburg. Forty-two fledging psychoanalysts were present, and they elected Carl Jung as their president. Freud had engineered this because he didn't want his new science to look too much like a Jewish club. Although Joyce and Svevo couldn't know it at the time, Freud and Jung were both to play important roles in their lives.

It was reading and talking about Freud and psychoanalysis that inspired Svevo to start writing a novel after twenty-one years of resisting that temptation. *The Confessions of Zeno* begins with Dr. S., Zeno's analyst, telling him to write down what he recalls of his early life. What Zeno writes for Dr. S. becomes the springboard for the novel. Svevo also had a close family connection with psychoanalysis. His nephew, Eduardo Weiss, a doctor, went to Vienna to study under Freud, and was later to return to Trieste and become the first analyst to practise in Italy. His connections were also of great help with a family problem. Svevo's brother-in-law, Bruno Veneziani, of whom the writer was very fond, had qualified as a chemist, but he was also a talented musician and decided to become a concert pianist. After a successful debut he began to suffer psychological problems largely because of his inability to accept his homosexuality. Through an introduction from Weiss, Bruno went to Vienna and started analysis with Dr. Tausk, a colleague of Freud. It was as well the family were wealthy because after a year Bruno felt he was making no progress. Weiss intervened discreetly and introduced Bruno to Freud, with whom he then had numerous sessions. Svevo learned a great deal about analysis from Bruno, but ended up a little sceptical about the cost of the treatment in relation to the benefits – at least in his brother-in-law's case. He may have become more reconciled to his sexual identity, but he was now addicted to psychoanalysis – an irony bound to appeal to Svevo. *The Confessions of Zeno*, originally inspired by psychoanalysis, ended up as a satire on the subject.

It is not known whether Joyce, at least while he was in Trieste, would actually have read any of Freud's work. He had read enough about it, though, to make it clear to Svevo that he did not share his interest or enthusiasm. When Joyce told Stanislaus that he was 'only interested in style', he meant it in terms of his literary life. He was consciously looking for a unique personal style that would enable him to write a totally new kind of novel. He had thought about it for many years, through the writing of *A Portrait of the Artist as a Young Man* and in the planning of *Ulysses*. By the time he actually came to write the book, he would have known that the basis of Freudian analysis was the attempt to release the patient's unconscious by free association. In fact, this was the technique that Joyce applied to his fictitious characters, Stephen Dedalus, Leopold and Molly Bloom, through the use of interior monologue. He had arrived at it by his own path, and the last thing he wanted said about his book was that it was heavily influenced by psychoanalysis. He wanted to be the James Joyce, not the Sigmund Freud, of literature.

Years later, it was Svevo himself who defended Joyce's true originality and achievement. Much as he disliked public speaking, Svevo gave a lecture about Joyce to a large audience in Milan in March 1927. Towards its end, he said:

> I can prove that Sigmund Freud's theories did not reach Joyce in time to guide him when he was planning his work. This statement will astonish those who discover so many traits in Stephen Dedalus that seem beyond doubt to have been suggested by the science of psychoanalysis: his narcissism which will probably be attributed not to his being an artist but to his being a first-born son, the adored mother who changes into a haunting spectre, his father despised and shunned, the brother forgotten in a corner like an umbrella, and finally in the eternal struggle in him between his conscious and his subconscious.
>
> Might not Joyce have borrowed from psychiatry the idea of communicating the thought of his characters at the very moment when they are formed in the disorder of a mind free from all control? On this head the contribution of psychoanalysis can be ruled out for Joyce himself has told us from whom he had learned this technique. In fact, his words were enough to confer celebrity on the venerable Edouard Dujardin, who had used this technique in his *Les Lauriers sont coupés*.
>
> For the rest I can bear good witness. In 1915 when he left us he knew nothing about psychoanalysis. Moreover, his knowledge of current German was too weak. He could read some poets, not scientists. Yet at that time all his works, including *Ulysses*, had already been conceived.

From Trieste, he went to Zurich, the second capital of psychoanalysis. Undoubtedly he became acquainted there with the new science, and there is reason to think that for a while he had more or less believed in it. But in 1919, when he returned, I found him in open revolt against it – one of those scornful rebellions of his by which he shook himself free of everything that hampered his thought. 'Psychoanalysis?' he said to me, 'Well, if we need it, let us keep to confession.' I was dumbfounded. It was the rebellion of the Catholic in him, enhanced with greater harshness by the unbeliever. Joyce's works, therefore, cannot be considered a triumph of psychoanalysis, but I am convinced they can be a subject of its study.[5]

Svevo showed his insight when he mentioned 'the Catholic in him'. Joyce may have lost his belief, but he never lost his attachment to the aesthetics and rituals of the Church. It was partially a nostalgic attachment, but also one that was vital to his creative imagination. In Trieste, his sisters noticed how he never went to Mass, but he would go into local churches and linger at the back during services.

Svevo's conviction that Joyce's work could be a worthy subject of psychoanalytic study has since been borne out a hundredfold. One of the first of these studies was by Jung himself. He wrote a preface to the second German edition of *Ulysses* in 1930, at the request of their joint publisher. It was not complimentary. He wrote that it was an example of 'the schizophrenic mind', and that one might as well read it backwards as forwards. Joyce responded to his German publisher, 'Why is Jung so rude to me? He doesn't even know me. People want to put me out of the church to which I don't belong. I have nothing to do with psychoanalysis.'[6] After this, Jung, no doubt prompted by their publisher, wrote Joyce a more conciliatory, warmer letter about the book. Some years later, Joyce was to meet Jung personally, for a sadder, non-literary reason. Joyce's daughter, Lucia, had first showed mental instability in her teens; looking for a diagnosis, Joyce had taken her to many doctors. There was no consensus among them about a diagnosis or a cure. When she was twenty-seven, Joyce travelled with her to Zurich to see Jung. He became Lucia's twentieth doctor, and she stayed in his clinic for a month. Jung then diagnosed her as schizophrenic.

CHAPTER EIGHT

Publication and Sarajevo

L'ITINERARI JOYCE, PRODUCED BY THE Tourist Information Office in Trieste, has a map showing all the places of Joycean interest, which includes all nine apartments where the family lived during their eleven-year stay. Each house has a plaque on the wall saying for how long the Joyces lived there and on what floor. The usual reason for constantly moving was an inability to pay the rent. One of their longest stays was on the third floor at via Alfredo Scussa 8, between late August 1910 and early September 1912. Here Joyce, Nora and their two children had rather more space than they were used to, for the Triestine branch of the wider Joyce family had diminished. Stanislaus had his own small apartment nearby, though he mostly ate supper with them. In July 1911, Eva went back to Dublin, despite the fact that there was only one cinema there. It was the Volta, her brother's brain-child, now owned by the British Provincial Theatre Company, but still a working cinema. Eileen was employed as a governess in Udine, a town about fifty miles north of Trieste. The only addition to the family was a dog called Fido – considering who his owner was, not a very imaginative name.

During this period Joyce was still being tormented by George Roberts's delays in sending the proofs of *Dubliners*, or giving him a definite publication date. Nonetheless, Roberts continued demanding changes. With these frustrations, Joyce felt unable to continue with *A Portrait of the Artist as a Young Man*. He was also tired of being an itinerant English language teacher, and decided to try to teach at a higher level in a school or college. He applied for a post at a school in

Como, and discovered that to teach in Italy he would need an Italian teaching diploma. He was advised to sit the necessary examinations at the University of Padua. Joyce went there for four days and sat eight different papers in Italian and English, in translation and in literature. He did amazingly well, scoring 421 points out of a possible 450, only to discover that there was a bureaucratic problem over reciprocity with his Dublin B.A. degree. He went back to Trieste and attempted to use what influence he could through various friends and pupils. In the end it came to nothing, but the unfairness of his situation gained him sympathy. With Svevo's help, and that of two aristocratic ex-pupils, Baron Ralli and Count Sordina, Joyce eventually ended up with an appointment at La Scuola di Commercio Revoltella, a commercial college in Trieste, where he taught English and basic literature courses in the mornings. He continued to give his private lessons on most afternoons. This was the period when he earned enough to employ Maria Kirn as a maid, so that now when Svevo came to visit, he was accompanied by Livia.

There was also sufficient money for Nora to contemplate a long-awaited trip back to Ireland. She had not seen her mother for eight years and wanted Lucia to meet her only grandmother. Joyce was in favour, since it would be an opportunity for her, en route to Galway, both to meet his family and for her to confront George Roberts about a final decision on *Dubliners*. Nora and Lucia, now aged five, left for Ireland in early July 1912, and were met off the ferry by the Joyce family. John Stanislaus Joyce became very emotional at meeting his first grand-daughter, but tactfully didn't enquire whether her parents were married or not. Nora spent the minimum of time with the Joyce family before setting off with Lucia to see her mother and surviving relatives, who included a rich uncle in Galway. Before leaving Dublin, she did go to Maunsel's offices to see George Roberts, but made the mistake of taking with her Joyce's father and brother, Charlie. Roberts had no trouble in brushing off this unliterary trio.

On the day Nora and Lucia left Trieste, Joyce wasted no time in rushing round to Svevo to announce how relieved he felt to have only men in the house at last. Giorgio, now seven, was at school all day. Anyway, in an emergency, there was always Stanislaus round the corner. It took Joyce only five days to realise that his life was insufferable without

Nora. His morale declined further when there was no immediate letter from her. He wrote her a furious letter and then visited Svevo to ask for an advance against twelve lessons to pay his and Giorgio's fare to Dublin. Once more Svevo gave him money. Then Joyce asked him to look after Fido while he was away. Joyce was extremely fortunate to have a friend of Svevo's generosity and forbearance who also loved animals. Fido repaid his host's hospitality by disappearing a few nights later. The next day Svevo sent a servant to look for him and found Fido up an alleyway, where 'he' had pupped a litter of six. Svevo took them all in – so much for Joyce's illusion of having an all-male household.

Joyce stopped in London, en route to Dublin, and went to visit Yeats in his flat, and introduce Giorgio to him. By now Yeats was recognised as one of Ireland's leading writers and poets, and had considerable influence in London literary circles. Joyce had a very mixed view of his work and opinions, but was not unaware of the advantages of keeping in touch with him. Yeats, another generous man, was impressed by what he knew of Joyce's work, rather than his personal experience of him. He was polite and hospitable to father and son. The two travelled on to Dublin, where Joyce discovered that Nora had just left for Galway. He saw his family and spent part of an afternoon with George Roberts at Maunsel, but basically got nowhere. Roberts, still nervous about being sued for obscenity and *lèse majesté*, wanted more changes and even suggested that Joyce publish the book under his own name. Joyce now just wanted to leave Dublin and see Nora and Lucia. Next morning, he and Giorgio took a train for Galway.

The next three weeks were probably the nearest Joyce and Nora had come to a proper summer holiday since they had left Ireland. They travelled around Galway and met various members of Nora's family, but not her father. When Joyce and Nora wanted to go off together, there was always his grandmother or an aunt with whom to leave Giorgio and Lucia. They went to Galway Races and took the ferry to the Aran Islands. There, Joyce wrote two pieces that were later published in *Il Piccolo della Sera*. For Nora's relatives and childhood friends there was inevitably a certain glamour surrounding this young family, who spoke several languages and managed to live and survive in foreign parts. The idea of relatives coming back from America or Canada to visit family was familiar, but Trieste in south-eastern Europe seemed even more strange and remote. The question of whether Joyce and Nora were married or not was somehow skirted around – after all, Joyce was an artist. Joyce found he had an affinity with Connemara and its rural people which he had never found in Dublin. He may even have managed to put the anxieties and frustrations about Roberts and *Dubliners* out of his mind for those few weeks. From Galway he sent Svevo a postcard of an elderly fisherman sitting on a rock. On the back he wrote 'A portrait of the artist as an <u>old</u> man.' He signed it 'Stephen Dedalus'.[1]

It was to be no happy return to Dublin. A telegram awaited him from Stanislaus telling him to come home immediately because the landlord was threatening to eject the family for non-payment of rent. Ejection or not, Joyce was not going to return until he had finished his business with Roberts. That did not take long. Roberts had consulted another solicitor, this time in London, and had a report advising him that the book was libellous on many counts. Roberts mentioned them all to Joyce and demanded changes on each count. All Joyce agreed to change were the names of characters and companies that were real. As a delaying tactic, Roberts again brought up the solution of it being published under Joyce's name, with the author paying most of the printer's bill. Joyce said he would consider this. At further meetings Roberts continued his game of trying to wring more changes out of Joyce. Fearing the worst, Joyce managed to sneak a copy of the proofs out of the office. It was as well that he did. The printer now intervened in the dispute, saying that he refused to print the book because it was blasphemous and unpatriotic. After three years of delays, Roberts now rejected the book, claiming that the printer had burned the pages. Whether this was true or not, it added drama to his story. Burning was the fate of heretics, and Joyce felt that was how his enemies saw his work – as heretical. He embellished his story later by saying that person, or persons unknown, had paid the printer to destroy his pages. Who were these enemies? They were three-fold. On his first return trip to Dublin, it was Cosgrave with his insinuations about Nora. On the second, it was the Catholic Church, which had condemned and undermined his cinema venture. Now it was Roberts and his printer who were trying to ruin his literary career. And there were also those 'persons unknown'. Like his hero, Parnell, Joyce saw himself as betrayed and humiliated. Some friends, perhaps justifiably, thought Joyce was becoming paranoid. Two years later, Joyce wrote to Grant Richards, a London publisher to whom he had just submitted *Dubliners,* 'I find it difficult to come to any other conclusion but this – that their intention was to wear me out and if possible strangle me once and for all. But in this they did not succeed.'[2]

Joyce's book was certainly no hagiography of Dubliners per se, and it had been written well before his recent visits. On 11 September 1912, he learned of the fate of his pages, Joyce and Nora boarded the mail boat at Kingstown, just as they had done eight years earlier, still unmarried, but now with their two children. Joyce never went back to Ireland. His father was to live for another nineteen years, but Joyce never saw him again. As for George Roberts, Joyce was determined to have the last word. On the train journey between the Hook of Holland and Salzburg, Joyce composed a long satiric poem, written in the first person as George Roberts, lampooning Roberts himself and some of the distinguished Irish writers whom he had published. He called it *Gas from a Burner,* an example of Joyce's weakness for multiple puns. In Ireland, gas was an alternative word for fun, or the Irish *craic,* as in 'He was great gas.' The Burner was, of course, George Roberts, and burners also burned gas. In the poem, the quatrain that was probably nearest to Joyce's heart was:

> This lovely land that always sent
> Her writers and artists to banishment
> And in a spirit of Irish fun
> Betrayed her own leaders, one by one.[3]

The allusion to Parnell would have appealed to Joyce's father too, but Joyce's plans for the pamphlet certainly did not. He had it printed in Trieste and sent copies to Charlie for distribution around Dublin. John Stanislaus read it and was shocked. He told Charlie not to distribute it. Charlie wrote to his brother quoting his father as saying the poem was the work of 'an out and out ruffian without the spark of a gentleman in him'. For Joyce's father, drunk or sober, feckless or not, 'being a gentleman' was all that mattered. Charlie asked for advice, and Joyce wrote back telling him to distribute the pamphlet. Charlie did. It would have entertained some and alienated others in Dublin literary circles, but it would serve Joyce's main purpose – to keep his name and provocative reputation alive in Ireland while he was elsewhere.

Within a year of this disgruntled return from Dublin, Joyce had started to write the first chapter of *Ulysses* from the notes he had been making on and off since he was in Rome six years before. He started to create those twenty-four hours in the life of a Dublin seen mainly through the eyes and mind of Bloom, Molly and Stephen Dedalus, his Ulysses, Penelope and Telemachus. W.B. Yeats read *Ulysses* when it was finally published in 1922, although he admitted to not actually finishing it. He had read enough, however, to sum up the central paradox of its author 'in flight from the objects of his hatred, bearing in mind always in minute detail, even to the names over the shops, the Dublin that he hated but would not forget.'[4]

By January 1913, Joyce was teaching all day, at the Scuola di Commercio in the mornings and his private pupils in the afternoons. It showed Joyce's remarkable energy that, even with this schedule and his already troublesome eyesight, he found any time at all to write. The years 1913 and 1914 were incredibly productive for him. He started his play *Exiles*, went back to working on *A Portrait of the Artist as a Young Man*, made further notes for *Ulysses* and wrote the first chapter, while he continued to badger London publishers about *Dubliners*. By the end of 1913, his luck began to change with the arrival of two letters. The first came in November from Grant Richards, the London publisher who, having originally rejected *Dubliners*, asked to see it again. The second arrived on 15 December. It came from Ezra Pound and was to have a seminal effect on Joyce's life. It began:

> Dear Sir,
> Mr. Yeats has been speaking to me of your writing. I am informally connected with a couple of new and impecunious papers ('The Egoist' which has coursed under the unsuitable name of the 'The New Freewoman' 'guère que d'hommes y collaborent', as the Mercure remarked of it – and

the 'Cerebrilist' which means God knows what – anyhow they are about the only organs in England that stand for free speech and want (I don't say get) literature….

This is the first time I have written to anyone outside of my own circle (save in the case of French authors). These matters can be better dealt with in conversation, but as that is impossible, I write….

Pound then went into details about the two magazines and their very minimal rates, but their excellent publicity value for any writer, particularly one whose work and opinions *The Spectator* might object to. He ends:

I am bonae voluntatis, – don't in the least know that I can be of any use to you – or you to me. From what W.B.Y. says I imagine we have a hate or two in common – but that's a very problematical bond of introduction.
Yours sincerely
Ezra Pound[5]

Pound was a 28-year-old American poet who had come to live in London in 1908. He had a brilliant academic background, and had learned eight languages in order to be able to appreciate and translate their poetry. He was flamboyant, eccentric and devoted to the arts. He much admired Yeats's poetry, introduced himself to him, became his friend and, for a couple of years, acted as his secretary. He was soon a highly influential figure in avant-garde literary circles and became enormously helpful to the careers of several then little-known writers: T.S. Eliot, Robert Frost, Ford Madox Ford, Joyce, and later, in Paris, Hemingway and Gertrude Stein. His own very modernist poetry was also attracting attention. Before Joyce could reply, Pound had sent another letter saying that Yeats had shown him a poem, 'I Hear an Army', which Joyce had once given him, and now wanted to include it in an anthology that he was editing. Joyce was happy to agree and took the opportunity to send him the first chapter of *A Portrait of the Artist as a Young Man*. Pound reacted with enthusiasm. He was now more formally 'connected' with *The Egoist*, as literary editor, and showed

Joyce's chapter to the editor, Dora Marsden, who agreed to publish it. As Richard Ellmann wrote, 'In Ezra Pound, as avid to discover as Joyce was to be discovered, the writings of Joyce found their missionary.'[6]

In the recent past, Joyce's bad news had come in battalions. In 1914 it was good news that came that way. On 29 January a letter arrived from Grant Richards in London saying that he would publish *Dubliners* and he would send a contract. This time a contract did arrive. The terms were not generous, no royalties on the first 500 copies, and the author had to take 120 copies himself. The first edition was to be only 1,250 copies, but, after the years of disappointment, Joyce was not about to quibble. This time the promised proofs arrived on time. Meanwhile, Pound had asked to see more of *A Portrait* and Joyce willingly obliged and sent him the other two chapters he had written.

Joyce was always fascinated 'by the loops and knots of coincidence'.[7] Now he was caught up in a series of them. In late June 1914, there was an editorial change at *The Egoist*. Dora Marsden retired to write her own books, and Harriet Shaw Weaver, who had been business editor, became the editor. She was born in Cheshire into a very proper family, her father a doctor, her mother from a wealthy family, from whom Harriet inherited an extremely large fortune. An attractive, highly intelligent woman, she never married or had a family. She espoused what she considered worthwhile, usually radical causes, and invested a lot of her own money in *The Egoist*. She was a staunch early feminist and later a communist. Harriet Weaver read and admired the first three chapters of *A Portrait* and wrote to Joyce, asking to see the next two chapters. It was her decision, enthusiastically supported by Pound, to serialise the entire novel. The only problem was that Joyce had not yet finished it. He was now encouraged to do so – and quickly too. It eventually came out in twenty-five episodes, each of around fifteen pages, over two years.

The coincidences now proliferated. The first episode of *A Portrait* in *The Egoist* came out on 2 February 1914, Joyce's thirty-second birthday. *Dubliners* was finally published on 15 June that year, the eve of the tenth anniversary of his first going out with Nora, the day memorialised in *Ulysses*. When the novel was finally published in 1922, Joyce insisted, it had to be on his birthday. Joyce saw serendipity in the links between these fortuitous events. It was his keeping in touch with Yeats that brought him the vital contact with Pound and then, through him, with *The Egoist* and Harriet Weaver. As important for Joyce, if not more so, than her literary role, was the fact that she was to become his financial benefactor for the rest of his life. Although they corresponded, they did not meet until 1922 in London. Joyce had met Pound in June 1920 at a hotel in Sirmione on Lake Garda. Both Pound and Weaver considered that they had discovered a genius, and meeting him did not alter their opinion.

If there had been a change in Joyce's luck, it was not reflected in his financial circumstances. He was still much in debt and struggling to find spending money. He had not received an advance from Grant Richards, nor any payment from *The Egoist*, and its editor's anonymous financial settlement had not yet begun. Again it was Svevo who came to the rescue, not by a loan, but by talking to his father-in-law, Gioachino Veneziani. Svevo persuaded him that the bulk of their mail from abroad was now so great that they needed a foreign correspondence clerk. Joyce, with his command of languages, would be the ideal man for the job. Veneziani had initially disapproved of his son-in-law's friendship with Joyce, whose drinking habits and bohemian ways were fairly well-known in Trieste. Svevo must have been very convincing because his father-in-law agreed to employ Joyce part-time at a hundred crowns a month. Joyce was now back doing the same work he had been doing seven years before in the bank in Rome, but this income became his survival money. The miracle was that he still found time to write, but at the expense of his family life. He clearly loved Nora, and was devoted to his children, but when he was at home, much of the time he would be merely a presence in a bedroom – writing. Cyril Connolly's literary dictum that 'There is no more sombre enemy of good art than the pram in the hall' did not apply to Joyce. Yet when there was an occasion Joyce knew how to enjoy himself with his family. There was drinking, singing around the piano and dancing. After all, Giorgio grew up to be a professional singer, and Lucia, briefly, a ballet dancer.

On 26 June 1914, Svevo wrote Joyce a letter expressing his heartiest congratulations on the occasion of two long-awaited events: the publication of *Dubliners* and of the first chapter of *A Portrait of the*

Artist as a Young Man and its forthcoming serialisation in *The Egoist*. Two days later, the Archduke Francis Ferdinand, heir to the throne of Austria-Hungary, and his wife, Sophie, were assassinated at Sarajevo by a Bosnian Serb nationalist. The two bodies were brought by boat to Trieste for a state funeral, and then taken on by train to Vienna. The events of the next few weeks in Europe fell into place like a disastrous game of dominoes. On 28 July Austria declared war on Serbia and within two weeks Serbia's ally, Russia, was at war with Austria – so was Germany with Russia; then Britain and France with Germany and Austria. Yet it was not totally one Triple Alliance against another. Italy, allied by treaty with Germany and Austria, declared its neutrality. The government, under its canny prime minister, Giovanni Giolitti, had decided to sit on the fence and see how events transpired.

Trieste, with its multi-national, multi-cultural population, was now a city of dangerously divided loyalties. The German-speaking population was anti-Slav,and vice versa, but, for the majority of Italian speakers, life could remain tolerably normal only as long as Italy stayed neutral. For individuals, some difficult choices had to be made. Joyce had a British passport, and, in early August, Austria went to war with Britain. Svevo had an Austrian imperial passport, but the Veneziani family were Italian. Later, Austrian naval officials came to inspect the Servola factory to see if it could increase its output, and there was an argument about the terms of the existing contract between the Imperial navy and the Venezianis. After that, Svevo set out on a prearranged visit to Germany. The German navy was one of the few European navies not to use the Moravia Anti-Fouling Composition, and Svevo met with naval personnel and a factory owner who were anxious to import the paint.

This trip caused Svevo great soul-searching. He was both Francophile and Anglophile, and already the Germans had invaded Belgium and were heading towards Paris. Over the past six years he had spent many months staying at 67 Church Lane, Charlton. He was fascinated by England, the English and their politics. He had written about them for *Il Piccolo della Sera* and his letters from London would eventually be published. Now he was an enemy alien, and as long as the war lasted, he could not visit Britain. On the other hand, he wrote to Livia that what he saw of the attitudes of the Germans impressed him. They seemed, despite the war, to be enthusiastic but exceedingly orderly and well-organised. Unhappily, he found it hard to imagine that such people would not be victorious. He wrote to Livia: 'You know how dear I hold the interests of the firm, but this time I cannot bring myself to desire its interests.'[8] Whatever Svevo's feelings, the Germans placed an order for eight and a half tons of the Veneziani paint. To all Svevo's other inner conflicts was now added divided national and professional loyalties. Further straining his scruples was his trip to Vienna to make sure that the naval authorities did not intend to take over the company, but to allow it to continue to be their supplier.

While Svevo was reluctantly involved in these business dealings, and avidly following the progress of the war, Joyce ignored it. He despised cruelty and violence of any kind and retired into his own world. As if to further illustrate his point to Stanislaus – 'I'm not interested in politics' – he decided to put *A Portrait* and *Ulysses* to one side, and develop a new idea. This harked back to two questions that Svevo had recently put to him: why was everything he wrote always set in Dublin? Why didn't he set something in Trieste for a change? Joyce could have riposted justifiably that everything Svevo wrote took place in Trieste. He pondered Svevo's questions, and, in the summer of 1914, decided it was indeed time that he wrote something with Trieste as a background. It would not be a book, but a long prose poem, an erotic love story.

In his journal, Svevo recorded an odd statement that an angry Joyce had made to him on his return from Dublin in 1912. He was still smarting from his treatment there and said 'what is certain is that I am more virtuous than all that lot – I, who am a real monogamist and have never loved but once in my life.'[9] The love of Joyce's life was undoubtedly Nora, but that did not mean he was not, from time to time, attracted to other women. He was particularly attracted to young Jewish women. He found them beguilingly Eastern and exotic, and there were several among his pupils in Trieste and later in Zurich. The one he seems to have most desired was Amalia Popper, the daughter of a wealthy businessman, to whom he gave lessons in the family home during most of 1913 and 1914. She becomes the subject of his poem, but though Joyce describes her and her origins, he never gives this pupil a name. She is: 'Rounded and ripened: rounded by the lathe of intermarriage and ripened in the forcing-house of the seclusion of her race.'[10]

What Joyce wrote was highly autobiographical. The frustrated suitor in the story was the young woman's teacher, who taught her at her home. Its style is highly free-associative and multilingual, its locations varied, but all associated with Joyce himself:

> 'I expound Shakespeare to docile Trieste: Hamlet, quoth I, who is most courteous to the gentle and simple, is rude only to Polonius.'[11]

Then the tutor is now in France:

> In the raw veiled spring morning faint odours float of morning Paris: aniseed, damp sawdust, hot dough of bread: and as I cross the Pont Saint Michel the steelblue waking waters chill my heart.[12]

He recalls Padua, where he had taken his teaching examinations a year before:

> Padua far beyond the sea. The silent middle age, night, darkness of history sleeps in the Piazza delle Erbe under the moon. The city sleeps. Under the arches in the dark streets near the river the whores' eyes spy out the fornicators. Cinque servizi per cinque franchi.[13]

And finally he is back with his seductive pupil:

> She coils towards me along the crumpled lounge. I cannot move or speak. Coiling approach of starborn flesh. Adultery of wisdom....
> –Jim, love![14]

That sounds like Nora's voice; she was the only woman who called him Jim.

> Soft sucking lips kiss my left armpit: a coiling kiss on myriad veins. I burn! I crumple like a burning leaf! From my right armpit a fang of flame leaps out. A starry snake has kissed me; a cold night snake. I am lost!
> –Nora![15]

Is that a cry for help? Who kissed his armpit? Or is it only a dream, and he wakes up in bed next to Nora? These lines are ambiguous, oblique, and much of the story reads as if Joyce is flexing his poetic muscles, a dry run for the epic to come. A consummation of the relationship between teacher and pupil never takes place either in the story or in reality. The actual lessons with Amalia Popper stopped early in 1914, before he started writing about her. It was written in his best calligraphic handwriting and stopped after sixteen pages. Not trying to disguise its unashamedly autobiographical nature, he called it *Giacomo Joyce* and put it in a drawer. It was found among his papers and finally published in 1968. Amalia Popper was to appear only once more in his life, but not until 1933. By then she was Signora Risolo and living in Florence. She wrote to Joyce asking permission to translate *Dubliners* into Italian. He granted it, clearly having great faith in the English he had taught her.

Joyce now went back to the reality of the Dublin of his earlier life and concentrated on writing the remaining chapters of *A Portrait of the Artist as a Young Man* for Harriet Weaver, Ezra Pound and *The Egoist*. Outside on the streets of Trieste, however, Joyce would have become aware of the realities of war. There were starting to be shortages of certain commodities, prices were shooting up, and the commercial life of the big port was running down. Britain and Austria were now at war and on 17 September 1914, as the new term was about to begin at the Scuola di Commercio, Joyce was informed that his post there had been suspended by the Ministry of Education on account of his being an enemy alien. Owing to conscription and to the more serious problems of wartime, people had other things on their mind than learning English. The number of Joyce's private pupils began to shrink. He was increasingly dependent on what he earned as the correspondence clerk at the Veneziani factory.

What Joyce and Stanislaus were unaware of was that the Austrian security police were taking an interest in them, as they investigated foreigners with known suspect political allegiances. Joyce was very quiet about his irridendist sympathies. Stanislaus was not. He spoke freely about them, and was a strident socialist to boot. On 9 January

1915, he was arrested and sent to an Austrian detention centre at the Schloss Kirchberg, north of Vienna, where he would stay for the rest of the war. Even though relations between the brothers had cooled considerably, this came as a great blow to the Joyces. Joyce tried to remain indifferent to the war, keeping his head down and writing. He went back to *Exiles* and pushed on with another chapter of *Ulysses*. He was interrupted by a family celebration. His sister Eileen, who was again living with them, had become engaged to Frantisek Schaurek, a Czech bank cashier working in Trieste. They were married on 15 April 1915. Joyce attended the ceremony in a borrowed morning suit. Soon after, with the possibility of war looming, Eileen and her husband went to live in the comparative safety of Prague. Joyce took on a bet, a case of wine, that Italy would not enter the war. The fifty per cent of the population of Trieste who were Italian felt the same way. Italy itself was divided on the issue of joining either side in the war.

The Italian government, still under Giolitti's premiership, continued to play both sides of the battlefield. Like the other major powers, Italy was greedy for empire. Though arriving late in the field, the capture of Libya and Cyrenaica in 1908 was a start towards making the Mediterranean *mare nostrum* again. Italy's ambition was to do the same with the Adriatic. Gioletti's government negotiated to join the Austrian-German side if, after victory, they were guaranteed the Trentino region and Trieste as a free city. The Austrians firmly rejected these conditions. Almost simultaneously, the Italians were talking to France and Britain about joining them for a bigger slice of the cake, not just the Trentino and Trieste itself, but Istria and a long stretch of the Dalmatian coast (today's Croatia). The allied powers agreed, and the secret Treaty of London was signed on 26 April 1915. Rumours were circulating around Trieste, defences began going up, and Italians started leaving the city. Italy declared war on Austro-Hungary and Germany on 23 May. That night there was extensive rioting in Trieste. Austrian and Slav mobs burned the offices of Italian companies and newspapers. Italian supporters responded by attacking public buildings. Troops were called in to suppress the violence. Joyce had lost his bet, and he and Nora felt increasingly insecure. Some of the population were being evacuated, and known Italian sympathisers were being arrested. Even Joyce realised it was time to leave. He went to the American consul who, because of the war, now represented British interests. Joyce's passport was in order and the consul could issue a visa, but the Joyces still needed permission from the Austrian authorities to leave the country for Switzerland. They had decided to go to Zurich where they knew a few families. In view of what had happened to Stanislaus and other expatriates, Joyce now knew he must leave quickly, and he needed help. He turned again to his two most influential ex-pupils, Baron Ralli and Count Sordina, and he waited while they tried to speed up the bureaucratic wheels.

Joyce was not to escape the Great War without hearing a shot fired. Only a week after war was declared, the Italian Army started its offensive across the River Isonzo, which marked the border between Italy and Austria. It was only 25 kilometres north of Trieste, and the rumble of the first artillery bombardments were clearly heard in the city. The Irridentists were confident the Italian Army would soon be in the streets of the city. This was excessively over-optimistic. In the three-and-half years of the war, there were to be twelve separate battles of the Isonzo, and the Italian army was never to reach Trieste.

All four Joyces were finally issued with visas and, leaving behind their furniture and most of their books, they left Trieste on 28 June 1915 for Zurich, the city where they had spent their brief honeymoon. They had been living in Trieste for eleven years. Joyce and Nora had never lived anywhere else together. Joyce later said: 'I met more kindness in Trieste than I ever met anywhere else.' In his 1926 lecture on Joyce in Milan, Svevo spoke touchingly of Joyce's life and works in Trieste since his arrival, quite by chance, in 1904:

> He had in his pockets, besides the small sum necessary for his long journey, various manuscripts: most of the poems that were to be published in *Chamber Music*, and some of the stories of *Dubliners*. All his other works down to *Ulysses* were born in Trieste. His two children were born here, so one can understand that we Triestines have a right to regard him with deep affection as if he belonged in a certain sense to us.... In his lively mind points of contact between the two cities

[Dublin and Trieste] were certainly established. That could easily be: Trieste was for him a little Ireland which he was able to contemplate with more detachment than he could in his own country....Joyce's outward life in Trieste can be summed up as a spirited struggle to support his family. His inner life was complex but already clear-cut: the elaboration of the subject matter offered him by his childhood and youth. A piece of Ireland was ripening under our sun. But the struggle cost him dear; for the life of a gerund-monger is not an easy one.[16]

Svevo himself was now giving the answer to the very question he had asked Joyce two years previously – why, living in Trieste, was he always writing about Dublin? Svevo went on to quote from one of Joyce's favourite philosophers, the sixteenth-century Italian Giordano Bruno:

'No man can be a lover of the true or the good unless he abhors the multitude; and the artist, though he may employ the crowd, must be very careful to isolate himself.' Thus was Stephen Dedalus born.... Thus too, I must add, was James Joyce born, the law of whose life was to be aristocratic solitude. A goodly measure of independence and – let me put it more bluntly – of arrogance accompanied him along the paths he was to travel alone, judged and restrained by no one.[17]

Svevo was summing up Joyce's character as a man and an artist with great insight. It must have cost him some soul-searching to do so. For these were the characteristics that Svevo most admired in Joyce and felt most lacking in himself. It was this lack that had always stopped him from committing himself sufficiently to writing. On this subject he was, to the end of his life, at odds with himself. The departure of Joyce from Trieste deprived Svevo of a friend who, whatever his 'arrogance', always stimulated him. He was not to see Joyce again for four years.

At a practical level, another departure affected Svevo even more, both for better and for worse. The Veneziani family were known for their irredentist sympathies. Gioachino and Olga were Italian citizens, and saw the writing on the wall just in time. On 24 June, four days before Joyce, they too headed initially for Switzerland. In July, the government decreed that all business concerns must be owned by Austrian citizens.

The factory was about to be requisitioned by the War Ministry and a naval engineer was put in charge, but Gioachino and Olga found a legal loophole. Livia was an Austrian citizen by virtue of her marriage to Svevo, and her parents now re-registered the Veneziani Company under the name of Ettore and Livia Schmitz. The Austrian navy needed their paint, so from now on they had to do business with Herr and Frau Schmitz.

'It's an ill wind that blows nobody any good', although Svevo might have contested how much good the wind of war actually brought him. An immediate good was that he was finally free of the professional pressure of his in-laws. Olga was endlessly demanding and Gioachino dangerously impulsive. Svevo was now almost his own master. Austrian officers and their families were billeted in the Villa Veneziani. One of them was an Imperial Commissioner whose duty was to oversee the factory and see that it met its government contracts on schedule. He was a Czechoslovak with anti-Austrian feelings and he and Svevo became good friends. Svevo was left alone to run the business. It was, however, only the business in Trieste. Gioachino and Olga Veneziani had by now moved to London and installed themselves at 67 Church Lane, Charlton, and were running the factory and offices there. In Murano, their nephew, Luigi Oberti, ran the Veneziani factory. Yet Svevo was the titular head of a highly profitable international company, supplying the navies of five of the six major combatants in the War. The Russian navy was alone in not using the Moravia Anti-Fouling Composition. Svevo was a political liberal and a pacifist who wanted to be a novelist, not a war-profiteering paint-maker. It was this inner conflict that finally bore fruit in his post-war novel. Not for nothing did he call it *La coscienza di Zeno*. Subsequent editions in English are called, depending on the translation, either *The Confessions of Zeno* or *Zeno's Conscience*.

Meanwhile in the peaceful cleanliness of Zurich – Joyce found it unbearably clean – he was observing almost exactly the same routine as he had in Trieste. He moved apartments five times in four years, gave English lessons, and he wrote. By October 1915 he had started on the third chapter of *Ulysses*.

CHAPTER NINE

Separated by Mountains

THE HISTORIC FOCUS OF THE Great War has always been on the four years of horrendous trench warfare between the British, French and German armies in Flanders and northern France, and their appalling casualty figures. With the spread of still and newsreel photography and the work of war artists, the visual images of life and death on the Western Front have survived vividly for subsequent generations. The conflict that took place between the Italian and Austrian armies along their border from June 1915 to November 1918 was largely forgotten. As Jan Morris wrote in her book on Trieste, 'It was a war that English-language history has largely left to Hemingway.'[1] Hemingway had been a nineteen-year-old American volunteer ambulance-driver with the Italian army and was badly wounded at the front in July 1918. He was to use his experience as the setting for his best-selling novel *Farewell to Arms*, published only twelve years later.

Known as The White War – it was fought mostly in snowy and sub-Alpine conditions – it more than rivalled the campaign on the Western Front in its hardship and slaughter. The tactics of attrition were very similar: an initial artillery bombardment, often lasting for twenty-four hours, announced the location of the coming attack. Then waves of infantry with fixed bayonets charged across the no-man's land that had been created, to be met by enemy artillery and machine-gun fire. Over several days, the casualties on both sides would mount into the thousands and only a kilometre of territory might have temporarily changed hands. On the first day of the Battle of the Somme in 1916, 19,000 British soldiers were killed and 30,000 wounded. It was to remain the record for one day's fighting in the Great War. The carnage on the Western Front raged back and forth over bleak flat fields and trenches, whereas on the Southern Front, Italians and Austrians were fighting each other in mountainous country, often in sub-zero temperatures. The Austrians invariably held the high ground, and were firing down on the Italians charging uphill, who inevitably sustained heavier casualties.

For the first two-and-a-half years of this war General Luigi Cadorna commanded the Italian army. In military terms he was so conservative as to make the Allied generals on the Western Front seem positively enlightened. He ignored the advice of his staff, bullied his subordinates, and believed in superior numbers rather than in adaptable tactics. The government found him, and the huge sacrifices he demanded of his troops, hard to control. Because of the uncertainty about whether or not Italy was going to join in the war and, if so, on which side, the majority of its soldiers were quickly assembled and poorly trained. Many were peasants from the south, illiterate, and with no idea of why they were fighting. Conditions in the Army were primitive. On the front lines there were shortages of food and warm clothing, and virtually no sanitation. Not surprisingly, morale was low and Cadorna hugely unpopular. The punishments meted out to the troops were of a severity unknown in the British, French or German armies. If an Italian battalion was deemed not to have acquitted itself bravely in action, one soldier in ten was taken out and shot by firing squad. Inevitably, there was much desertion and, if caught, deserters were summarily executed. Italians taken as prisoners of war were promptly forgotten about – even the food and clothing parcels sent by their families were not forwarded to them. They became totally dependent on their Austrian captors, and of the 600,000 Italian prisoners of war, 100,000 died in captivity.

Many of the pitched battles took place on the Carso, the long, high limestone plateau that runs behind Trieste, most of which is now in Slovenia. It stretches fifty kilometres northwards to the river Isonzo, and became the most disputed territory in the war, with casualty figures which almost rivalled the British record on the Somme. For the people of Trieste, nearly all the artillery bombardments could be heard in the distance and seen as flashes in the night sky. For three years this made the war a constant presence, like some unpredictable and angry neighbour. It quickly took its toll on the everyday life of the city. The population was almost halved, basic commodities were in short supply, businesses shut down and commercial activity in the port shrank. There was censorship of all mail coming into and out of the city, as well as of newspapers. Close as the action was, it was still hard to get any overall impression of what was happening. One day there would be gossip that the Italian army was advancing on Trieste; a few days later it had fallen back after yet another battle along the Isonzo.

In Svevo's posthumously published novel *The Nice Old Man and the Pretty Girl*, his protagonist is always referred to as the Old Man. When he hears the artillery fire in the city, the Old Man asks: 'Why haven't they yet invented a way of killing each other without making so much noise?'[2] Since the Villa Veneziani at Servola was close to the port and the refuelling depot, Svevo and Livia frequently had to take shelter from Italian air raids. With the family and many of their friends scattered, Svevo and Livia now led a somewhat isolated life, concentrating on running the factory efficiently to prevent it being totally requisitioned by the Austrian authorities. Although Svevo deplored the war and its increasingly terrible consequences, he saw no alternative but to continue as titular head of the family business. In *The Nice Old Man and the Pretty Girl* he writes, 'Every sign of war that the Old Man witnessed reminded him with a pang that he was making plenty of money out of it. The war brought him wealth and degradation.'[3] Svevo found it impossible to concentrate on writing a novel and went back to playing the violin for comfort. It was also the only activity he had found that could not be combined with smoking. For Svevo, one of the great crises of the war occurred in March 1916 when the city ran out of tobacco. There was rioting, and when supplies were finally resumed, tobacconists' shops were broken into as smokers made sure of their fair share. Svevo did not join in the violence, but managed to buy a year's supply. He hoped this would last him for the duration of the war. He was being unduly optimistic. Meanwhile he and Livia kept up a correspondence with

James Joyce in Zurich in 1915.
(COURTESY: BEINECKE RARE BOOK AND MANUSCRIPT LIBRARY)

Italo Svevo in 1892. Photograph by Umberto Veruda.
(MUSEO SVEVIANO, TRIESTE)

TOP LEFT: *Plaque to Leopold Bloom at 52 Upper Clanbrassil Street, Dublin.* (AUTHOR PHOTO)

BOTTOM LEFT: *With a branch in London, the Veneziani product was in huge demand in the naval build-up to the Great War.* (AUTHOR PHOTO)

RIGHT: *Wall plaques at 32, via San Nicolò, Trieste.*
1. *Joyce and his brother Stanislaus lived together on the third floor in 1907.*
2. *The Berlitz School opened here in 1905 on the first floor.*
3. *Italo Svevo arranged his English lessons here with James Joyce.* (AUTHOR PHOTO)

RIGHT: *The wedding of Italo Svevo and Livia Veneziani on 30 July, 1896. It was a civil ceremony. A year later Svevo agreed to be married in church.*

(MUSEO SVEVIANO, TRIESTE)

Nora, Giorgio and Lucia Joyce in Zurich,
where they spent most of the 1914-1918 War.

Livia, Letizia and Svevo in 1906. Letizia was nine. 1906, Trieste.
(MUSEO SVEVIANO, TRIESTE)

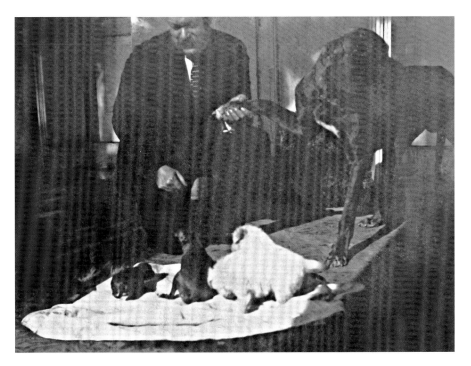

Joyce left his dog, Fido, with Svevo when he went on a trip to Dublin.
Two days later Fido had a litter of puppies.
(MUSEO SVEVIANO, TRIESTE)

Paris, 1924: A studio portrait of the Joyce Family, James, Nora, Lucia and Giorgio. Joyce had become a celebrity after publication of Ulysses *in 1922.*

Nora Barnacle, James Joyce and their solicitor, on their way to their marriage in the Registry Office, Kensington on 4 July 1931. They had been living together for twenty-seven years.
(COURTESY: GETTY IMAGES)

LEFT: *The statue of Joyce, unveiled in October 2004, on the bridge over the Canal Grande in Trieste.*
(AUTHOR PHOTO)

RIGHT: *Anna Livia Plurabelle in its original location in O'Connell Street, Dublin. Joyce asked permission from Svevo and Livia to use her name and long hair for the spirit of the river Liffey in Finnegans Wake.*
(PHOTO BY PIOLINFAX CC BY-SA 3.0)

BELOW: *Anna Livia Plurabelle. In 2011, as it was attracting rubbish, Anna Livia was re-designed and moved to a safer location by the Liffey.*
(PHOTO BY WILLIAM MURPHY CC BY-SA 2.0)

their daughter, Letizia, who was still staying with her aunt and uncle in Florence. Despite the censorship, they also tried to keep in contact with other relations and friends abroad. Two of Livia's married sisters and their families had joined the considerable Triestine community in Zurich, and through them Svevo had news of Joyce, from whom they were still taking English lessons.

In fact, in Zurich the Joyce family's life continued much as it had done in Trieste. They moved hotels and apartments several times. Giorgio and Lucia learned German to go to school. Nora also tried in order to find some social life in the expatriate community. When not teaching, Joyce found new drinking friends and continued working on *Ulysses*. In fact, Zurich was the perfect place for anyone trying to escape the general European catastrophe and get on with their own lives. It seemed symbolic that the city was virtually equidistant from the Western and the Southern Fronts. Here, Joyce stayed in touch with the outside world, but also to insulate himself from it. Several of the English people he met commented on how uninterested he was in the war, to the point of not seeming to care who won. One outside political event, however, did affect him emotionally – if only briefly. In April 1916, he heard the news of the Easter Rising in Dublin. He followed it with very mixed emotions. Patrick Pearse, the leader of the Rising, had been Joyce's first teacher of Irish. Joyce had never liked him or agreed with his narrow, nationalistic ideals, but later he was appalled to hear of his former teacher's execution. Joyce was also shocked to learn that his friend from college days, Francis Sheehy Skeffington, with whom he had written his first published essay, 'The Day of the Rabblement',[4] had been killed. A firm pacifist and idealist, Skeffington had been trying to stop the poor from looting Dublin shops when he was arrested by a British officer and shot without trial. The officer was later found guilty of murder but judged to be insane. This was small comfort to friends and family. Joyce had been friendly with the whole Skeffington family and wrote them a long letter of condolence. He deplored the violence in Dublin and felt it would lead to nothing. Richard Ellmann describes Joyce's attitude to Ireland at the time as 'balanced between bitterness and nostalgia'.[5] He declined invitations from the Swiss press to write any analysis of the Rising. Joyce seemed determined to maintain his own political and emotional neutrality, and concentrate on his own work.

In August 1916, Joyce's complex attitudes to Ireland and its place in the British Empire were to be further complicated by the activities of his great supporter Ezra Pound. Pound had discovered that there was a benefit for worthy individuals called Civil List pension. It was granted at the personal behest of the prime minister, and very occasionally granted to deserving artists. W.B. Yeats had recently received one. Pound decided that the impoverished Joyce, with his growing reputation, and living abroad in a neutral country, would be a worthy beneficiary. Pound now had to pull the right strings, but he was nothing if not well-connected. He started with W.B. Yeats, who agreed that it was a good idea. The next string was the literary socialite Lady Maud Cunard, who knew about Joyce's work. She loaned what she had – *Dubliners*, *Chamber Music* and some extracts from *A Portrait* in *The Egoist* – to her friend Eddie Marsh, who just happened to be the personal secretary to the current prime minister, Herbert Asquith. Marsh was a highly influential literary dilettante. He took a few informed soundings and then recommended Joyce to the prime minister. On 16 August 1916, Joyce was awarded a Civil List pension of £100 per annum (equivalent of about £3,500 today) for the rest of his life. His British passport was now complemented by government patronage.

This was only the beginning of a much-needed change to Joyce's financial circumstances in Zurich. In February 1917, he received a registered letter from a firm of solicitors in London:

> We are instructed to write to you on behalf of an admirer of your writing, who desires to be anonymous, to say that we are to forward you a cheque for £50 on the 1st May, August, November and February next, making a total of £200, which we hope you will accept without any enquiry as to the source of the gift.
>
> We trust that this letter will reach you, the address having been taken by our client from 'Who's Who' for 1917.
>
> Yours faithfully,
> Slack Munro Saw & Co.[6]

Joyce was intensely curious about the identity of his admirer, but Harriet Shaw Weaver had covered her tracks very carefully. Despite numerous enquiries, Joyce did not discover that it was her until three years later. At a stroke Joyce's income had increased, at today's value by £10,000 per annum. Harriet Weaver's contribution continued over the years and included the purchase of government war bonds in Joyce's name. It has been estimated that over his lifetime Harriet Weaver contributed nearly £2 million to Joyce, an extraordinary act of literary philanthropy. As Richard Ellmann was neatly to express it, 'Harriet Weaver's benefaction did not make Joyce rich, but it made it possible for him to be poor only through determined extravagance.'[7]

Concurrent with his financial improvement – though he still thought of himself as impoverished – Joyce's reputation was growing in literary circles. In London, the serialisation of *A Portrait* and its subsequent publication led to reviews in various literary magazines. H.G. Wells gave it a glowing review in *The Nation,* and Pound, naturally, did too, with enthusiastic quotes from Yeats and T.S. Eliot. There was now interest in his work from America too. As if to prove that lightning could strike twice, on 27 February 1918 Joyce was invited to call on the manager of the Eidgenössische Bank of Zurich, who informed him that a client who admired his work wished to give him a fellowship of a thousand francs a month. This amount at today's value would be worth around £4,000 per annum. This time Joyce managed to discover the identity of his benefactor. She was Mrs. Edith McCormack (née Rockefeller), an American resident of Zurich. Because of the war, the neutral city had become a cosmopolitan centre of art and culture, and Mrs. McCormack had become one of its most generous sponsors. Joyce personally thanked her and presented her with autographed copies of his work.

Mrs. McCormack also subsidised the work of Carl Jung at the clinic he helped to run in the city. It was Jung, however, who was to cause a rift between Joyce and his new benefactor. After six months of her regular cheques, Mrs. McCormack told Joyce that, despite her conviction that he was a great artist, she still felt he would benefit enormously by an analysis with Dr. Jung, for which she would gladly pay. Joyce's views on psychoanalysis had not mellowed and he politely declined. Shortly after this, Mrs. McCormack's monthly payments ceased. Two years later, Joyce was to refer to this experience in a letter to Harriet Weaver. He was anxious to an almost paranoid degree, as money was involved, that she might hear rumours about his behaviour, particularly about his drinking habits:

> A nice collection of legends could be made of legends about me. Here are some. My family believe that I enriched myself in Switzerland during the war by espionage work for one or both combatants....The general rumour in Dublin was (till the prospectus of *Ulysses* stopped it) that I could write no more, had broken down and was dying in New York. A man from Liverpool told me that I was the owner of several cinema theatres all over Switzerland. In America there appear to be, or have been, two versions: one that I was almost blind, emaciated and consumptive, the other that I am an austere mixture of the Dalai Lama and Sir Rabindranath Tagore.... A batch of people in Zurich persuaded themselves that I was gradually going mad and actually endeavoured to induce me to enter a sanatorium where a certain Doctor Jung (the Swiss Tweedledum who is not to be confused with the Viennese Tweedledee, Dr. Freud) amuses himself at the expense (in every sense of the word) of ladies and gentleman who are troubled with bees in their bonnet.[8]

As Joyce's literary reputation grew, so too did the gossip about his eccentricity. Never averse to publicity, Joyce both encouraged and denied it. There is no record of an answer to this letter, but Harriet Weaver's financial support did not falter, although she was never reconciled to Joyce's drinking.

Joyce's closest friend in Zurich was Frank Budgen. The same age as Joyce, Budgen was English, a self-educated, ex-sailor turned painter. He became Joyce's most frequent drinking partner. Joyce would talk to him, in great detail, about *Ulysses* and its creative problems, and soon even became indispensable as a sounding board. Joyce also took advantage of Budgen's studio for one of his more bizarre adventures. His eyesight had continued to deteriorate in Zurich, and he had two delicate and painful operations there in 1917. However, in December

1918 his sight was still just good enough for him to spot, through his study window, an attractive young woman in the apartment across the courtyard. He could see her in her bathroom and bedroom. She was in her early twenties, and had the dark and seemingly exotic look that always attracted Joyce, and which he associated with Jewish women. He discovered that her name was Marthe Fleischmann and that she was in fact Jewish. She was also the mistress of a local engineer, Rudolf Hiltpold. Joyce saw her in the street, found her glamorous, and followed her. He noticed she had a slight limp, a small detail that was to have literary consequences. He wrote her an admiring letter and sent her a copy of *Chamber Music*. Marthe, flattered by the attention of a published writer, agreed to meet him. He asked for a date, and she suggested 2 February. Joyce was delighted by the coincidence that it was his birthday. He needed a discreet, artistic location for the assignation, and Frank Budgen's studio was the obvious place. Initially, he was reluctant to help. Budgen liked Nora and had scruples about being complicit in Joyce's planned infidelity. Joyce eventually prevailed upon him with the line, 'If I permitted myself any restraint in this matter, it would be spiritual death to me.'[9] As a great admirer of Joyce's spirit, Budgen presumably did not want the responsibility for any diminution of it.

Joyce now planned appropriate lighting for the event. He had recently visited a Jewish friend, Rudolph Goldschmidt, and remembered seeing in his apartment a menorah, the eight-branched ceremonial candlestick used for celebrating the festival of Chanukah. Joyce felt nothing could be more appropriate than this for lighting the studio when he met his Jewish guest. He borrowed the menorah, and Marthe was shown Budgen's paintings by candlelight. What else happened is not totally clear. Joyce later boasted that he had 'explored the hottest and coldest parts of a woman's body'.[10] Budgen does not seem to have enquired what the 'coldest parts' were, but seemed convinced that no greater consummation had taken place. Joyce and Marthe did not meet again for some time, but exchanged letters. A few months later, Joyce received an angry letter from Rudolf Hiltpold asking him to stop his attentions to Marthe. By then, Joyce had already decided that discretion was the better part of valour.

In early 1918 Joyce and another Zurich friend, Claud Sykes, co-founded the English Players, a semi-professional acting group based at the British Consulate. Sykes was the producer-director, while Joyce, reincarnating himself as an entrepreneur, became the business manager. Their first production, chosen by Joyce, was Wilde's *The Importance of Being Earnest*. After the opening night, Joyce became involved in a furious row with Henry Carr, who was playing the leading role of Algernon Moncrieff. Carr had been an amateur actor, had served in the Great War, been wounded and invalided out of the army. He was now a minor consular official. He apparently gave a brilliant performance, and was deeply offended that Joyce did not reimburse him fully for the hiring of his costume. He brought a lawsuit against Joyce, who riposted by counter-suing for Carr's non-payment for five house-tickets and also for libel. The cases took six months to come to court. Joyce won the first case and finally withdrew from the second. He was ordered to pay costs, which he never did. He did, however, make a lifelong enemy of Henry Carr.

This farcical lawsuit came to the attention of the playwright Tom Stoppard, and he uses it at the end of Act One of *Travesties*, his play set in Zurich in 1917/18. Carr is describing his cross-examination of Joyce in court. He disdainfully asks him: 'And what did you do in the war, Mr. Joyce?'

'I wrote *Ulysses*. What did you do?'

The stage direction reads BLACK OUT.[11]

CHAPTER TEN

Enter Zeno

IF SVEVO HAD TO ANSWER THE question of what he had done in the war, he would have had to admit that, despite his pro-Italian irredentist sympathies, he had supplied maritime paint to the Imperial Austro-Hungarian navy. Much as he deplored the war and its ever-growing slaughter, Svevo saw no alternative to continuing his business, so that his family would survive. He could not, like Joyce, exonerate himself by claiming that he was writing a great novel. That had to wait, but at least he was now, as Joyce had always been, his own man, steering his way through extraordinary times. Because his political sympathies were suspect, Svevo was occasionally taken in by the security police for questioning. He always talked his way out of it, and he had friends in high places, especially among the senior officers now billeted in the Villa Veneziani. Since these officers came from different parts of the Habsburg Empire, their own loyalty to Vienna was by no means total.

In December 1915 Svevo ignored the censorship to reply to birthday greetings from Letizia in Florence. He was fifty-five.

> The best wish would be to see this period over. It is far too long. Do you remember how you left after a few moments' discussion? You seemed to be going off on holiday and instead you were off for a long spell at school. I no longer write fairy tales. Reality is far too distracting for my daydreams – if one can put it that way. I'm becoming a very serious businessman.... Up to a couple of weeks ago I played the violin a little while every day. Then fresh preoccupations came up, nothing serious, just business difficulties which had to be tackled, and that too was abandoned.[1]

But, during the war, Svevo always kept himself occupied intellectually. He returned to reading Freud, and in this he was stimulated by one of his favourite nephews, Aurelio Finzi, a doctor with an interest in psychology. Finzi had been conscripted into the Army, was wounded and came to stay to recuperate at the Villa Veneziani. Together they set about translating Freud's *On Dreams* into Italian. At the same time, Svevo embarked on a self-analysis. It was not a procedure of which Freud, or any of his colleagues, would have approved. Svevo did not pursue it for long, but it was an encouraging sign that the seeds of *Zeno* were starting to sprout.

Svevo may not have been writing fairy tales or a novel, but he was an inveterate scribbler, in notebooks and on bits of paper. In June 1917, he started on a memoir:

> An old man is almost bound to be an orderly man. Now I am 56 I have three kinds of spectacles to look after – a great training in tidiness. So I can take up this volume of memoirs with the firm knowledge I shall carry it through to its end. So many things that were important to me have vanished from my mind; it's a great cause of regret to me….I shall end up imagining I too have always been as I am today, though at present I can still remember loves and hatreds I have long stopped feeling…. The essential thing is not what one desires, but how one desires it. I don't know whether I lost the things I was attached to out of laziness or because of fate, or whether the things I hated dogged me because I was too feeble or because they were too strong….Four years ago, before the world war, I took a long journey all over Europe. On my way, I wished all the fields I passed a good harvest and the peasants, in all their different costumes, a good reward for their labour. I felt I had done a great thing by this, and that Napoleon might have envied me. So when the War broke out, each new terror and disaster seemed a pointless waste; I had no need for a war to unload my hatreds.[2]

By the autumn of 1917, the White War had reached a stalemate at an enormous cost in casualties. Fifty kilometres north of Trieste the battlefields moved a few kilometres back and forth across the river Isonzo. With grandiose appeals to their Italian patriotism and honour, General Cadorna threw more and more men into futile attacks. On both sides there were manpower and raw material shortages. Because of all its increasingly disaffected nationalities, the war was also threatening the cohesion of the Habsburg Empire. On the Western Front, there was a similar stalemate. The Austrian Emperor appealed to the German Kaiser for military help.

In October 1917 the Bolshevik Revolution took Russia out of the war, and the German Army was able to withdraw most of its troops from the Eastern Front. Six divisions, with artillery support, were transferred to join the Austrian Army on the Southern Front. On 24 October the combined force attacked at Caporetto, a small village in the foothills of the Alps. General Cadorna was not properly prepared for the speed and weight of this attack. The Italians retreated. The retreat soon turned into a rout, despite Cadorna's exhortation that 'whoever does not feel that he wins or falls with honour on the line of resistance is not fit to live.'[3]

The defeat at Caporetto became the greatest humiliation in Italian history since reunification. The word became synonymous with disaster. In Hemingway's *Farewell to Arms*, his protagonist, Frederick Henry, a Red Cross volunteer, looks back at all the over-blown Italian rhetoric of the time:

> I was always embarrassed by the words sacred, glorious, and sacrifice and the expression, in vain…. I had seen nothing sacred, and the things that were glorious had no glory….There were many words that you could not stand to hear and finally only the names of places had dignity….Abstract words such as glory, honor, courage, or hallow were obscene beside the concrete names of villages, the numbers of roads, the names of rivers, the numbers of regiments and the dates.[4]

When the novel came out in 1929, Mussolini made sure it was not distributed in Italy or translated into Italian. He found it detrimental to the armed forces. Its anti-militarist attitude did not suit the heroic mythology he was creating out of recent Italian history. Hemingway had already made an enemy of Mussolini. In 1923, as a correspondent for the *Toronto Daily Star*, he had been granted, with several other journalists, an interview with Mussolini at the Lausanne Conference. Hemingway wrote:

Mussolini sat at his desk reading a book, his face was contorted into the famous frown. He was registering Dictator…. I tiptoed over behind him to see what book he was reading with such avid interest. It was a French-English dictionary – held upside down.[5]

In a later piece, Hemingway referred to Mussolini as 'the biggest bluff in Europe'.

After Caporetto, the Italians were driven back into Lombardy as far as the river Piave. A war, entered into for territorial expansion, had forced them to surrender a large area of north-east Italy. Venice, Padua and Verona were now almost in the front line, and their civilian populations, as well as the occupying army, were running short of food. Despite his bungling, General Cadorna refused to resign. It took pressure from the British and French finally to persuade the Italian government to dismiss him. When British reinforcements eventually arrived, the expression 'doing a Cadorna' passed into their slang for 'coming unstuck, perpetrating an utter fuck-up and paying the price.'[6] Cadorna was replaced by General Armando Diaz, an efficient and popular commander, who spent the next nine months refitting and reforming the demoralised army.

In late 1917, the frequently hungry population of Trieste began to realise that victory by either side still lay in the distant future. What any post-war settlement would entail for the city's mixture of Austrians, Italians and Slavs remained a mystery. On the night of 9 December 1917, two large explosions rocked Trieste. The imperial battleships, the *Wien* and the *Budapest*, had just moored at the southern end of the harbour, close to the Villa Veneziani at Servola. In one of the more heroic exploits of the war, two Italian torpedo-boats, commanded by a Lieutenant Rizzo, penetrated the defences of the harbour, and fired their torpedoes. In her memoir of her husband, Livia described what happened:

The frightful explosions were followed for about ten minutes by the howling of crazed voices and then a tragic silence: it was the seamen of the *Wien* drowning in the tempestuous seas. Ettore, touched to the depths of his human feelings, and in spite of the strict blackout regulations, immediately ordered all the powerful lights in the garden to be turned on so as to allow the floundering men the encouragement and the guidance of the illumination in that stormy night.[7]

The *Wien* sank and fifty of the crew were killed or drowned. The *Budapest* was severely damaged. The Villa Veneziani and the factory became a frontline hospital. Triestines took it as an omen that the ships bore the names of the twin capitals of the Austro-Hungarian Empire.

With the withdrawal of Russia and the increasing amount of American troops and supplies arriving on the Western Front, the balance of the war was rapidly changing. For the first time a German attack was turned back and their army forced to retreat. The Habsburg Empire was experiencing nationalist revolts as well as acute domestic hardship. By mid-1918 the Allies had enough men and munitions to supplement the Italian forces in the south. Finally, there was a feeling among the Allies that the Central Powers would soon have to negotiate surrender. General Diaz, with his reinforced and reconstituted army, waited and watched the Austrian Army, ragged and hungry, on the other side of the river Piave. The German divisions that had supported them at Caporetto had now been withdrawn to fight on the Western Front. After the terrible casualties of the past year, Diaz had no enthusiasm for risking his army in another battle. He would sit it out until the start of peace negotiations. The government, however, under its new prime minister, Vittorio Orlando, had different ideas. He ordered Diaz to prepare for a new offensive. Italy's allies, forewarned of this, had been persuaded to contribute several divisions of British, French and Commonwealth troops.

Orlando's government had a variety of motives. One was certainly a matter of national pride. After the terrible *brutta figura* (loss of face) of Caporetto, the Italians could not bear that humiliation to be their last major battle. They had entered the war for territorial gain, for the Adriatic to become *mare nostrum*. Now, if peace was imminent, their negotiating position would be considerably weakened unless they could secure a last victory. A new rival was already making territorial claims along the Adriatic. If the Habsburg Empire was to break up, their ethnic entities in the Balkans – Slavs, Croats and Slovenes – were demanding, in any peace settlement, a national entity called Yugoslavia.

General Diaz had no alternative but to obey his government's orders. At least the arrival of the Allied divisions gave him superior numbers. The battle started on 23 October and lasted a week. The Austrian soldiers were hungry and demoralised. Outnumbered, outgunned, realising that peace was imminent, many deserted and headed back to Vienna and their varied Habsburg homelands. On the last day of October, the town of Vittorio Veneto, which gave its name to the battle, was captured and the whole Italian line swept forward. Two days later a ceasefire was agreed, and General Diaz wrote to his wife that the battle had been '…Caporetto in reverse. I have won the war more by my strength of heart and nerves than by any intellectual gifts, and I feel stronger, more balanced, than all of them'.[8] By 'them' he meant the politicians who had been so willing to sacrifice his soldiers' lives, and who had deplored his caution.

In Trieste, a large proportion of the population did not wait for the official armistice with the Austrians. On 30 October a large crowd of students marched through the city chanting *Viva Italia, Viva Trieste Italiana.* This became the signal for a general uprising and a crowd stormed the Municipal building and raised the Italian tricolour on the roof. On 3 November an Italian destroyer and a small flotilla of torpedo boats arrived in the harbour. General Petitti di Roreto, the governor of Venezia, disembarked and proclaimed, 'In the name of His Majesty the King of Italy, I take possession of the city of Trieste.' Svevo joined the enthusiastic crowd to witness this event in the Piazza Grande, and there is a photograph of him, contentedly smoking a cigarette, with an Italian soldier standing behind him.[9]

The feeling of liberation and exhilaration on the part of the irredentists did not last long. Conditions in the city were bad, and within weeks the ethnic and political divisions of its population flared into violence. The country had paid an enormous price – over a million dead – for entering the war, and her only reward, so far, was the dubious prize of a deeply divided and impoverished Trieste. The antipathy between Italians and Slavs had increased, as had the political gulf between the Left and the Right. A recently formed Fascist party was rapidly gaining support. In Trieste, a new Italian-language newspaper, *La Nazione*, was launched, and Svevo agreed to be on its editorial board and to write articles for them. He was careful to avoid political subjects because he was becoming increasingly pessimistic about the outcome of the peace settlement at Versailles, and its effect on the country.

In the first weeks of the peace, Svevo and Livia went to Florence to be reunited with their daughter, Letizia, and her fiancé, Antonio Fonda, now a decorated war hero. The couple returned to Trieste and were married in early 1919. The scattered members of the family gradually came home. Olga and Gioachino returned from London, and the Villa was full of family again. For Svevo, the most personal effect of all these political and domestic changes happened in March 1919. He did something he had not done for twenty-one years – he started work on a novel. He made a note in his diary about his personal 'liberation':

> It is certainly true that if Italy had not come to me I should never have thought of being able to write my novel four months after the arrival of our troops, as if it were a perfectly natural thing for a man of fifty-eight to do. With the arrogance of all released prisoners, it seemed to me I had suddenly acquired the right of an '*incolato*' [resident] for myself and my patois. [10]

Svevo turned his back on the horrors of the war, the difficult realities of the peace, and created Zeno Cosini, businessman, husband, lover, and amateur violinist. Like the protagonists of his two much earlier novels, Zeno is a highly autobiographical creation. But now, as a 'released prisoner', Svevo found he had a far richer fund of life's ironies and compromises on which to draw. It is his interest in Freud, however, that gives the novel its original viewpoint and final twist. The literary establishment may have previously rejected Svevo, but now he saw himself as making a major contribution to Italian literature. He was introducing the subject of psychoanalysis into the novel for the first time. The novel begins with an ingenious preface signed by Dr. S.:

> I am the doctor who is sometimes spoken of in unflattering terms in this novel. Anyone familiar with psychoanalysis will know to what he should attribute my patient's hostility.
>
> About psychoanalysis I shall here say nothing, for there is quite enough about it elsewhere in this book. I must apologise for having persuaded

my patient to write his autobiography. Students of psychoanalysis will turn up their noses at such unorthodox proceeding. But he was old and I hoped that in the effort of recalling his past he would bring it to life again, and that the writing of his autobiography would be a good preparation for the treatment. And I still think my idea was a good one, for it gave me some quite unexpected results, which would have been better still if the patient had not suddenly thrown up his cure just at the most interesting point, than cheating me of the fruits of my long and patient analysis of these memoirs.

So Svevo is writing in the role of both doctor and lapsed patient, but he still has a trick up his sleeve. Dr. S. continues:

I take my revenge by publishing them, and I hope he will be duly annoyed. I am quite ready, however, to share the financial spoils with him on condition that he resumes his treatment. He seemed to feel intense curiosity about himself. But he little knows what surprises lie in wait for him, if someone were to set about analysing the mass of truths and falsehoods which he has collected here.[11]

Here was a doctor, who showed no concern for the Hippocratic Oath, and sought to justify himself by offering to share the royalties with his patient. It was a preface that enabled the actual author to show his originality and wit from page one. Svevo starts by introducing psychoanalysis, and ends up by satirising it.

The novel is carefully constructed so that each chapter – Zeno's father's death, his marriage, his mistress, his business affairs – is effectively a short story in its own right. Yet it is written as though it is Zeno's actual 'confession' for his analyst. Dr.S., realising the importance of smoking for his patient, now asks him to write about how he started and how he tries to renounce it. The first chapter is called 'The Last Cigarette'. Zeno is persuaded by his wife to enter a private clinic that will cure him of his addiction. Under the eye of a bullying nurse, he replaces the torments of withdrawal with those of jealousy. He convinces himself that his wife wants him in the clinic only so she is free to have an affair with the good-looking doctor who runs it.

There is, of course, no one better qualified to write about giving up smoking than Svevo. One wall of his study was covered with the dates he had scrawled there every time he renounced cigarettes.

> I am sure a cigarette has a more poignant flavour when it is the last. The others have their own special taste too, peculiar to them, but it is less poignant. The last has an aroma all its own, bestowed by a sense of victory over itself and the sure hope of health and strength in the immediate future. The others are important too, as an assertion of one's own freedom, and when one lights them one still has a vision of that future of health and beauty, though it has moved a little off.[12]

Zeno, like his creator, is addicted to giving up things, whether it is cigarettes, a mistress, or a particular food. He has discovered that the last of anything always provides the most pleasurable and 'poignant' sensation.

Since his son-in-law, Antonio Fonda, had now joined the business, Svevo was relieved of much of the everyday work. Obsessive by nature, once he started writing, he found it hard to stop. He wrote for as long as he could every day without becoming completely anti-social, or totally neglecting his business. By the end of chapter one, Zeno has yet again failed to give up smoking, but at least he has the comfort of discovering his wife's fidelity. In chapter two, Zeno sets down for Dr. S. his relationship with his father, and faces the sense of guilt and inadequacy this has given him. The climax of this episode comes in the black comedy of the deathbed scene with his father. It is Svevo's talent for moving so seamlessly from the tragic to the comic that gives *The Confessions of Zeno* its uniquely ironic quality. Early in the novel, Zeno says:

> 'One need only remind oneself of all we men expect from life to see how very strange it is, and to arrive at the conclusion that man has found his way into it by mistake and does not really belong there.'[13]

After a twenty-one-year silence, Svevo had found his voice and was off to a flying start.

CHAPTER ELEVEN

The Plight of Trieste

THE JOYCES ALWAYS INTENDED to return to Trieste when the war was over, but it took Joyce longer to wind up his affairs in Zurich than he had intended. By 1918, thanks to the generosity of both the British government and Harriet Weaver, Joyce had achieved a measure of financial security. His literary reputation had also grown. During his time in Zurich, he had written over half of *Ulysses*, and sent it episode by episode to Ezra Pound in London. Acting as a combination of admirer and agent, Pound used his American connections to forward the chapters to *The Little Review*, a quarterly, avant-garde literary magazine edited by Margaret Anderson and Jane Heap, in New York. They were immediately enthusiastic and ran the first episode, 'Telemachus', in March 1918. They were to continue serialising *Ulysses* until December 1920, when the magazine was shut down.

The Joyces returned to Trieste in mid-October 1919. This meant that Nora had to give up her agreeable social life in Zurich and go back to speaking Triestine. For Giorgio and Lucia it meant changing schools again. More immediately, the family faced an accommodation problem. Because of a housing shortage, their old flat had been requisitioned, and their furniture and possessions put in storage. Nor were they the first Joyces to return to the city. As soon as the war ended, Eileen and her Czech husband, Frantisek Schaurek, came back from Prague with their two small children. They managed to find themselves a large flat, and were soon joined by Stanislaus, just released from his four-year internment in Austria. The experience had toughened him considerably. He had maintained an intermittent, but censored, correspondence with his brother, and had had plenty of time to consider his past relationship with him. When Joyce wrote him from Zurich in May 1919 to say that his family intended to come back to Trieste, Stanislaus replied:

> Some eight years ago I took the quarter for you, moved in and paid the first rent. Now I have paid the last rent for you and moved out. The packing up and moving out of a flat ankle-deep in dust has been a week's dirty work for Frank and Eileen. It has cost me nearly three hundred lire. I have just emerged from four years of hunger and squalor, and am trying to get on my feet again. Do you think you can give me a rest?[1]

Despite receiving this letter, Joyce, Nora, Giorgio and Lucia left Zurich in mid-October, and sent a telegram to Stanislaus to say they were on their way only when they reached Milan. It was Eileen who felt she couldn't turn them away, but her husband, Frantisek, and Stanislaus were not happy with the arrangement. It meant there were now eleven people living in the flat, including a children's nurse and a cook, and Stanislaus had to give up his large room to Joyce and Nora. It was back to the overcrowded conditions of their early years in Trieste. Because of all the Italian Triestine exiles returning home, Joyce and Nora were unsuccessful in finding another affordable flat. Stanislaus had the same problem when he tried to move out. Joyce and Stanislaus did not get on as they had before. Both men had changed. Joyce could not adjust to his brother's tougher, more independent spirit. Stanislaus no longer had any tolerance of his brother's attitudes to money or drink. To add to the tensions, it was clear that Eileen's marriage to Schaurek was not working out. The two families began to eat their dinner separately. Stanislaus ate with the Schaureks.

Joyce still had some old friends in Trieste, and Svevo was one of the first he saw. For the first time, both men were simultaneously doing the same thing in the same place – writing a novel. Joyce was delighted that his friend was making good progress and was enthusiastic about what he was writing. Svevo was anxious to catch up with Joyce's news, particularly about life in Zurich, which was, after all, the second city of psychoanalysis. Joyce was not forthcoming on the subject – 'Well, if we need it, let us keep to confession'.² Joyce was more anxious to talk about *Ulysses*, despite the linguistic difficulties. Even though Joyce had taught Svevo, the language of *Ulysses* presented special problems. The two men, preoccupied with their work, did not meet as frequently as they had done before. It was Bloom and Zeno who kept them apart.

Joyce always had a great need to talk about his work while he was creating it. He showed Stanislaus the chapters of *Ulysses* he had completed in Zurich. Their relationship was further strained when Stanislaus did not give the reaction Joyce was used to – admiring, but, if critical, at least constructive. Stanislaus showed too obviously that he was becoming bored with the novel's linguistic complexities. He had his own social life now in Trieste and didn't want to be dragged back into being his brother's sounding board or his keeper. He was never to doubt Joyce's genius, only the direction it was taking. In these circumstances, Joyce increasingly missed the friendship of Frank Budgen. He wrote him:

> Need I tell you what a great privation it is to me to have not within earshot your over-patient and friendly self? …. Not a soul to talk to about Bloom. Lent two chapters to one or two people, but they know as much about it as the parliamentary side of my arse.³

Before he left Zurich, Joyce had made Budgen promise that he would come and visit him in Trieste. Now he wrote him plaintive letters, urging him to come, and when Budgen admitted that he could not afford the fare, Joyce offered to pay half and made efforts to find him a studio they could share. There was never a falling out between the two men, but Budgen stayed in Zurich, getting on with his painting and his own life. They continued to correspond, at first mostly about the details of *Ulysses*, and to see each other whenever there was an opportunity.

Joyce was becoming increasingly disenchanted with Trieste. It was not the city he remembered with such affection. He had been spoilt by the cleanliness and Swiss efficiency of Zurich. At one point, an old friend greeted him in the street and asked him how he was finding the city. Joyce replied, 'like a dunghill'. No doubt a Joycean exaggeration, but Trieste was visibly battle-scarred, and many streets were overgrown with grass. Joyce regretted the passing of the old Empire. He later lamented that no one who had not lived there before the war could know the real charm and sophistication of the old Austro-Hungarian Empire. It had been called 'a ramshackle empire', but Joyce's view was 'I wish to God there were more such ramshackle empires'.[4] The Italian government was not going to allow another port on the Adriatic to compete with Venice and, as a consequence, the thriving commercial and maritime life of Trieste was much diminished. For Joyce and other expatriates, it was becoming just another provincial Italian town. When Pound wrote to enquire how he was finding Trieste, Joyce replied:

> Without saying anything about this city (*de mortuis nil nisi bonum*) my own position for the past seven months has been very unpleasant. I live in a flat with eleven other people and have great difficulty in securing time and peace enough to write both those chapters. Since I came here I suppose I have not exchanged 100 words with anybody. I spend the greater part of my time sprawled across two beds surrounded by mountains of notes....I could give private lessons here (most people expect it of me) but I will not. I have a position in that school which the government has now raised to the rank of a university. My pay is about 3 shillings an hour for 6 hours a week. This I shall resign as it wastes my time and nerves.[5]

When Joyce became self-pitying, he could lay it on with a trowel. In fact, he had spoken thousands of words with many people. He was seeing Svevo and other old pupils, and had spent several drunken and highly talkative evenings with his old friend Francini Bruni.

Yet, despite all his complaints and distractions, Joyce had managed to finish 'Nausicaa', the episode of *Ulysses* he had started in Zurich. This was the episode that was the main cause of offence in the United States and led to the obscenity charges against the book. The problem was Joyce's introduction of the seventeen-year-old Gerty MacDowell at the beginning of the episode. She is sitting on the beach at

Sandymount Strand, slightly apart from her two girlfriends, who are looking after three little children, two of whom are playing with a ball. Gerty is gazing into the distance, lost in thought.

> She was in very truth as fair a specimen of winsome Irish girlhood as one could wish to see. She was pronounced beautiful by all who knew her.... Her figure was slight and graceful, inclining even to fragility but those iron jelloids she had been taking of late had done her a world of good much better than the Widow Welch's female pills and she was much better of those discharges she used to get and that tired feeling....There was an innate refinement, a languid queenly hauteur about Gerty which was unmistakably evidenced in her delicate hands and high-arched instep. Had kind fate but willed her to be born a gentlewoman of high degree in her own right and had she only received the benefit of a good education Gerty MacDowell might easily have held her own beside any lady in the land...patrician suitors at her feet vying with one another to pay their devoirs to her. Maybe it was this, the love that might have been, that lent to her softly featured face at whiles a look tense with suppressed meaning and that imparted a strange yearning tendency to the beautiful eyes a charm few could resist.[6]

One of Joyce's gifts, amply illustrated in *Ulysses*, was that he could parody any style in English literature. Before he wrote the Gerty MacDowell scenes, he did his homework by reading the sort of romantic novelettes that Nora frequently read.

Having described Gerty's clothes in great detail, a 'neat blouse of electric blue, self-tinted by dolly dyes', a three-quarter length skirt and new hat – Joyce had a great interest in women's clothes – he brings the focus of the scene back to the two boys playing with the ball. One of them kicks the ball down towards the seaweedy rocks:

> … but luckily the gentleman in black who was sitting there by himself came gallantly to the rescue and intercepted the ball....The gentleman aimed the ball once or twice and then threw it up the strand...but it rolled down the slope and stopped right under Gerty's skirt.... she just lifted her skirt a little, but just enough and took good aim and gave the ball a jolly good kick....[7]

Gerty leans back against a rock, and is aware that 'the gentleman in black' is looking at her, and finds her cheeks flushing.

> ....Till then they had only exchanged glances of the most casual kind but now under the brim of her new hat she ventured a look at him and the face that met her gaze there in the twilight, wan and strangely drawn, seemed to her the saddest she had ever seen....Yes, it was her he was looking at and there was meaning in his look. His eyes burned into her as though they would search her through and through, read her very soul. Wonderful eyes they were, superbly expressive, but could you trust them? People were so queer. She could see at once by his dark eyes and his pale intellectual face that he was a foreigner....If ever there was undisguised admiration in a man's passionate gaze it was there plain to be seen on that man's face. It is for you, Gertrude MacDowell, and you know it....Even if he was a protestant or a methodist she could convert him easily if he truly loved her. There were wounds that wanted healing with heartbalm.[8]

Then the fireworks show begins, and Gerty's two friends and the children go off to watch it. Gerty and the gentleman in black remain as they are, indulging their own separate fantasies. As Gerty leans farther back against the rock, looking up at the fireworks, he, hands in his pockets, is looking up her skirt. Then a 'Roman candle burst and it was like a sigh of O!'

> He was leaning back against the rock behind. Leopold Bloom (for it is he) stands silent, with bowed head before those young guileless eyes. What a brute he had been! At it again? A fair unsullied soul had called to him and, wretch that he was, how had he answered? An utter cad he had been! He of all men! But there was an infinite store of mercy in those eyes, for him too a word of pardon even though he had erred and sinned and wandered....Should a girl tell? No, a thousand times no. That was their secret, only theirs, alone in the hidden twilight and there was none to know or tell save the little bat that flew so softly through the evening to and fro and little bats don't tell.[9]
>
> –Gerty! Gerty! We're going. Come on. We can see better from farther up.

She drew herself up to her full height. Their souls met in a last lingering glance and the eyes that had reached her heart, full of a strange shining, hung enraptured on her sweet flowerlike face. She half smiled at him wanly, a sweet forgiving smile, a smile that verged on tears – and then they parted.

Slowly, without looking back, she went down the uneven strand…. It was darker now and there were stones and bits of wood on the strand and slippy seaweed. She walked with a certain quiet dignity characteristic of her but with care and very slowly because Gerty MacDowell was…

Tight boots? No. She's lame! O!

Mr. Bloom watched her as she limped away. Poor girl![10]

Joyce had stored away Marthe Fleischmann's handicap in Zurich for Gerty MacDowell's exit at Sandymount Strand.

The Little Review was distributed by mail and, unfortunately, the issue that contained 'Nausicaa' came into the hands of the secretary of the New York Society for the Suppression of Vice. The scene at Sandymount Strand was enough to offend any member of a society for the suppression of vice. Whatever their private habits, voyeurism and masturbation were not something they had ever encountered before on the printed page. Even more heinous, the object of Bloom's fantasy was still a minor, and a handicapped one at that. A prosecution was brought against the editors and publishers of *The Little Review*, which came to court in 1920. The defendants were found guilty of disseminating obscene material. They were fined, but avoided a prison sentence. Under the Tariff Act, this meant that the still unpublished book, or any part of it, could no longer be handled by the U.S. Post Office, or imported into the United States by any other means. Copies of the magazine that the Post Office already held were burned. Joyce later wrote to Harriet Weaver: 'This is the second time I have had the pleasure of being burned while on earth so that I hope I shall pass through the fires of purgatory as quickly as my patron St. Aloysius.'[11] Aloysius was James's middle name, an old family one.

In Britain, Harriet Weaver had also been printing extracts in *The Egoist*. She had published four before she found that, under the shadow of the U.S. obscenity case, no British printer was willing to print further episodes. This also put paid to her plans to publish *Ulysses* as a book, or to find a publisher who would. In 1922, the book was banned by the Home Office after the Director of Public Prosecutions had actually read only forty of its 724 pages – apparently it was Molly's soliloquy at the end of the book that attracted his attention. The book remained banned in Britain until 1936.

By the late spring of 1920, after being back in Trieste for only eight months, Joyce decided it was time to leave Trieste. He was desperate to find somewhere quiet and peaceful, and above all cheap, where he could finish *Ulysses*. Joyce planned for Bloom and Stephen Dedalus to visit Bella Cohen's brothel in Nighttown. This became 'Circe', the highly complicated fifteenth episode. By now, Joyce could see the end in sight – Bloom's return to Molly corresponding to Ulysses' return to Penelope. He and Nora discussed going to stay in England for a while, or even Ireland. Joyce had read enough newspapers to know that Ireland was neither quiet nor peaceful at the time. However, after sixteen years, he had an urge to see his father again, maybe for the last time. Nora also wanted to visit her family, but any visit was ruled out after a letter from his Aunt Josephine, who wrote, 'There is nothing but raids and murder here'. It was a succinct description of the brutal repression of the Black and Tans and the reprisals of the IRA in the dying days of British rule. Further discussions about locations were interrupted by a letter from Ezra Pound, who was coming to Venice and suggested that he and Joyce meet there. When Mrs. Pound fell ill, the Pounds moved, for her recuperation, to Sirmione on Lake Garda. There, on 8 June, Joyce finally met his composite publicist and fairy godfather.

The two men got on well. Their main topics of conversation seem to have been the progress of *Ulysses* and the identity of Joyce's benefactor. It is a sign of Harriet Weaver's discretion and reticence that, despite working so closely with her, Pound had no idea she was the benefactor. He and Joyce again decided it had to be Lady Cunard. Apart from saying later, to the novelist Wyndham Lewis, that he found Pound 'slightly mad', Joyce left no written description of him. Pound wrote one of Joyce in a letter to John Quinn, a rich New York lawyer, book collector and admirer of Joyce's work:

Joyce – pleasing: after the first shell of cantankerous Irishman. I got the impression that the real man is the author of *Chamber Music*, the sensitive. The rest is the genius; the registration of realities upon the temperament, the delicate temperament of the early poems….Also great exhaustion, but more constitution than I had expected, and apparently good recovery from an eye operation. He is, of course, stubborn as a mule or an Irishman, but I failed to find him at all unreasonable. Thank God, he has been stubborn enough to know his job and stick to it. [12]

Joyce may have been slightly constrained by the presence of Giorgio, now fifteen and already six feet tall. Joyce was frightened of thunder and lightning and told Pound that he had brought Giorgio along as 'a lightning-conductor'. Pound may have found Joyce eccentric, but, after the two days they spent together, he had no doubt about his genius. His main concern was that it should be allowed to flourish in the right setting so Joyce could finish *Ulysses* and write more ground-breaking books. Pound extolled the post-war attractions of Paris to him, now restored as the cultural capital of Europe. Most important for a writer, it was a cheaper place to live than either Trieste or London. He insisted that Joyce should at least come on a visit. Pound had tempted his genius, and would go back to Paris to spread the word that Joyce was coming.

On his return to Trieste, Joyce solved a mystery. He had received a letter from Slack, Munro, Saw & Co. informing him that his benefactor was transferring to him a £5,000 war bond that yielded five per cent interest a year. After his conversations with Pound, he was now convinced that his benefactor was Lady Cunard. He wrote to the solicitors telling them he had guessed his benefactor's identity. He respected her delicacy and self-effacement, and wished to write and express his gratitude. He was also curious to know what it was about his work that so inspired her generosity. Still keeping her anonymity, the solicitors reported his benefactor's answer – 'your piercing spirit, your scorching truth, the power and startling penetration of your intense instants of imagination'.

Harriet Weaver now decided it was pointless to maintain her anonymity. She was concerned that Joyce may not have guessed correctly, and it was all becoming too complicated. Weaver finally wrote to Joyce, not to claim credit, she said, but to prevent any embarrassment:

> It was I who sent the message through Messrs Munro, Saw & Co., and I am sorry I sent it in the way and in the form I did. It is rather paralysing to communicate through solicitors. I fear you will have to withdraw all words about delicacy and self-effacement. I can only beg you to forgive me for my lack of them.[13]

To offer an apology for helping support someone for the rest of his life – even paying for his funeral – was an extraordinary sign of Harriet Weaver's modesty and altruism. Given her inherited wealth and socialist principles, there may well have been an element of guilt behind her philanthropy.

Having resolved that mystery, and being confident in Harriet Weaver's financial reliability, Joyce now set about convincing Nora that it was time to leave Trieste. She did not take a lot of convincing. She shared Joyce's feelings about how the city had changed, and about the discomforts of their present living conditions. However, Nora did hate the idea of another upheaval, particularly for the children. They would have to change schools again and be educated in yet another language. Much as Joyce undoubtedly loved his family, *Ulysses* came first. He decided to accept Pound's offer to find them somewhere to stay for a couple of weeks in Paris en route to London. If the situation in Ireland improved, they would go on and visit their families there. Joyce handed in his resignation to the 'university', but put in a plea that they replace him with Stanislaus. This they eventually did, but relations between the brothers remained strained. They saw each other again on only three further occasions, but they continued a correspondence. Joyce, Nora, Giorgio and Lucia left Trieste on 2 July 1920 and none of them ever returned. The city may have changed and lost its appeal for Joyce, but it did leave him with one abiding memory – 'I have never met such kindness as I met in Trieste.'[14]

CHAPTER TWELVE

Bloom and Zeno

IN TRIESTE, WHILE JOYCE had been writing about Bloom's and Gerty MacDowell's encounter, Svevo was turning Zeno Cosini's thoughts towards marriage. Joyce and Svevo were working only three kilometres away from each other, but their circumstances were very different. Joyce was living in an overcrowded flat with eight other members of the family, four adults and four children, near the centre of the city. He still had to write in a bedroom. Svevo lived with Livia in a large apartment in the Villa Veneziani and worked in his study. Their only child, Letizia, lived with her husband, Antonio, in another separate apartment in the villa. Joyce was thirty-seven and Svevo fifty-eight. Both writers had talked with each other about what they were writing. Whereas Joyce's novel was set on that one particular day in 1904, Svevo's covered a period from 1904 to 1915. There is a unique and unusual relationship between the protagonists of both novels. Joyce's Bloom was partially modelled on Svevo, and owed much of his Jewish background and culture to what Joyce had learned from him. Svevo certainly did not model Zeno on Joyce, and naturally Zeno has many of his creator's characteristics. Yet Bloom and Zeno are both kindly, thoughtful men, prone to getting involved in awkward and embarrassing situations which they somehow manage to survive. They are not quite brothers under the skin, but certainly first cousins.

Both novels are finely blended mixtures of autobiography and imagination. As Svevo wrote about *The Confessions of Zeno* in a letter to a sympathetic critic, the poet Eugenio Montale:

...It is an autobiography, yet not my own. Far less than *Senilità*. I took three years to write it in my spare time. And this is how I proceeded: When I was alone I tried to persuade myself that I was Zeno. I walked like him, I planted into my own past all his adventures that might resemble my own only because the re-evocation of an adventure of your own is a reconstruction that easily turns into a completely new construct when you succeed in setting it within a new atmosphere. And it does not thereby lose the flavour and the value of memory, nor its sadness.... I know of one or two points where Zeno's mouth was replaced by my own and is jarringly loud.[1]

In his long exile from novel-writing, Svevo had plenty of time to think about its structure and techniques. He also had the benefit of talking about these subjects with Joyce. In practice, they found a variety of solutions to the questions of chronology, narrative and the authorial voice. Svevo also played with the idea of the unreliable narrator. Whom do you believe – the psychoanalyst or his patient? Svevo often talked about how little he had read. Montale saw how absurd this was. He wrote that 'Svevo has more insights than most of our men of letters have any inkling of.... He can discuss numerous foreign writers, right up to Kafka, with rare penetration.'[2] This was a barb aimed at the literary establishment, who had ignored or patronised Svevo because he wrote largely in the Triestine dialect and not the classical Italian of Dante. Something else he had in common with Joyce was that both men were attacked for their linguistic style. Joyce wrote in perfectly good English, but he was criticised for making it too idiosyncratic, complicated and often incomprehensible.

At the beginning of the chapter 'The Story of my Marriage', Zeno admits that he had reached an age, his early thirties, when the rhythm of his life suddenly felt unchanging and monotonous.

Perhaps it was the tedium of producing and hearing that solitary note which put into my head the idea of getting married. Those who have not experienced it are inclined to think marriage is more important than it really is. We persuade ourselves that the mate we choose will bring about our renewal – a curious illusion which the facts in no way support. In fact one may live together quite unchanged, except that one may come to feel dislike for a being so different from oneself…. The odd thing about my matrimonial adventure is that it began by making the acquaintance of my future father-in-law, and feeling a great admiration and affection for him before I knew that he had daughters of a marriageable age.[3]

The future father-in-law, Giovanni Malfenti, was a wealthy businessman, who had three daughters of marriageable age. There was a fourth but she was only eight, and thus safe from Zeno's intentions. All their names began with A – by seniority, Ada, Augusta, Alberta, and Anna. Svevo got this idea from neighbours who had four daughters whose first names began with that letter. More significant was the fact that his own wife, Livia, was one of the four daughters of Gioachino Veneziani, the very successful businessman for whom Svevo worked. He was also a strong, dynamic character, similar to the fictional Malfenti. Fortunately, Livia's three sisters did not have first names that began with L, but Svevo had to be subtly inventive about the Malfenti family not to offend either his wife or her family.

Zeno had been told that the girls were all good-looking, and before he even met them

> I dreamt about those four girls linked together so closely by their names – Ada, Augusta, Alberta, Anna. I almost felt they were a bunch of flowers. But that initial meant something else too. My name is Zeno, and I felt as if I were about to choose a wife from a far country.[4]

When Zeno first visits the Malfentis' home, he is shown into the drawing-room, and his dreams are wrong from the start. Only the second oldest, Augusta, is there. She shakes hands shyly with him, and goes off to call her mother and sisters.

> Well, that was the end of one of the four girls with the same initial, as far as I was concerned. How could they have called her pretty? The first thing I noticed about her was that she squinted, and so badly sometimes that if one had not seen her for a while that squint seemed to sum up her whole personality. Her hair was not very thick and of a

dull shade of blondness without any lights in it; and though she had not exactly a bad figure she was rather broad for her age. In the few moments I remained alone I thought to myself; 'If all the others are like this one…!'[5]

Fortunately, the others are not. Anna, aged eight, is a very pretty girl. Alberta, who is seventeen, is very attractive, and the oldest, Ada, in her early twenties, is beautiful. Even Signora Malfenti is a handsome, elegant woman with an imposing personality. Zeno immediately decides that Ada is the one he wants as a wife. He sets about impressing the whole family. He tells amusing anecdotes, talks about his time in England, how odd the English are, and how he mainly mixed with foreigners there because he had lost the letters of introduction he had been given. Alone with five women, Zeno cannot help showing off, and when the conversation turns to the subject of grief, he talks about how deeply he was affected by the death of his father, and tells a funny but morbid story.

My reason in talking this way was that I wanted to show them I had a sense of humour, which had often in the past made me popular with women.[6]

It soon becomes clear to him that Ada does not appreciate his humour as much as the others. She is a serious young woman, but Zeno will not be discouraged.

She shall stay just as she is, for that is how I like her; but if she wants it, I will change to please her. I was, on the whole, very modest, for it is undoubtedly easier to change oneself than re-educate somebody else.[7]

Zeno's visits to the house increase. He even brings his violin to entertain the family. As he admits, he is no virtuoso, but is disappointed when it is Augusta, and not Ada, who happily accompanies him on the piano. In his company, Ada is polite, but no more. He remains enamoured of her, but still unable to declare his passion. The Malfenti family become the centre of his life, until one day Signora Malfenti takes him aside in her sitting-room to tell him that he is welcome in their home, but the frequency of his visits is compromising Augusta. Zeno thinks she must be muddling her daughters' names. Surely not Augusta! 'Yes. Augusta. You are putting ideas into her head and compromising her.' Zeno is baffled. All he has done is let Augusta accompany him on the piano, and has told her a few anecdotes that he hopes she will pass on to Ada.

–Tell me what I must do so as not to offend anyone.
   –It would be better if you came here less often for the present; let us say two or three times a week, instead of every day.
   Her words, which were milder than I expected, gave me courage to show my resentment.
   –If you wish I shall never set foot in this house again. I shall go immediately.
   The Signora laughingly protested: 'There can be no fear of you compromising *me*, so you may stay on a little'.
   –Does the whole family know that you have asked me to stay away?
   –Stay away? Only for a few days. I shall say nothing about it to anyone. Not even my husband.[8]

So Zeno stays away from the house for five days. It is now time for the author to transfer his own hypochondria on to his character. Zeno is distraught at being barred from the house, even temporarily, without having declared his feelings to Ada, or at least to her mother. Unable to sleep one night, he goes to a bar and meets an old friend, Tullio, who is on a crutch. Zeno asks him what happened. Tullio explains that his leg problems started six months ago with a bad attack of rheumatism. Tullio has now become an expert on the illness, and found that drinking a great quantity of lemon juice daily has relieved some of the pain. Tullio has also studied closely the anatomy of the leg and foot.

He told me with amusement that when one is walking rapidly each step takes no more than half a second, and in that half second no fewer than fifty-four muscles are set in motion. I at once directed my attention to my legs and tried to discover the infernal machine. I discovered something terrifically complicated, which seemed to get out of order directly I began thinking about it. I found that I was limping as I left the café, and for several days afterwards walking became a burden to me and even caused me a certain degree of pain.[9]

Zeno starts drinking lemon juice, and contemplates the mystery of his banishment:

They told me I was compromising Augusta, but in fact it was she who was compromising herself by loving me. I saw it all quite clearly in a flash. Ada did not love me and never would, as long as she thought her sister did....With all my efforts I had only succeeded in doing what the famous marksman did – hitting the bulls-eye, but of the target next to the one he was aiming at.[10]

On the much-anticipated fifth day, a Sunday, Zeno rushes into town, hoping to bump casually into the Malfenti family returning from church. He bumps into only one of them – Ada. At least she smiles at him, but says she is in a hurry. He walks with her a short distance, but she makes no comment either on his absence or his limp. As he is about to express his feelings, they are joined by Guido Speier, who greets Ada warmly. A successful businessman, recently arrived in Trieste, Guido has obviously been entertained already by the Malfenti family. Zeno is instantly suspicious, and inspects him closely:

He was a very handsome young man. His slightly open lips revealed a set of perfect white teeth. He had bright, expressive eyes, and when he took off his hat I could see that his brown, curly hair covered the entire space provided for it by Nature, whereas a great part of my own head had been usurped by my forehead. I should have hated him even if Ada had not been there. I tried to get rid of him and my hatred, but failed.[11]

Guido, with his advantage in age, eyes, teeth, hair, and without a limp, becomes the villain for virtually the rest of the book. Guido and Ada are talking about spiritualism, and Zeno learns that Guido has introduced table-turning into the Malfenti household. There is to be a seance at the house that evening, and Ada invites Zeno to come.

This is not the way he would have wished to return to the bosom of the Malfenti family, but he accepts.

With the seance, Svevo turns the story from sharp comedy into high farce. Svevo had not written plays, even if unproduced, for nothing. The threat of Guido determines Zeno to declare his love to Ada that evening. Unfortunately, he arrives a little late, and the seance is already in progress. The maid ushers him into a darkened room. Zeno can just discern the company assembled at the round table. Darkness is the vital dramatic device necessary to make Svevo's plot work. Zeno finds a vacant chair, presumably left for him, between two women, whom he dimly recognises as Ada and Augusta. He sits down and mumbles his apologies. Guido, sitting opposite, is trying to make contact with the spirit world. Zeno seizes his opportunity. He puts his arm gently round Ada's waist, and whispers, 'I love you, Ada.' After a pause, he gets a soft reply, 'Why have you not been here for so long?' It is not Ada's voice, it is Augusta's. Zeno, horrified, recovers enough to say, 'I am glad to have confided in you, Augusta.' Guido calls for silence. He thinks he has contacted someone 'on the other side'. Trapped in the dark between the woman he loves and the woman who loves him, Zeno realises there is nothing he can do. He is increasingly irritated by Guido's calls for more concentration, and when Guido proclaims that he is in touch with his own grandfather, Zeno interferes with the occult contact, using his knees to help the table rise and fall to give positive or negative answers. Guido realises there is a counter-force at work under the table and the seance comes to an end. As the lights come on, Augusta assures Zeno she will not tell anyone about what has passed between them. He appreciates that she is a good woman:

> …and I felt certain affection for her waist, round which I had so lately put my arm and which I found smaller than I expected. Her face was really quite pretty, but for that eye which had gone off on a path of its own. I had certainly exaggerated her deformity.[12]

The evening now continues disastrously for Zeno. Wherever he turns he seems to put his foot in it. He admits to Guido that it was his knees that were the culprit and apologises for his bad taste joke, allowing Guido to behave magnanimously. Signor Malfenti now calls on Guido to play his violin. He does, playing the Bach Chaconne quite brilliantly. Zeno realises his own puny musical efforts are not in the same class, and decides never to play to the Malfentis again. He is still determined, however, to press his suit with Ada, and finally has a moment alone with her.

> I could not leave that house without the assurance I needed for my peace of mind. I tried to be as simple as possible. 'I love you, Ada. May I speak to your father?'
>
> She stared at me in horror and amazement.
>
> 'Surely you must have understood!' I said. 'You couldn't have thought I was courting Augusta.' In my confusion I put my emphasis in the wrong place, and ended by pronouncing poor Augusta's name in a tone of contempt. She could not countenance this insult to her sister.
>
> 'Why do you think yourself better than Augusta? I don't for a moment suppose that Augusta would consent to be your wife. As for me, I wonder that such a thing entered your head.'[13]

Zeno is cast down by her rejection. He has lost all his *witze*. Then he remembers his father's advice: 'Choose a young wife; it will be easier for you to educate her to suit you'. Later in the evening, he is talking with the seventeen-year-old Alberta, and realises how attractive she is – almost as beautiful as Ada. He proposes to her. She treats it as a joke. Anyway she doesn't want to get married She wants to go to university.

Still gripped by his obsession to be a part of the Malfenti family, he decides he must face reality. Can he be third time lucky? He looks around for Augusta. He finds her in the corridor outside the kitchen.

> 'Listen, Augusta! Would you like us to get married?' It was a rough-and-ready proposal, but I felt I was only doing what they all seemed to expect from me.
>
> The eyes she lifted to me were wide with astonishment. This seemed to make her squint worse than ever. In a voice I could hardly hear, she said: 'You are joking. It is unkind of you.'
>
> I was afraid she would cry. I thought I might comfort her by telling her my troubles: 'I am not joking,' I said, gravely and sadly. 'I proposed

to Ada, who refused me angrily. 'But I am very, very unhappy.'

She grew calmer as she saw my grief, and looked tenderly at me. Her look was like a caress. She was evidently thinking hard. 'So you want me to understand and always remember that you don't love me?'

It was on the tip of my tongue to say that I could not bear the thought of never meeting Ada again, and having to leave this house, but I only said: 'I can't face living alone any longer.' She remained silent. I went on talking. 'I am not a bad fellow. I think I should be easy enough to live with, even if it wasn't very romantic.'

She sighed and still said nothing, but with a dignity I have never forgotten, she stood erect, no longer needing the wall to support her. She said: 'You need a woman, Zeno, to live with you and look after you. I will be that woman.'

She put out her hand, which, as if by instinct, I kissed. I don't mind confessing that at that moment a feeling of immense satisfaction pervaded me. I had no decision to make. Everything was decided for me. At last I had obtained certainty. And so I became engaged.[14]

Zeno hardly comes out of this serial courtship well. Augusta may have had a squint in one eye, but was Zeno such a catch? He was over thirty, going bald and had a psychosomatic limp. Yet Svevo is merely portraying the sexist standards of his day with ironic honesty.

When Zeno and Augusta announce their engagement, they receive endless congratulations.

My success was something like Guido's on the violin. Giovanni kissed me and said he had looked upon me as a son ever since he had begun to give me advice about my business. My future mother-in-law held out her cheek, and I kissed it as lightly as I could.

'You see I guessed everything,' she said with incredible assurance.

Ada said: 'Bravo, Zeno!' then, more quietly, 'I want to tell you this: you may think you have been too hasty, but no one has ever acted more sensibly than you have this evening.... I want you to love me as a sister. Let us forget all that has happened.'

When the party broke up Augusta said to me gaily, 'Till tomorrow then.'

I had attained my end, nothing was over. It would go on just the same tomorrow. She looked into my eyes, and found them respond warmly to her invitation. I went down the stairs, my limp was gone, and I said to myself:

'Who knows? Perhaps I do love her after all.'

This uncertainty has never left me during the whole of my life, and today I am compelled to believe that true love is compatible with such a doubt.[15]

Despite his endless analysing, Zeno never realised the extent to which his engagement was discreetly orchestrated by the Malfenti family. Their plan had resolved the difficult problem of Augusta loving Zeno who loves Ada who loves Guido. Augusta herself was not a party to it. Nor was her youngest sister, the eight-year-old Anna, who had expressed her own views directly to Zeno. A few days earlier, having listening to some of his opinions, she had whispered in his ear, 'You're mad, you are quite mad.'[16]

More important for Svevo, however, was the fact that he had managed to create a family who were sufficiently different from his wife's – the Malfentis were not the Venezianis. There was no marine paint factory and Zeno did not work for his father-in-law. The respective heads of the families, Giovanni and Gioachino, may have been similar, but Gioachino Veneziani died in 1921, two years before Svevo's novel was published. The two mothers also had some similar characteristics – both were shrewd and controlling – but Svevo may have been settling old scores with his formidable mother-in-law, Olga. He portrayed the four sisters as differently as he could, and there was no gay, concert pianist brother in the family. There also seems to have been no Guido in Svevo's life. In the novel, Guido inevitably joins the Malfenti family by marrying Ada. Most importantly, Livia is nothing like Augusta. Judging by her photographs, as a bride, and later in middle age, Livia was a very attractive and elegant woman. She had no squint, and her hair was anything but 'a dull shade of blondness and not very thick'. In fact, it was Livia's crowning glory, and Joyce was to immortalise it as Anna Livia Plurabelle's in *Finnegans Wake*. Besides, Livia was no third choice, and there was no question of Svevo not falling in love with her. He loved her from the moment she handed him a drink at his dying mother's bedside, but, like Zeno, he never regretted marrying her.

Of course, Svevo's marriage into the Veneziani family had great advantages for him. He had the warmth and security of an extended family life more comfortable than his own. In the Villa Veneziani he and Livia coped reasonably well with the proximity of her parents. His position and his travel for the family company gave him financial security, as well as interest, after his years of boredom in the bank. There were rarely problems with the family until their reunion back in Trieste after the war. Their problem was basically political, and reflected the increasing divisions and violence in Italian politics, especially in Trieste, in the early post-war years. As almost everywhere else in Europe, except the Soviet Union, the political split was basically Left versus Right. The Veneziani family, with their successful business interests, looked politically to the Right, to protect themselves from what became increasingly known as the Bolshevik threat. In 1919, after much rioting in Budapest, only 250 kilometres from Trieste, Béla Kun set up his Hungarian Soviet Republic. It lasted four months before being overthrown by the right-wing dictatorship of Joyce's old pupil, Admiral Horthy. His regime lasted for twenty-four years.

Politically, Svevo was the odd man out in the Veneziani family. He had always voted for the Liberal Party, but the party's influence was shrinking, squeezed between the political extremes of the Right, soon to become fascist, and the Left, eventually to turn communist. Svevo's political ideas were Utopian rather than socialist, but he could not ignore self-interest, and it was the socialists who organised the excessive wage claims and frequent workers' strikes that affected the Veneziani factories in Trieste and Murano. Svevo, like Joyce, had always tried to avoid any serious commitment in politics or religion. Even his writing basically avoided those subjects. Svevo tried to turn a blind eye to the growing political and social unrest around him in Trieste and elsewhere in Italy. There is no better example of this than the series of four witty articles he wrote, as promised, for *La Nazione*. They were about trams, and entitled 'We of the Servola Tramway'. After that, he got on with writing *The Confessions of Zeno*.

In 1919 at the Versailles Peace Conference, Italy, despite being on the winning side, did not gain territorially what its allies had promised in the Treaty of London in 1915. In the north, they wanted to annex the Trentino, South Tyrol and Trieste, and down the Adriatic coast, Istria and most of Dalmatia, to which they now added an additional claim for Fiume (now Rijeka). Thirty years before, after a conference in Berlin about Italy's borders, Bismarck had said: 'Italy has a large appetite but very poor teeth'. The Allied leaders, who gathered at Versailles in 1919 to divide the spoils of victory, came to feel very much as Bismarck did about their Italian allies. The historian Christopher Duggan writes: 'Stereotypes and prejudices abounded in the deliberations of the three most senior figures – Woodrow Wilson, Lloyd George and Clemenceau. The old idea that Italians were charming but utterly unscrupulous, played through the minds of many of the delegates.[17] Clemenceau said, "The Italians met me with an enormous *coup de chapeau* of the seventeenth-century type, and then held out the hat for alms at the end of the bow". '[18] The British and French still nursed their grudge against the Italians for joining them late, and only after much cold calculation. They had had to give them numerous wartime loans, which would probably never be repaid. The Italian fleet had hardly left port to patrol the Mediterranean, as they had promised. The allies had found fault with the leadership of the army, and had sent heavy reinforcements for their final victory at Vittorio Veneto, which afterwards the Italians claimed to have won single-handedly. The fact that Italy had sacrificed 600,000 men to the allied cause seems to have been conveniently overlooked at the peace conference.

The Italian prime minister, Vittorio Orlando, found himself between the proverbial rock and a hard place. The rock was the majority of public opinion in Italy. Having been divided about entering the war in the first place, the Italian people were now demanding some tangible reward for their huge sacrifice. Nationalistic, grandiloquent rabble-rousers like Mussolini, in his newspaper *Il Popolo d'Italia*, and Gabriele d'Annunzio, in his writings and speeches, warned the public that their former allies were patronising them, and that their own politicians were about to betray them. The hard place was Versailles. Orlando knew that it was more than his political life was worth to compromise his country's major demands. At one point in the increasingly acrimonious negotiations, he burst into tears, and left the conference table. The conference secretary, the suitably named Sir Maurice Hankey, later said that 'I would have spanked my son for such a disgraceful show of emotion'.[19] Orlando and his foreign minister, Sidney Sonnino, stuck to their demands, based on all they had been promised, plus Fiume. An impasse was reached and the temper of the normally calm and patient Woodrow Wilson began to fray --'It is curious how utterly incapable these Italians are of taking any position on principle and sticking to it,' he announced angrily. Desperate, but dry-eyed, Orlando appealed personally to Lloyd George:

> -'I must a have a solution. Otherwise I will have a crisis in parliament or in the streets of Italy.'
> -'And if not, who do you see taking your place?'
> -'Perhaps d'Annunzio.'[20]

Like most of Europe, Lloyd George would have heard of D'Annunzio. The implication of Orlando's forecast was clear – if Lloyd George thought he was difficult, wait till he met d'Annunzio. Orlando was wrong about his successor – but only just.

Gabriele d'Annunzio was one of Italy's most celebrated writers in the pre-war years, a poet, novelist and playwright. Svevo was not among his admirers, and was appalled to discover that Joyce was. He had a bet with Joyce that if he opened any of d'Annunzio's books at random, he would come across phrases that were pretentious and meaningless. Svevo had a d'Annunzio novel, and Joyce opened it and found a sentence: '*Il sorriso che pullulava inestinguibile, spandendosi fra i pallidi meandri dei merletti burandesi*', which translates as 'the smile which pullalated inextinguishably, spreading among the pallid meanders of Burano lace'. Joyce agreed that Svevo had made his point. As as a writer preoccupied with words, Joyce, however, continued to admire the poetic quality of d'Annunzio's language. Yet d'Annunzio was far more than just a writer. He was a fearless aviator, a war hero, who, aged fifty-two, had led a squadron of planes over Vienna and dropped 40,000 propaganda pamphlets he had written himself. Despite being the lover for several years of the great Italian actress, Eleonora Duse, he was also a tireless Lothario. Everything he did made headlines. In his time – he lived to be seventy-six – he was a one-man celebrity culture.

As a fervent and mystical nationalist, d'Annunzio's aim was to mythologise the Italian nation in his writing and speeches, much as Wagner had done in music for the Germans. It is relevant that both countries had been nation-states for less than sixty years. For Italians, their huge sacrifice of life in war had merely gained them Trieste. Inevitably, they turned on those who had negotiated the peace. D'Annunzio wrote a celebrated poem that ends:

> Who is it today that arises as arbiter of all future life, over our wailing and smoking land?
> Who would transform the greatness and beauty of this violence into a long debate between old men, in a senile council of trickery?
> The ink of scribes for the blood of martyrs?
> Oh victory of ours: you will not be mutilated. Nobody will bend our knees or clip our wings.[21]

Italians now referred to the outcome of Versailles as 'the mutilated victory'. Orlando resigned as prime minister, and his two successors held the post very briefly. The Liberal Party that had led them into the war was completely discredited. D'Annunzio labelled them traitors, and continued fanning the fires of violent nationalism. He accused their former allies of conspiring to keep Italy poor and isolated. At Versailles, the three 'old men, in their council of trickery' were aiming to resolve the Italian-Slav problem by creating the kingdom of Serbs, Croats and Slovenes, a title as unwieldy as the country. Its name was changed to Yugoslavia in 1929. Trieste was now Italian, but not Fiume, or any of the rest of the Dalmatian coast. D'Annunzio continued his violent rhetoric from town hall balconies and in the press. The Italian nation needed to assert its glorious manhood under a strong leader, a saviour who would restore its former glory, which meant going back a very long way. For many Italians, this second Caesar and saviour would now be the short (5ft 4in.), dandified, shaven-headed, one-eyed, fifty-six-year-old d'Annunzio.

In Milan, however, there was another prospective saviour who shared d'Annunzio's mystic nationalist views. Benito Mussolini also made violent speeches from balconies and was not to be outshone in abuse by d'Annunzio. In 1914, in an early editorial in his paper, *Il Popolo d'Italia*, he wrote:

> The Italian people is a mass of precious minerals. It needs to be forged, cleaned, worked. A work of art is still possible. But a government is needed – a man. A man who, when the situation demands it, has the delicate touch of the artist and the heavy fist of the warrior. Sensitive and determined. A man who knows the people, loves the people, and can direct and bend it – with violence if necessary.[22]

This highly emotive, almost emetic, style was soon *de rigueur* for all literate fascists. Mussolini had been a schoolteacher, a journalist and a socialist. He had served in the Army and fought in the trenches before being wounded and discharged with the rank of corporal. His future ally, Adolf Hitler, had fought in the trenches on the Western Front, been wounded, and also left the Army as a corporal. In 1919, Mussolini was thirty-six, and had returned to his editorial desk in Milan. He immediately began abusing those he saw as Italy's enemies, internal and external. He called Orlando 'an invertebrate who gets propped up on strong zabagliones'. The new prime minister, Francesco Nitti, was 'His excrescency'. The British were 'the fattest and most bourgeois nation in the world'. Then there were 'the Bolsheviks, 80% of whose leaders were Jews operating in the service of Jewish bankers in London and New York'.[23] This rather gives the lie to the apologists who tried to excuse Mussolini's anti-Semitism by claiming that Hitler forced it on him later. Words were followed by deeds. Mussolini founded the Fascist Party in Milan in March 1919, and began recruiting his *squadristi*. These were trained, mobile gangs, usually ex-soldiers, who wore black shirts and carried large truncheons. Their main duty was to beat up any socialists they could find, individually or in groups. (The black shirts were adopted later as a uniform by Hitler's S.S. units, as well as by Sir Oswald Mosley's Fascists in Britain.)

Since Italy was not to be granted Fiume in the peace treaty, D'Annunzio decided there was only one solution. He personally would take it for Italy. He recruited 200 of the toughest army veterans he could find, and advanced on Fiume. By the time he got there, he had 2,000 men behind him, and the garrison of largely Italian troops would not fire on him, despite orders from Rome. He and his very motley crew turned the town into a bizarre cross between an army camp and an early hippy commune. His occupation of Fiume lasted for fifteen months, and it became an international problem. Not to be upstaged by d'Annunzio, Mussolini took advantage of the publicity by visiting him there.

D'Annunzio believed that he had taken Fiume for Italy. In the end, he found that he had taken it only for himself. The Italian government ordered him and his troops to leave. When he refused, the city was surrounded by units of the regular Italian Army and a battleship was moored in the harbour. There ensued a not very serious battle in which thirty-three men were killed. Two shells fired from the battleship solved the Fiume problem, at least for the time being. D'Annunzio's men surrendered and he retreated to his apartment in Venice. The government took no further action against him. Fiume became an internationally guaranteed independent city and, after a four-year negotiation, it was annexed by Italy. After World War II it was ceded to Yugoslavia and renamed Rijeka.

D'Annunzio remained a patriotic hero until his death in 1938. In the melodrama of Fiume, however, he had shot his political bolt, and was no longer a serious rival to Mussolini for the leadership of the Fascist movement. Yet, because of d'Annunzio's hero-status, Mussolini always found it advisable to keep him as a close ally. His inflated rhetoric and theatricality had its effect on the national psyche. Svevo came closest to summing it up when he wrote to his friend the poet Eugenio Montale in 1927, 'We are a living protest against the ridiculous conception of the superman which has been foisted upon us, and especially upon us Italians.'[24]

In nearby Trieste, Svevo had been keeping a close eye on the farce of Fiume as it turned into violence. Soon there was violence on his own doorstep. Now they were part of Italy, a large section of Trieste's irredentist movement felt their new country would be best served by the Fascist Party, their only bulwark against Bolshevism taking over. Already fascist gangs were attacking Slavs as well as socialists, and burning down their property. In January 1921, the Italian Communist Party was founded in Livorno. The classic confrontation between fascists and communists, which was to dominate the inter-war years in Europe, was now well under way on the streets of Trieste. After local elections, the Fascist Party took over the running of the council as the dominant force in a right-wing coalition. It was its first political victory in Italy, and one soon repeated all over the country.

Svevo now found himself trapped between his own pacifist and liberal beliefs and the fascist sympathies of the Veneziani family. Livia was in an even more difficult position, because her views were midway between her husband's and her family's. The Venezianis' views, shared by most of the middle-class business community of Trieste, were basically self-interested. They saw around them their prosperous city degenerating into chaos. A strong government was needed to restore and maintain order. Svevo found it impossible to divorce himself from his family or their business. His friend Joyce had always proclaimed his disinterest in politics. Except for his abortive venture into the Dublin cinema business, Joyce had always managed to preserve his uncompromising single-mindedness as a writer. Svevo admired and often envied him, but could never have endured the insecurity of living off writing and someone else's generosity. It was in Svevo's nature to compromise. The best he could do was close his study door, shut out an unsympathetic world and return to his alter ego, Zeno Cosini.

CHAPTER THIRTEEN

Ulysses *in Paris*

IN JANUARY 1921, SVEVO RECEIVED a letter from Joyce from his latest address – 5 Boulevard Raspail, Paris VII. The Joyces moved almost as often in Paris as they had in Trieste. The letter arrived a month after the Joyces' usual Christmas card. It was warm and friendly, if slightly facetious in its formality and detail. Joyce wanted a favour. Inevitably, most of the letter is about the writer and his work rather than enquiries about the recipient's writing or well-being:

> Dear Mr. Schmitz, The Circe episode was finished some time ago, but four typists refused to copy it. At last a fifth one turned up, but she works very slowly, so the work will not be ready till the end of the month….

The 'Circe' episode covers the events and fantasies of Bloom's and Stephen Dedalus's visit to Mrs. Cohen's brothel in Nighttown. Mixed in with explicit and surreal descriptions, Joyce has his revenge on some of the English people he so disliked in Zurich. He gives their real names to his characters. The British Consul, Percy Bennett, makes an appearance and is dismissed in a couple of obscenity-packed lines: 'God fuck old Bennett. He's a white-arsed bugger. I don't give a shit for him.' [1]

In fact, the fifth secretary did not deliver the whole episode because her husband had read some of it and threw it on the fire in disgust. Burning was to play a major part in the publishing history of *Ulysses*. Fortunately, Joyce managed to obtain copies of the dozen or so burned pages from *The Little Review* in New York. Joyce's letter goes on to tell 'Mr. Schmitz' in detail of the plans to publish the book in the United States. As a result of the upcoming prosecution for obscenity, however, this never happened. Joyce continues:

> Now for the important thing: I cannot move from here (as I thought I could) before May. In fact for months and months I haven't got to bed before two or three in the morning, working without a break. Soon I shall have exhausted the notes I brought with me here to write these last two episodes. In Trieste, in the district where my brother-in-law lives, there is a flat marked Via Sanita 2, and on the third floor of the said building, in the bedroom at present occupied by my brother, at the back of the building overlooking the house of public insecurity (police station), there is an oilcloth brief-case fastened with a rubber band the colour of a nun's belly and measuring approximately 95 cm by 70 cm. In this brief-case I placed the written symbols of the flashes which sometimes flickered languidly across my soul.
>
> The weight is estimated at 4.78 kg. Having urgent need of these notes, I am turning to you, my most esteemed colleague, asking you to let me know if anyone from your family is proposing to come to Paris soon, it would be the greatest boon to me if they could bring that bundle....

Joyce goes on to recommend, in the same facetious tone, a hardware store, where Svevo could buy a small case to contain the papers:

> ...and my brother, who is professor at the *Berlitz Cul* will pay. At all events send us a couple of lines – how we eat them up.
>
> Cordial greetings and forgive me if my small brain sometimes plays me up a bit. Please write soon, I beg you.
> James Joyce [2]

Shortly after receiving this letter, Svevo had to make a business trip to London. Since the post-war return of his in-laws to Trieste, the responsibility for the Charlton factory had reverted to him. Svevo dutifully stopped over in Paris to deliver his precious package in a small suitcase, which he had paid for himself rather than bother Stanislaus. It is amazing serendipity that the model for Bloom should personally deliver the notes for 'Ithaca', the penultimate episode, in which Bloom finally returns to his home at 7 Eccles Street just as Ulysses returned to his in Ithaca. The chief difference between the two returning travellers was that Ulysses's journey took him ten years, whereas Leopold Bloom's odyssey in Dublin was accomplished in 24 hours. Also in that package was 'Penelope', the final episode. Without Svevo's help, the eight sentences that comprise the forty pages of Molly's interior monologue might have been much shorter. After that delivery of notes, Joyce finished the novel by mid-summer 1921.

Probably the most concise of the many attempts to synopsise the content and intention of *Ulysses* was written by its author at about the time he finished it. It was written to a friend, Carlo Linati, who had been asked to write about it for an Italian magazine:

> It is an epic of two races (Israelite-Irish), and at the same time the cycle of the human body as well as the little story of a day (life). The character of Ulysses has fascinated me ever since boyhood....For seven years I have been working on this book – blast it! It is also a sort of encyclopaedia. My intention is to transpose the myth *sub specie temporis nostri*. Each adventure (that is, every hour, every organ, every art being interconnected and interrelated in the structural whole) should not only condition but even create its own technique.[3]

Joyce makes it sound as though he had worked with a complex template in mind, bringing all the pieces together in a literary jigsaw puzzle. He was not concerned, after seven years' hard work, to make *Ulysses* an easy read. With his usual touch of paranoia, Joyce ends his letter by warning Linati that there was already a groundswell of opinion against the book, led by 'Puritans, English Imperialists, Irish Republicans, Catholics – what an alliance! For achieving that I deserve the Nobel Peace Prize.'[4]

Joyce had originally intended to stay in Paris for two weeks, but stayed for twenty years. Now, after a year, without *Ulysses* even being published, he had become a literary celebrity. Ezra Pound had diligently paved the way for him. When the Joyces arrived in Paris on 8 July 1920, Pound had met them at the Gare de Lyon and escorted them to a hotel on the

Left Bank, where he had made reservations for them. He had already circulated copies of *A Portrait of the Artist as a Young Man* in literary circles, and persuaded his friend Ludmila Bloch-Stavitsky to translate it into French. She was later to offer the Joyces free accommodation in the servants' quarters of her house at Passy. Within a few days of his arrival, Pound arranged a supper party in Joyce's honour to meet some influential *littérateurs*. Among them was Sylvia Beach, an American, who ran Shakespeare & Co., the bookshop that had become a Mecca for English-speaking literary expatriates in Paris. Many were Americans escaping the new Prohibition laws at home and taking advantage of the exchange rate of the dollar against the franc. Beach was already a great admirer of Joyce and had copies of *Chamber Music* and *A Portrait* in the bookshop window. In a memoir, she described Joyce at this first meeting:

> He was of medium height, thin, slightly stooped, graceful….His eyes, a deep blue, with the light of genius in them, were extremely beautiful. I noticed, however, that the right eye had a slightly abnormal look, and that the right lens of his glasses was thicker than the left….He gave an impression of sensitiveness exceeding any I had ever known. His skin was fair with a few freckles, and on his chin was a small goatee. His nose was well-shaped, his lips narrow and fine-cut. I thought he must have been very handsome as a young man.[5]

Beach also took notice of Nora Joyce:

> She was rather tall and neither stout nor thin. She was charming with her reddish curly hair and eyelashes, her eyes with a twinkle in them, her voice with its Irish inflections, and a certain dignity that is so Irish also. She seemed glad to find that we could speak English together. She couldn't understand a word of what was being said.[6]

In Paris Joyce may have almost immediately become a literary lion, but for his wife and children it was again the experience of having to learn yet another foreign language from scratch, in addition to moving house five times in their first two years in the city. In this period Joyce also had to endure two more eye operations from a leading Parisian ophthalmologist.

Soon after Joyce's arrival in Paris, T.S. Eliot, now living in London, wrote to his friend Ezra Pound, 'Is there any chance of Joyce staying in Paris, or coming to London, so that he could be seen?'[7] Pound arranged a meeting. He felt they would get on well together, as they had more than poetry in common. Both had worked as bank clerks, Joyce in Rome, and Eliot still at Lloyd's in London. Eliot brought with him his friend the acerbic writer Wyndham Lewis, as well as a parcel that Pound had given them for Joyce, who opened it in front of them. He was humiliated to find it was a gift of some second-hand clothes. They asked Joyce out to dinner. He went with them, and, because he had just received a little money from America, he insisted on paying for a hugely expensive meal as a way of restoring his pride. He frequently did this, behaving like the best-selling author he thought he ought to be. Both Eliot and Lewis commented on Joyce's politeness. Others, who knew him better, felt this was Joyce's way of withdrawing into himself. After his work, his two main concerns were with his family and his sight, and currently both were giving him problems. It was usually very late in the evening, after dinner and a couple of bottles of wine, that Joyce came out of himself and was easily encouraged to sing Irish songs – still in a fine tenor – and, after even more wine, do his spider dance and show off his extraordinary breadth of knowledge.

Eliot wrote to his friend Robert McAlmon, another American writer in Paris:

> Joyce I admire as a person who seems to be independent of outside stimulus, and who therefore is likely to go on producing first-rate work until he dies.[8]

After spending more time with Joyce, Eliot wrote to John Quinn, who was in the process of buying the episodes of *Ulysses*. (It was probably this money that paid for the dinner that Joyce bought Eliot and Lewis.)

> I can see that Joyce is certainly a handful, with the true fanatic's conviction that everyone ought to forward the interests of his work.

However, it is the conviction of the fanatic, and not the artfulness or pertinacity of ordinary push: and the latter part of *Ulysses*, which I have read in manuscript, is truly magnificent. I hear that he has captured some of the French literary elite who profess to know enough English.[9]

The use of the word 'profess' is telling. Knowing something about the eccentric writer and his work had become fashionable on the Left Bank, a fashion that soon spread across the Channel to literary London.

After his initial meeting with Sylvia Beach, Joyce began to pay regular visits to Shakespeare and Co. Apart from classic fiction, the bookshop sold and loaned many current American and English novels, and Joyce took out a subscription to borrow books. He began spending more time there, and Sylvia Beach was even more impressed when Joyce told her that he spoke or read eleven languages. The two he seemed most proud of were Hebrew and Yiddish. The walls of Shakespeare & Co. were covered with the photographs of her favourite living writers, French, British, American and Irish. Joyce's photograph took its place there alongside Hemingway, Scott Fitzgerald, Proust, André Gide, Eliot, Pound, Ford Madox Ford and many others. Joyce became friendly with Hemingway and Fitzgerald, friendships that each required a considerable intake of alcohol. By 1921, Paris was once again the undisputed capital of the arts. Joyce called it 'the last of the human cities'. The extraordinary array of creative talent assembled in the Twenties in Paris was not, of course, limited to writers. There were painters, composers, sculptors and architects, much of whose work survives, and has been of enormous influence ever since. The American critic Harry Levin, a leading Joyce scholar, called this gathering 'a constellation of genius'.

For once, Joyce found himself in the right place at the right time, but he was not there purely by chance. Ezra Pound had persuaded him to make the move and promoted his work to help him on his way, but Joyce was not the only artist whom Pound helped over the years. Hemingway was another, and his tribute to Pound was published a few years later in an issue of *Poetry Magazine* devoted to Pound's work:

Ezra was the most generous writer I have ever known. He devoted about a fifth of his time to his own writing, and the rest to advancing the careers of other artists....He defends his friends when they are attacked, he gets them into magazines and out of jail. He writes articles about them. He introduces them to wealthy women. He gets publishers to take their books. He sits up with them all night when they claim to be dying. He advances them hospital expenses and dissuades them from suicide. And, in the end, a few of them restrain from knifing him at the first opportunity.[10]

Joyce had in mind that Paris would be a good base for visits to London and Dublin. He had not seen his father for eight years and Nora wanted to take Giorgio and Lucia to visit her family in Galway. However, the news from Ireland was making headlines even in foreign newspapers, and greatly discouraged any visit. In 1920, the British government had recruited an irregular force of tough ex-soldiers and ex-convicts, who became known by their uniforms as the Black and Tans. Both in their uniform and violent behaviour, they closely resembled Mussolini's *squadristi.* They were there ostensibly to curtail the activities of the IRA but soon civilians were suffering from the reprisals taken against life and property by both sides. At one point the Black and Tans burned to the ground much of the centre of Cork, and arrested the Lord Mayor, Terence MacSwiney, a writer and nationalist, for sedition. He was tried by a military court and sentenced to two years' imprisonment. Shipped over to Brixton Prison, he went on hunger strike in protest of his trial by a military court. Despite attempts to force-feed him, MacSwiney died after a seventy-two-day fast. His case attracted worldwide attention. There were protests in many European countries, and Joyce would not have been unaware of them in the centre of Paris. Two weeks after this, the IRA took its revenge, murdering twelve British Army intelligence officers, most of them asleep in their quarters in Dublin. The next day, Black and Tans in armoured cars drove into Croke Park, the Gaelic Athletic Association stadium in Dublin, and turned their guns on the spectators, killing fourteen of them. The 21 November 1920 became known as 'Bloody Sunday'. A month later, almost a continent away, in Fiume, there was 'Bloody Christmas'. Only two years into the post-war world, and the word 'bloody' was back in the headlines.

In Paris, there was no way that Joyce could hide the fact that he was not Irish, nor did he try to. Inevitably, he was asked his opinions about the Irish 'Troubles'. Again Joyce would reiterate his lack of interest in politics – 'I don't talk about them, and these days they are getting into everything'. By mid-1921, Joyce had personal problems on his mind that far outweighed the Irish troubles. In April he had heard about the outcome of the obscenity trial in New York. Now, just as as he was on the verge of finishing his magnum opus, it looked as though it would never be published. He was about to have another operation on his eyes. Lucia's relationship with her mother was noticeably deteriorating. She was a bright, talented girl who wanted to be a dancer, but she was already experiencing increasing mood-swings that eventually were diagnosed as schizophrenia. As so often, when in a low mood, Joyce took himself to Shakespeare & Co. and bemoaned his fate to Sylvia Beach. On that particular occasion in early May, she said, quite spontaneously, 'Would you let Shakespeare and Company have the honour of bringing out your *Ulysses*?' It was perhaps the most important question Joyce had ever been asked. He took only a moment before saying the last word in *Ulysses*—'Yes'.[11]

Sylvia Beach, worried that she may have acted precipitately, went home to discuss the project with Adrienne Monnier, her partner, who also ran a bookshop, a French one. Because of her long, dark flowing dresses, Monnier was known as the 'The Nun of Literature'. She was enthusiastic about the idea, and said she would help. It was pure coincidence that initially all Joyce's first publishers were women. In the U.S. the editors of *The Little Review*, Margaret Anderson and Jane Heap were also a couple. In London, Harriet Weaver lived on her own. However, the most celebrated female couple in Paris were Gertrude Stein and Alice B. Toklas, who ran a literary salon to which Joyce was pointedly never invited. Stein had read the episodes of *Ulysses* in *The Little Review*, and felt her own early novels had anticipated its free-associative style by years – her first and best-known novel, *Three Lives*, was published in 1908. She deplored all the attention being given to Joyce. He had merely followed her lead, and in an obscene fashion too. Stein was also a habitué of Shakespeare & Co., and when she heard that Sylvia Beach was going to publish Joyce, in a pique she withdrew her bookshop subscription. However, Stein's protégé Ernest Hemingway called *Ulysses* 'a most goddamn wonderful book' and wrote to a friend:

> But the report is that he and all his family are starving, but you can find the whole Celtic crew of them every night in Michaud's where Binney [Hemingway's wife] and I can only afford to go at most once a week.[12]

Plans were now laid for a speedy publication of *Ulysses*. For Sylvia Beach, it was an extraordinarily daring undertaking. Shakespeare & Co. had been open for just over a year, and she had never published a book before. Joyce seemed to admire her and trusted her implicitly. The deal he made with her was very much in his favour-- a royalty of 66% on the profits. Behind their contract lay the fact that Joyce desperately wanted his book published and Sylvia Beach very much wanted to publish it. She chose a printer in Dijon, Darantière, the only one she knew who was capable of dealing with Joyce's text. There would be a first edition of 1,000 copies to be subscribed to in advance, and they sent out 3,000 leaflets about the book. There were also a limited number of autographed, de luxe copies, that Joyce sent to his special benefactors; the first went to Harriet Weaver, the second to Sylvia Beach, and the third to Margaret Anderson in New York. Initially they had a positive response of around three hundred orders, mainly from the literary world in Paris and London. Among the orders was one from Winston Churchill. George Bernard Shaw did not order the book, but gave his reasons to Sylvia Beach – at some length:

11 June 1922

Dear Madam,

I have read several fragments of *Ulysses* in its serial form. It is a revolting record of a disgusting phase of civilisation; but it is a truthful one; and I should like to put a cordon round Dublin; round up every male person between the ages of 15 and 30; force them to read it; and ask them whether on reflection, they could see anything amusing in all that foul-mouthed, foul-minded derision and obscenity. To you, possibly, it may appeal as art.... But to me it is hideously real; I have walked those streets, known those shops, and have heard and taken part in those conversations. I escaped from them to England at the age of twenty; and forty years later have learnt from the books of Mr. Joyce that Dublin is still what it was, and young men are still drivelling in slackjawed blackguardism just as they were in 1870. It is, however, some consolation to find that at last somebody has felt it deeply enough to face the horror of writing it all down and using his literary genius to force people to face it. In Ireland they try to make a cat cleanly by rubbing its nose in its own filth. Mr. Joyce has tried the same treatment on a human subject. I hope it may prove successful....

I must add, as the prospectus implies an invitation to purchase, that I am an elderly Irish gentleman, and that if you imagine that any Irishman, much less an elderly one, would pay 150 francs for a book, you little know my countrymen.
Yours faithfully,
G.Bernard Shaw[13]

Shaw must have been fairly certain that Joyce would read the letter. It was a case of one exiled Irish writer pitting his ego against another's. It later transpired that Shaw had never finished reading the book. Although if he did not enjoy all its contents, he never had any doubts about the author's gifts. Seventeen years later, in 1939, in a letter to the editor of *Picture Post*, Shaw wrote:

In your issue of the 13th May, Mr. Geoffrey Grigson, in an interesting article on Mr. James Joyce, states that 'Shaw was disgusted by the unsqueamish realism of *Ulysses,* and burned my copy in the grate.'

Somebody has humbugged Mr. Grigson. The story is not true. I picked up *Ulysses* in scraps from the American *Little Review*, and for years did not know that it was the history of a single day in Dublin. But having passed between seven and eight thousand single days in Dublin I missed neither the realism of the book nor its poetry. I did not burn it; and I was not disgusted. If Mr. Joyce should ever desire a testimonial as the author of a literary masterpiece from me, it shall be given with all possible emphasis and with sincere enthusiasm.
G. Bernard Shaw
Ayot St. Lawrence, Welwyn, Herts.[14]

Another distinguished Irish writer who later revealed he had not finished reading the novel was W.B. Yeats, one of Joyce's earliest benefactors. Yet, in 1932, Yeats wrote from Dublin:

My dear Joyce,
Bernard Shaw and I are busy founding an Academy of Irish Letters. We are nominating the first members, twenty-five, who have done creative work with Ireland as their subject matter....Of course the first name that seemed essential both to Shaw and myself was your own, indeed you might say of yourself, as Dante said 'If I stay who goes, if I go who stays?' Which means that if you go out of our list it is an empty sack indeed.

The Academy will be a vigorous body capable of defending our interests, negotiating with government, and I hope preventing the worst forms of censorship. All the writers here who are likely to form the council are students of your work.
Yours sincerely,
W.B. Yeats[15]

He then sent Joyce the Academy's rule-book and a signed nomination to complete. Friends advised him to join, but Joyce, the self-imposed exile, was also a born non-joiner. He returned the rule-book with a covering letter:

Dear Yeats,
Many thanks for your letter and the kind words you use. It is now thirty years since you first held out your helping hand. Please convey my thanks also to Mr. Shaw whom I have never met.... My case, however, being as it was and probably will be, I see no reason why my name should have arisen at all in connection with such an Academy; and I feel quite clearly that I have no right whatsoever to nominate myself as a member of it.

I hope your health keeps good. For myself I have to go back to Zurich every three months about my eyes. Still, I work on as best I can
Yours sincerely,
James Joyce[16]

Since the idea of Ulysses and Bloom first came into Joyce's mind while he was a bank clerk in Rome, it had taken fifteen years for the novel to gestate. Now that he had found a publisher, it was a quick birth, but not a painless one. There had been considerable argument between Sylvia Beach and Joyce about the date of publication. Joyce's superstitions asserted themselves and he decided against bringing it out at the end of 1921, because those figures added up to thirteen. It was finally decided that publication would be on 2 February 1922, his birthday. He always tried to have important events happen on that day. However, on 1 February, the books had still not arrived from Dijon. Because of the state Joyce was in – he had been rewriting until the last minute – Sylvia Beach phoned Darantière, who personally went to the station and handed two de luxe copies to the guard on the Dijon-Paris express. Sylvia Beach was waiting to collect them at the Gare du Lyon. She took a copy to Joyce in his apartment, and she put the other copy in the window of Shakespeare & Co. Family and friends had a dinner that night to view the book and toast it, but Joyce kept his copy under his chair until after the dessert and the arrival of the champagne.

The rest of the copies arrived over the next few weeks, and began to sell quickly. Meanwhile Harriet Weaver was very supportive to both Joyce and Beach. She had sent them 2,000 more leaflets and came to an arrangement with Beach that, after her edition had sold out, there would be a reprinting in Dijon at her expense, with the addition of her own imprint, The Egoist Press, added to it. This was also to be sold by private subscription. Because of the censorship problems, *Ulysses* was distributed rather like a *samizdat* in Soviet Russia. Just after Weaver had started sending out copies, the book was banned by the Home Office, and 499 copies were confiscated by Customs at Folkestone. In the U.S., around 500 copies, sent separately, were impounded by the Post Office and burned.

The critical reaction to *Ulysses* was very mixed and appeared only gradually. In Paris, the writer and leading critic Valéry Larbaud called Joyce 'the greatest living English writer', and wrote that with this book, 'Ireland is making a sensational re-entrance into European literature'.[17] In Ireland there would be many to disagree with him, usually on the grounds of the book's obscenity. Joyce's old friend and now jealous rival Oliver St. John Gogarty was reported to have said: 'That bloody Joyce, whom

I kept in my youth, has written a book you can read on all the lavatory walls of Dublin.'[18] Ezra Pound wrote a glowing review in the *Mercure de France*, bestowing the ultimate accolade by calling Joyce Flaubertian. He advised any serious writer to read it. There were other good reviews from the Paris literati, and Joyce was well on the way to becoming a celebrity there. These reviews drew the attention of the English reviewers, but they came out only in a trickle and were a great deal more varied. In the literary magazines, Arnold Bennett, Middleton Murry, and Wyndham Lewis were more complimentary about the book's style than its content. After a long pause, T.S. Eliot weighed in with a long plaudit in *The Dial*. The more popular press concentrated on the frequent obscurity, the explicit sex and the obscenity of the language. The *Daily Express* delivered itself of the verdict 'reading Mr. Joyce is like making an excursion into Bolshevik Russia: all standards go by the board.' 'Artemis', the cultural columnist in the *Sporting Times* (they actually had one) was the most graphic: 'In *Ulysses*, Mr. Joyce has ruled out all the elementary decencies of life….The main contents of the book are enough to make a Hottentot sick.' Opinion was broadly divided along generational lines. The old guard were mostly shocked and upset by Joyce's style and content, whereas the avant-garde welcomed something so original and challenging.

The Puritan backlash was inevitable. Appropriately, it came at its strongest from the man whom Joyce had called 'the puritan'. He had sent Stanislaus the book and, before that, a typescript of the 'Circe' episode. It was the latter that Stanislaus concentrated on, when replying:

> I suppose 'Circe' will stand as the most horrible thing in literature, unless you have something on your chest still worse than this 'Agony in the kips'. Isn't your art in danger of becoming a sanitary science? I wish you would write verse again….I should think you need something to restore your self-respect after this last inspection of the stinkpots. Everything dirty seems to have the same irresistible attraction for you that cow-dung has for flies.[19]

Joyce was hurt by this letter. Clearly his once admiring brother had lost respect for him and thought he was misusing his genius. Relations between them, now only postal, became strained, and Joyce was to make it worse. A month after publication, Joyce received a gift of £1,500 (approximately £60,000 today) from Harriet Weaver. He was delighted, and wrote to tell Stanislaus about it. He could not resist adding that the total money she had now given him came to £8,500 (today, approximately £250,000). His motive in divulging this is difficult to assess. Was it revenge for Stanislaus's criticism, to put his ill-paid, over-worked brother in his place? Or just to show that he had no shame about having a wealthy patron because he thoroughly deserved one? However, Stanislaus had the last word, when he wrote and asked for the £10 he had lent James two years before in Trieste, saying that 'he could hardly have need of it now'.[20]

What most upset Joyce about the reviews, on both sides of the Channel, was that they almost totally ignored his ingenious parallels with the *Odyssey*. *Ulysses* was published at the beginning of 1922 and T.S. Eliot's *The Waste Land* at the end. The two books stand like bookends to the year that Ezra Pound, to whom Eliot dedicated his poem, called 'Year One of the new era'. In all the arts, 1922 saw the birth of Modernism. For the general reading public, however, whether in Britain or the U.S., *Ulysses* was not easily obtainable, even though Joyce and his reputedly 'dirty book' had become a household word. It was never actually banned in Ireland – just not available. Usually the book would be bought in France, brought home, read and passed on. Anyone reading it purely for prurient reasons would be quickly disappointed. It is many pages before Bloom even goes, fairly graphically, to the toilet. Such readers would have done better to read the last episode, 'Penelope', first.

Meanwhile Joyce was pressing Sylvia Beach to send out more leaflets with critical quotes on them to try to get more reviews, as well as to reprint the book. He became what is known as 'a publisher's pest', and his relations with her became temporarily strained. Another woman was also growing impatient with Joyce – his wife. Nora had spent the greater part of her married life in the shadow of *Ulysses*. She and the now exhausted Joyce were experiencing the disadvantages of celebrity – eating out in restaurants, people would stare at them, or want to shake Joyce's hand and ask for his autograph. His picture had been in the newspapers, and people stopped him in the street. There were not too many men in Paris who looked like Joyce. Nora was desperate to put all that and Paris behind them for a while. With Harriet Weaver's recent gift, they could afford to travel. Nora wanted them to go to Ireland and take the children to see her family. They argued furiously about this, but, underneath this row, Joyce was angry for another reason. When all the books had arrived, Joyce gave her the thousandth numbered copy. Nora, jokingly, offered to sell it to Arthur Power, a friend who was visiting them at the time. Joyce was not amused, or by her slowness in reading the book. He wrote to his Aunt Josephine in November that 'Nora has got to page 27, counting the cover.'

Joyce argued that it was not safe for them to go to Ireland. The Anglo-Irish Treaty that created the Irish Free State had been signed in December 1921, and he foresaw the conflict looming between those who had voted in the Dáil for the Treaty and those who hadn't. He felt Dublin would be a particularly unsafe place for an anti-nationalist, apostate, expatriate, Irish writer on a pension specially granted by the British government. His paranoia about Ireland, particularly Dublin and its literary set, lasted for the rest of his life. If Dublin did not need him, he did not need Dublin. What he needed of it was already in his head. It had provided him with a book of short stories and two major novels, and a third, based on the river Liffey, was beginning to take shape in his head. Anything else he needed he could get by writing to his Aunt Josephine.

Nora now asserted her independence and left for Ireland with Lucia and Giorgio on April Fool's Day 1923. Her recent row with Joyce had been so acrimonious that her goodbye included the threat that she might not come back. After thirty-six hours on his own Joyce was bereft, and cabled to London for her to spend only a few days there and come home. Nora had no intention of doing that. She went on to Dublin to visit her rich uncle, Michael Healy, and her father-in-law, John Stanislaus. She then took the train to Galway to see her family.

Before leaving Dublin, she had received a letter from Joyce which tells her how sick and lonely he feels. The most telling sentence in it stands out very clearly – 'O my dearest, if you would only turn to me even now and read that terrible book which has broken the heart in my breast, and take me to yourself alone....'[21] Her friends in Paris thought that Nora had read more of the book than she had let on. Whether she had read it or not, she still thought Joyce would have been more successful as a singer. To their rich American friend, Robert McAlmon, she admitted, 'He may be a genius, but what a dirty mind he has, surely!' A few years later, and much to Joyce's annoyance, McAlmon quoted this in *Being Genuises Together*, a memoir of his life in Paris.[22] Nora had matched Joyce letter for letter in their erotic and scatological exchange on the two occasions when he had been away in Dublin. Those letters make it clear that she shared some, if not all, of Joyce's tastes. It is not surprising that Nora disliked the idea of the reading public knowing about what went on in her husband's mind. She was, after all, a woman of her time with no literary background – her main reading was still romantic novels – and it must have seemed to her that Joyce was exposing the most private parts of their relationship. Those particular letters were not destroyed, and eventually appeared in Richard Ellmann's three volumes of Joyce's collected letters. Nora would not have liked that either.

Nora and the children had spent two enjoyable weeks in Galway when the civil war between the Free State Army and the IRA caught up with them. Nora faced the reality of the conflict when Free State soldiers took over her bedroom, in the boarding-house, to set up a machine-gun post. A few hours later, the Joyce family were on the Galway-Dublin train. En route their carriage was fired on. Nora and Lucia dived on the floor, but Giorgio, now seventeen, remained upright in his seat, as did the old man next to him. The man asked him if he wasn't going to duck down. 'No,' said Giorgio.

'You're right,' said the old man; 'whichever side they're on, they never shoot straight.'

Giorgio was to dine out on that story for many years.[23]

Nora's uncle, Michael Healy, met the train and escorted them out to the mail-boat at Kingstown. Nora never went back to Ireland again. Two days later she, Giorgio and Lucia were in Paris. Joyce was delighted to see them again, and to be proved right about Ireland being a dangerous place to visit. It took Nora some time to recover from her experience of civil war. In August, they decided to visit London. The children were now old enough to go away with their friends, and Joyce knew the time had come for him to meet Harriet Weaver. He also hoped to use his literary contacts in London to encourage more reviews. Joyce and Nora stayed at the Euston Hotel and met Harriet Weaver on two occasions. He was impressed by her integrity and kindness. Despite her natural modesty and thrift, Joyce did not modify his own extravagance, even though it was largely at her expense. She travelled by bus and Joyce insisted on taxis, and she watched him over-tip the drivers as well as waiters. Harriet Weaver seemed able to accept his eccentricities and was fascinated by his conversation. When she asked him what he was going to do next, he replied, 'I think I will write a history of the world.'[24] If she thought that was a little over-ambitious, she didn't say so. Joyce did show his appreciation of her when, after the London trip, he wrote: 'Your extraordinary beneficence must be unique in the history of literature. I only hope I can justify it, and that fortune continues to favour me.'[25] Presumably he meant the fortune of his talent, and not Harriet Weaver's fortune. That would continue to favour him for the rest of his life.

Joyce knew that his Aunt Josephine's daughter Kathleen was a nurse in a London hospital. He contacted her and invited her out to dinner. She came with her sister, who also worked in London. It was an enjoyable evening of family reminiscences, spoilt only when Joyce asked his cousins why their mother had not commented on the copy of *Ulysses* he had sent her. His cousins looked embarrassed. Kathleen was forced to admit that her mother had said 'It was not fit to read.' Joyce replied: 'If *Ulysses* is not fit to read, life isn't worth living.'[26]

London seemed to aggravate Joyce's eye condition and he consulted three Harley Street ophthalmologists. They all gave different diagnoses – iritis, conjunctivitis, incipient glaucoma, or a combination of all three. Joyce was referred to the Westminster Hospital where they applied leeches to his eyes to purge excessive blood. Joyce decided to cut their holiday short and return to Paris to see Dr. Borsch, his ophthalmic surgeon, but he was still on his *fermeture annuelle*. When Joyce finally saw him, Borsch told him the one thing he did not want to hear – he needed another eye-operation. Furthermore, after an x-ray, Borsch decided that the eye condition was partially due to root-abscesses in the teeth. He advised Joyce to have them all removed before he had the eye operation. It need not all be done immediately, Borsch said, and Joyce could have the holiday he and Nora had arranged in Nice in the hope that warmth and sunshine would improve his health. After only two days of sunshine, the Côte d'Azur did not stay Azur for the Joyces: storms and rain arrived, Joyce's eyes were more painful, and the couple returned to Paris. He wrote about all this to Harriet Weaver, who had now become a cross between his confidante and his literary manager. He signed his letter James Job Joyce. 'Year One of the New Era' was coming to a gloomy end for him, and Year Two had some very unpleasant procedures in store. Job's comforters might have told him not to worry. After all, he was not going to go totally blind like Homer and Milton. He could always get a set of dentures. And although it had been prosecuted, banned and burned, *Ulysses* had finally been published.

CHAPTER FOURTEEN

Svevo and Psychiatry

AFTER SVEVO HAD SEEN JOYCE IN Paris and delivered the briefcase 'fastened with a rubber band the colour of a nun's belly', he went on to London. He settled back into 67 Church Lane, Charlton, and supervised the production of the Veneziani marine paint. In this post-war period, the factory was back to normal business and staffing was at its pre-war levels. Svevo renewed acquaintance with local friends. Since it was winter, on Saturday afternoons he would go with one or other of them to watch and cheer for Charlton Athletic. He returned to practising his violin and rejoined the violin trio. He went to concerts and the theatre and deplored the plays he saw there. For a country that had produced Shakespeare as well as such fine contemporary novelists, he felt now that the only good playwrights were Irish, but the plays of Wilde and Shaw were to be found more in bookshops than on the stage. Svevo worked only sporadically on *The Confessions of Zeno*, but was writing increasingly about England and the English in his journal and in several pieces for *La Nazione*. They were later published in *This England is so Different*, a collection of his many letters and essays that covered the 1920 Miners' Strike, Guy Fawkes Day, etiquette on public transport, and British social and political mores in general:

> English kindness and good manners are something very special;
> they constitute almost an unwritten law that complements civil and
> criminal law that, as far as I know, in England is not written down

either. The fact that it looks to a foreigner like a law whereas ours, at home, when it exists, looks like it is imposed on a naturally coarse people by upbringing and coercion. It is clear here that it was borne on the playing fields. For example, the violent game of rugby without 'kindness' would degenerate into fisticuffs and it was developed in the great urban centres where, without it, the movement of immense crowds would be more difficult and dangerous.[1]

Unlike Joyce, Svevo had no qualms about writing or talking about politics. He studied the British political scene closely, and found most of it admirable and, for an Italian, enviable. His own sympathies lay with the Labour Party. He was delighted to learn that when the Labour leader, Ramsay MacDonald, became prime minister in 1924, he and his cabinet went to the opening of parliament 'in top hats and wigs'. Svevo was slightly misinformed, as wigs would have been worn only by the Lord Chancellor and the Attorney General.

The aspect of British politics to which Svevo most objected was its policy towards Ireland. No doubt influenced by his many conversations with Joyce, he saw it as a continuing colonial occupation. He was in London in 1920 and 1921 at the height of the 'Troubles' and at the start of Ireland's civil war. After the death of Terence MacSweeney and the murder of the British officers, Svevo was fascinated by the reaction of the British public. Here was one aspect of that conflict where British kindness 'toned down the struggle', as he wrote in *La Nazione*.

> The coffin of the Lord Mayor of Cork was carried through London to his final rest accompanied freely by his supporters dressed as soldiers of the Irish Republic, and surrounded by the weeping and respect due to the hero.... Then we had the funeral of the English officers barbarously massacred in Dublin. It is as kind as the previous one, and its kindness is not revealed by the mourning due to those you agree with, but a feeling of deep emotion for those with whom you do not. A Sunday newspaper says: 'Emotions such as these cannot fail to bring about reconciliation between our two people.' In other countries the funerals of the victims of a popular uprising is the most dangerous moment of that uprising.[2]

For Svevo, the politics of the new Italy made an unpleasant contrast with those of the old Britain. Yet, although he remained a steadfast Anglophile, he was not blind to her shortcomings. He deplored English insularity and the lack of any attempt to learn other languages. Svevo reports that during the war, their generals, several of whom were in command of French officers and men, could not speak French. He had heard that Lloyd George understood French, but only when it was spoken by his foreign secretary, Lord Grey. Then there was Britain's well-known hypocrisy:

> Perfidious Albion has always consisted of *Gentlemen*. She is so perfidious that a *Gentleman* of the last century, revealing his country's dual quality, said: 'If we were honest for a single day, we would be lost.' But that is how countries come to know all about another country's politics. But we are all perfidious when dealing with foreign countries. Remember, we Italians are all descended from Machiavelli.[3]

In this post-war period Svevo made several trips to London, sometimes accompanied with Livia, who had also become an Anglophile. Wherever Svevo travelled, he was a sharp observer of the details of national difference. He enjoyed his London life and the contrast it made with his Trieste routine, but he was beginning to find this double life tiring. It was not just the travel, but in both places he divided his time between business and writing, and put in long hours at both.

When he returned to Trieste at the end of 1921, Svevo had just turned sixty and was bothered about his health. As a hypochondriac, this was not unusual. Now, however, he had a genuine reason. He discovered he had a heart problem, as well as a chronic catarrh and a frequent cough. His doctor advised him to go on a diet and lose weight – Svevo cut out having lunch. The doctor had given up trying to stop him smoking. When Svevo was writing he smoked even more heavily, and he was never going to stop writing. By the end of 1921, he was more than halfway through *Zeno*, and the rest of the book had been carefully planned. Zeno was now married to Augusta, and Guido had married Ada. They were to be the eternal quadrilateral of the book. Zeno's marriage was a happy conjunction of opposites, a positive with a negative, chalk with cheese. Augusta was a good Catholic with a cheerful, healthy outlook. Zeno was a non-believer, a constant questioner of his own and Nature's motives. He admired and envied his placid wife. This was strongly autobiographical.

> I occasionally went to mass with her, to see what effect the contemplation of pain and death had on her. For her it seemed not to exist, and the visit was a source of quiet refreshment to her that would last the whole week.... If I had been religious I should have ensured my everlasting happiness by staying in church all day long.[4]

Despite his wife being such a fine advertisement for the comforts of religion and the prospect of life eternal, Zeno could not accept them – on the contrary:

> At that time I was attacked by a slight illness from which I was never to recover. It was a mere trifle; the fear of growing old, and above all the fear of death. I think it rose from a kind of jealousy. While I was alive I was sure Augusta would never betray me, but I pictured to myself that directly I was dead and buried, no sooner had she provided for my tomb to be kept in good order and the necessary masses said, than she would look about for my successor.[5]

Svevo, like Joyce, had read Schopenhauer. They had discussed his work and both been influenced by his broadly pessimistic view of the human condition. Svevo did not call his protagonist Zeno without reason. He was well aware that Zeno was the father of Stoicism, which had influenced Schopenhauer. He was also familiar with Darwin's work. If Svevo had any belief, it was a form of latter-day stoicism, a struggle between man's will and Nature's implacability, the application of the old saying – 'Man proposes, God disposes', and even if one didn't believe in God, there was a great deal of unpleasant disposal going on.

> The law of Nature does not confer the right to be happy; on the contrary it condemns us to pain and suffering.... If Nature chooses you as a

victim, what is the use of complaining? Yet all do complain. They die complaining about the injustice of nature, those who feel they have not had enough, and those who have enough but still want more.[6]

An ecologist ahead of his time, Svevo was concerned about how we treat Nature as much as how it treats us.

Mother Nature created pleasure to guarantee reproduction. That obtained, if she allows the capacity for pleasure to go on existing, she only does so out of absent-mindedness, just as certain insects go on wearing their mating colours after the mating season is over. Running a firm of that size, you can't attend to every detail.[7]

Svevo was particularly impressed by Schopenhauer's view that comedy resides in the incongruity between our concepts and objective reality. The protagonists in his three novels all exist in this incongruity – none more so than Zeno.

The fourth of the six chapters of *Zeno* is called 'Wife and Mistress', and shows Zeno again trapped in an awkward situation of his own making. While he appreciates his contented marriage, he decides he needs more adventure; to live his life with more intensity. Zeno falls in love with Carla, a much younger woman with ambitions to become an opera singer. No matter of the heart is ever straightforward for Zeno. He torments himself about being unfaithful to Augusta for the first time.

I had deplored my own infidelity so much beforehand that you would have thought I might easily have avoided it. It is easy to laugh at anyone for being wise after the event, but it is almost as useless to be wise before it.... For a brief moment I was full of good resolutions. I even called to mind some curious advice that had been offered me in order to help me give up smoking, and which might come in useful on this occasion: sometimes it is quite enough if one lit a match and then threw away both the match and cigarette.[8]

Zeno was never able to throw away the cigarette, and now, with the match alight, he cannot bear to throw away the lovely and soon compliant Carla.

He finds her a new music teacher and becomes her patron. It is very much like the Pygmalion situation in *Senilità*, except Zeno is married and Emilio was not. Zeno tells Carla the story of his marriage and how he resigned himself to marrying Augusta, his third choice. When Carla asks him if his wife is pretty, he replies 'That is a matter of taste.'[9]

Svevo now develops a series of dramatic ironies plotted like a Feydeau farce. Zeno is torn between wife and mistress. When Zeno draws a more sympathetic portrait of Augusta, Carla is seized with a curiosity to see her. She persuades him to arrange an opportunity where she can view his wife unobserved. He finds a way to do this, but with a devious twist. His vanity leads him to pass off the beautiful Ada as his wife.

> I don't know even now what led me to do this. Maybe I felt the need of attaching Carla more closely to me, and the lovelier my wife seemed to her the more she would love the man who, in some sort, had sacrificed such a woman to her. [10]

So Carla goes to the prearranged position and sees Zeno's 'wife'. Later she tells him:

> –'Nobody could have mistaken her. You had described her features so accurately. Oh, how well you know her.'
> She was quiet for a moment, trying to control her emotions. Then she went on:
> –'I don't know what has happened between you, but I don't want ever again to betray that woman. She is so beautiful and so sad!' Zeno was astonished. 'Sad? You must have made a mistake. Maybe her shoes were hurting.'
> –'No, it was not her shoes.'
> Carla told me with ever-growing agitation that she had even had a few words addressed to her by Ada. The latter had dropped her handkerchief and Carla picked it up and gave it to her. Her brief word of thanks had been very moving to her. Carla realised why she had dropped her handkerchief. She could see that she had been crying. Everything was plain to Carla; my wife knew that I was unfaithful to her, and was suffering.[11]

Zeno is now in a total dilemma. There is no way to explain to Carla that 'his wife' is actually his sister-in-law – the woman who was his first choice as a wife. Because of his elaborate plan, he is about to lose the mistress he has come to love. Zeno wanted adventure, to live his life more intensely. Now he is doing that, but at the cost of his peace of mind – a fine example of the old maxim that answered prayers cause more tears than unanswered ones. That evening, over dinner with Augusta, the mystery of Ada's tears is solved. Augusta has just heard from Ada that she had caught Guido kissing a maid, and from the way she was responding, it was not the first time. The maid is promptly sacked, and Ada is now talking of separating from Guido. To pile irony on irony, in bed that night Augusta says:

–'Ada would have done better to have married you.'
As I was dropping off to sleep I murmured:
–'What a scandal! Deceiving his wife – and in her own house!'
I had sufficient decency to reproach Guido only with that part of his conduct of which I had no need to reproach myself.[12]

Since so much of Svevo's work is autobiographical, the question inevitably arises of whether or not there was a Carla in his life. There was, of course, Giuseppina Vergol, later the well-known circus equestrienne. But Svevo was not married then. None of his biographers have ever managed to discover whether in his married life there was a Carla. If there was, Svevo was careful to destroy any evidence of her, and, if not, Livia did so after his death.

In the novel, Guido has meanwhile become Zeno's business partner. Their partnership is also a disaster. Guido turns out to be a compulsive gambler and philanderer. He is even inept enough to commit suicide accidentally. It is Zeno who muddles through to save the family fortunes. Now as the eternal triangles and quadrilaterals draw to a close, Svevo returns Zeno to where he started – with Dr. S. The name of the final chapter is *Psychoanalysis*.

...I have finished with psychoanalysis. After practicing it assiduously for six whole months I find I am worse than before. If I could be sure of laughing instead of getting into a rage, I should not mind seeing him again. But I'm afraid I should end by assaulting him. Since War broke out, this town has become more tedious than usual, and to fill up the time I used to give to my treatment, I have returned to my beloved notebooks.[13]

Zeno has packed off his family to their country villa, farther away from fighting, while he remains in war-torn Trieste, still buying and selling. In the evening he turns to his notebooks. Zeno is no longer writing his notes for Dr. S., but for himself. And he has a lot to get off his chest.

Svevo has been credited with introducing psychiatry into the twentieth-century novel. He had read much of Freud's work, but, like his old friend Joyce, he did not want the critics to think he had been unduly influenced by him. On the other hand, he could not resist the comic potential of the psychoanalytic process.

I had abandoned myself to the doctor with such entire confidence that when he told me I was cured I believed him absolutely, and gave no credence to the pains in my legs which still continued to torment me. I said to them: 'You are not really there!' But they were. But that is not the reason I am giving up the cure…. I can no longer endure to be in the company of that ridiculous man, with his would-be penetrating eye, and the intolerable conceit that allows him to group all the phenomena in the world round his grand new theory…. I ought to be cured, for they have found out what was the matter with me. The diagnosis is exactly the same as the one that Sophocles drew up long ago for poor Oedipus: I was in love with my mother and wanted to murder my father. I listened enraptured…. My disease exalted me to a place among the great ones of the earth. It could even trace its pedigree back to the mythological age![14]

Earlier, Zeno has confessed to Dr. S. his infidelity with Carla, and also mentioned his interest in two of Augusta's sisters, before he married her:

He said that, if I had been able, it was clear that I would have seduced Ada and Alberta. I did not deny it, but it made me laugh when, in saying it, he put on an air of Christopher Columbus discovering

America. He must be the only person in the world who, hearing that I wanted to go to bed with two lovely women, must rack his brains to try and find a reason for it.[15]

Having given up his analysis, Zeno, out of the blue, receives a letter from Dr. S., who has evacuated himself to Switzerland. He asks to see all Zeno has recently written. Zeno decides he will send his final notes to Dr. S. They will show what he really thinks of him, and how well he has been since he abandoned his treatment. 'It was my business that cured me, and I should like Dr. S. to know it.' Zeno will now ask for his whole manuscript to be returned. However, the reader knows from the first page of *The Confessions of Zeno* that Dr. S. will not return any notes. Dr. S. has written in the preface:

> I take my revenge by publishing them, and I hope he will be duly annoyed.... He little knows what surprises lie in wait for him, if someone sets about analysing the mass of truths and falsehoods which he has collected here.

Svevo has written a book within a book. In its final pages, the reader cannot be quite sure whether what Zeno is writing is going to become part of the doctor's book, or if Zeno is just writing for himself. One may even forget that Dr. S. is, after all, a fictional character. *Zeno* is full of surprises, nowhere more than in its last two pages, where Zeno, with extraordinary prescience, has written in his notebook:

> Our life today is poisoned to the root. Man has ousted the beasts and trees, has poisoned the air and filled up the open spaces. Worse things may happen. That melancholy and industrious animal – man – may discover new forces and harness them to his chariot. Some such danger is in the air. The result will be a great abundance – of human beings. Every square yard will be occupied by a man. Who will then be able to cure us of the lack of air and space? The mere thought of it suffocates me.[16]

The note is dated 26 March 1916. The war was to continue for another two and a half years, the casualties would triple in that time.

Not surprisingly, Zeno's final notes are preoccupied with disease and disaster.

> Health can only belong to the beasts, whose sole idea of progress lies in their own bodies. When the swallow realised that emigration was the only possible life for her, she enlarged the muscles that worked her wings. The mole went underground, and its whole body adapted to its task. The horse grew bigger and changed the shape of his hoof.

Svevo knew his Darwin. He loved animals, and over the years had enjoyed writing his fables. His animals, well adjusted to their environment, are always puzzled by the behaviour of men:

> Bespectacled man invents implements outside his body, and if there was any health or nobility in the inventor there is none in the user. Implements are bought or sold or stolen. It is natural that his cunning should increase in proportion to his weakness. The earliest implements only added to the length of his arm, and could not be employed except by the exercise of his own strength. But a machine creates disease because it denies what has been the law of creation throughout the ages. The law of the strongest disappeared, and we have abandoned natural selection. We need something more than psychoanalysis to help us. Perhaps some incredible disaster produced by machines will lead us back to health.
>
> When all the poison gases are exhausted, a man, made like all other men of flesh and blood, will in the quiet of his room invent an explosive of such potency that all the explosives in existence will seem like harmless toys beside it. And another man, made in his image, and in the image of all the rest, but a little weaker and sicker than them, will steal the explosive and crawl to the centre of the earth with it, and place it just where he calculates it would have the maximum effect. There will be a tremendous explosion, but no one will hear it and the earth will return to its nebulous state and go wandering through the sky, free at last from parasites and disease.[17]

Svevo foresaw the twenty-first century's greatest nightmare – a nuclear device in the hands of terrorists – and then Armageddon.

CHAPTER FIFTEEN

Repaying a Debt

SVEVO FINISHED HIS FINAL DRAFT OF *The Confessions of Zeno* in the autumn of 1922. When he had started writing it three years before, he had said that if Italy had not come to him, he would never have thought of writing another novel 'as though it was a perfectly normal thing for a man of fifty-eight to do.'[1] As he emerged from that imaginary world of *Zeno* and its final gloomy predictions, there was little comfort Svevo could take from the real world around him. Italy may have come to him, but, apart from his novel, it had brought very mixed blessings. Like Trieste, many cities in Italy now had Fascist councils. A general strike in September played into the hands of the Fascists, and their *squadristi* went around strike-breaking and beating up workers. A coalition government was formed under a very uncharismatic liberal, Luigi Facta. The opposition was composed of a violently incompatible mix of fascists, socialists and communists. The country was increasingly polarising between the Far Right and the Far Left. For the fourth anniversary of the country's victory at Vittorio Veneto on 4 November, the government planned a day of national reconciliation. D'Annunzio was to be lured from his retirement to make a patriotic speech calling on all Italians to unite behind the flag. It was a reconciliation day that never took place. Mussolini saw that his fascist rival was about to steal a march on him. He acted quickly and planned a real march – on Rome. In the event, d'Annunzio was no threat as a rival leader. At his villa on Lake Garda, with one or several of his mistresses and apparently high on cocaine, he fell out of a window. He was seriously injured, and for several months was unable to march anywhere.

Mussolini reacted promptly with both deeds and words. In the peculiarly emotive and emetic style, that he shared with d'Annunzio, he gave a speech calling for the spiritual regeneration of Italy:

> And it is our intention to make Rome the city of our spirit, a city that is purged and disinfected of all the elements that have corrupted it and pulled in into the mire. We aim to make Rome the beating heart, the galvanizing spirit of the imperial Italy that we dream of.[2]

Mussolini mobilised his well-drilled squads and, on 27 October, they began occupying public buildings, telephone exchanges, town halls and prefectures. Now the only way to stop a fascist take-over was for the government to call out the Army. For this, Facta and the Army generals needed the royal signature. The King, Victor Emmanuel III, refused to sign. His motives were never known. One would certainly have been his fear of starting a civil war and, like many of his subjects, he must have wondered if a fascist government could be any worse than the ineffectual and unpopular ones with which he had been saddled since the war. This was Mussolini's opportunity, and he seized it with alacrity. On 29 October, he wrote in his editorial in *Il Popolo d'Italia*: 'Much of northern Italy is already under fascist control. Central Italy is completely controlled by Blackshirts.' Then, adapting a line of d'Annunzio's, he concluded 'The victory must not be mutilated. The government must be unequivocally Fascist.'[3]

The traditional image of the march on Rome has always been of Mussolini, at the head of his fascist supporters, entering the city. The reality was that Victor Emmanuel, unable to find any politician willing to lead a government under these circumstances, turned to Mussolini. Christopher Duggan writes: 'The march on Rome was an exercise in political blackmail rather than a revolutionary or military operation. It was a *coup de théâtre* rather than a *coup d'état* that brought the fascists to power.' Mussolini did not lead his men into the capital. He caught the night train from Milan and arrived in Rome on the morning of 30 October. He was driven to the Quirinal and, wearing a black shirt, had an audience with the King. He reputedly said, 'Sire, I bring you the Italy of Vittorio Veneto.'[4] He was invited to form a government and disband his now armed supporters. Mussolini accepted the invitation, but insisted that his *squadristi* should be allowed a victory parade. Reluctantly the King agreed and the *squadristi* marched through the streets of Rome singing their song 'Giovinezza', which was to become the national anthem. That night, a group of them broke into the house of the former prime minister, Nitti, and ransacked it.

Nitti was also the name of the hero, or rather anti-hero, of Svevo's first novel *Una Vita*. Its author did not see this as a happy coincidence. As a liberal and a pacifist, he was appalled that his new country was to be governed by imperialist fascists. Within two years, and with some constitutional changes, Italy produced the twentieth century's first fascist dictator. It was a decade before Hitler took power in Germany, as did Salazar in Portugal in 1934, and Franco in Spain in 1939. Closer to home, what distressed Svevo most was that the Veneziani family approved of Mussolini, and registered their company with the Fascist Confederation of Industry. Like many Italians of the upper and middle classes, the Venezianis felt that the fascists were restoring law and order and protecting their interests. Mussolini even had supporters among the intelligentsia. One was the country's most celebrated playwright, Luigi Pirandello. Svevo had greatly admired him until he did not reply to a letter, or acknowledge the book he had sent him. In September 1924, after the constitutional changes that made him effectively a dictator, Pirandello sent Mussolini a telegram:

> Excellency, I feel this is the moment to declare a faith that has been nurtured and adhered to in silence.
>
> If your Excellency deems me worthy of entering the National Fascist Party, I will consider it the greatest honour to occupy the post of your most humble and obedient follower. Luigi Pirandello.[5]

Svevo had no such 'faith', and 'adhered in silence' to his own views, except with trusted friends. They were all well aware that many of the *squadristi* were now *Il Duce*'s security police, and they used their truncheons freely on opponents of the regime who, when taken into custody, were often force-fed a litre of castor oil.

The vicissitudes of the literary life added considerably to Svevo's frustrations. His experience with *Zeno* was repeating the pattern of his first two novels – the difficulty of finding a publisher who would accept their style and content. In the end, he took the same solution as before. He found a publisher in Bologna who would print and distribute the novel, but only at the author's expense. Once again, Svevo the business-man had to pay for Svevo the writer. *The Confessions of Zeno* was published in May 1923. The local critics gave it generally favourable reviews; several praised its psychological insight, while largely ignoring its style, but even those reviews came out very slowly, while the national press ignored the book completely. The stress of getting the book published, the anti-climax of its publication and waiting for the reviews, took its toll on Svevo's health, and aggravated his heart trouble. He castigated himself for not taking his own advice –'Write one must, what one need not do is publish.'[6] Was there to be another twenty-five-year gap before he wrote another novel? Svevo knew there was not that amount of time left. Livia became very concerned about him. In December, Svevo, or maybe it was Livia, came up with the idea of sending the book to Joyce. They both knew of the success that he was having with *Ulysses* in Paris. Svevo wrote a covering note asking for advice on how to interest the Italian critics. On his next trip to London, he would come via Paris and he suggested they met.

Joyce was continuing to have a *succès d'estime* in Paris. *Ulysses* was much praised as a trail-blazer in this cultural hothouse, and it was no disadvantage for its author to be a tall, multi-lingual Irish polymath who frequently wore a black patch over his left eye. He was talked about almost as much as Marcel Proust, and certainly was seen more often. Proust, owing to his asthma and general poor health, rarely left the cork-lined study of his apartment on the Boulevard Haussmann. It was inevitable that the two men would meet. When they did, 'high bohemia', as this milieu came to be known as, was agog to hear reports of their elevated literary conversation – the clash of two great minds. They first met at a dinner at the Majestic to celebrate the premiere of the Ballet Russe production of a Stravinsky ballet, directed by Diaghilev. Both composer and director were there, as well as other icons of modernism, Picasso, Gide, and Cocteau. Joyce arrived late and rather drunk, Proust arrived shortly after him. They were introduced and talked briefly. The reports of what they said to each other are varied. The American poet, William Carlos Williams, sitting nearby, reported that the two men exchanged news about their maladies – Joyce about his sight, Proust about his lungs and digestion. A little later, Proust asked Joyce if he liked truffles and Joyce said he did. There was only one other meeting; this time at a late night party also full of artistic celebrities. Joyce told a friend that 'Proust would only talk about duchesses and I wanted to talk about chambermaids.'[7] He expanded further in a letter to his friend in Zurich, Frank Budgen:

> Our talk consisted solely of the word 'No'. Proust asked me if I knew the duc de so-and-so. I said 'No'. Our hostess asked Proust if he had read such and such a piece of *Ulysses*. Proust said 'No'. And so on. Of course the situation was impossible. Proust's day was just beginning. Mine was at an end.[8]

Neither writer appeared to have read the other's work. Joyce soon remedied this. On holiday in Nice in October 1922, he wrote to Sylvia Beach that he had read the first two volumes of what he called 'A la Recherche des Ombrelles Perdues and Du Côté de Swann et Gomorrhée et Co. par Marcelle Proyce and James Joust.'

A month later, Joyce attended Proust's funeral at the Père Lachaise Cemetery. More or less the entire cast of the dinner at the Majestic was there, but this time dressed in black. Of the four great modernist writers, Proust was the first to die, aged fifty-one. Kafka died of tuberculosis in Prague two years later, aged forty-one. Joyce and Svevo were to go on writing a little longer. In Paris, Joyce was dividing his attentions between the French translation of *Ulysses,* for which he had assembled and supervised a team that included Sylvia Beach's partner, Adrienne Monnier, Valéry Larbaud, and an unlikely collaborator, Stuart Gilbert, an English expatriate married to a Frenchwoman, who had worked for the Colonial Office and retired after being a judge in Burma. However, Gilbert did have very fluent French. He became a good friend to Joyce, but was not blind to Joyce's manipulative qualities – 'I have never known anyone with such a gift for getting people to do things for him. I used to call them "Joyce's runabout men".'[9] Gilbert knew he was one of them, but then he saw Joyce as a genius and was grateful to him for providing fascinating work to do in his retirement. This was not an uncommon pattern with Joyce's friends and collaborators. Gilbert's comment is a discreet echo, as befits an ex-diplomat, of Stanislaus's entry in his Dublin Diary of twenty-five years before. Having first lauded his brother's frequent kindness and openness 'with those who are open with him', Stanislaus adds: 'But few people will love him, I think, in spite of his graces and his genius whosoever exchanges kindnesses with him is likely to get the worst of the bargain.'[10] It is a harsh prophesy from a brother who frequently felt hard done-by. In the places where Joyce had lived, Trieste, Zurich, Paris, he had found many helpful friends. Did few of these love him? Many of them knew Joyce's vulnerabilities, physical and emotional, and certainly felt very protective about him. Would Stanislaus not have admitted this as a form of love?

The French translation took five years and was finally published in 1929. Meanwhile Joyce was spending long hours, when his sight allowed, on his *Work in Progress*. It was to be seventeen years before he unveiled it as *Finnegans Wake*. The apostrophe was omitted because it meant both the death of Finnegan, and the resurgence of all Finnegans. The action of *Ulysses* had taken place over one day in Dublin. This book covers one night in Dublin. It takes the interior monologue of *Ulysses* a stage further – into the dreams of certain of its sleeping citizens, and reconstructs their nocturnal life with its dreams and sudden awakenings.

The book's chief protagonist is Anna Livia, the River Liffey itself. Joyce had written to Svevo and received permission to use his wife's name. Her fine head of blonde hair becomes the personification of the river running through Dublin to the sea, joining all other rivers, even the canal in Trieste, in a great circular flow. This also corresponds to the cyclical nature of the book itself. No writer has ever given fairer warning, from the first sentence, of what to expect. The sentence begins in the middle:

> riverrun, past Eve and Adam's, from swerve of shore to bend of bay, brings us by a commodius vicus of recirculation back to Howth Castle and environs.[11]

To emphasise this 'recirculation', the missing beginning of that sentence becomes the last words of the book – 'a way a lone a last a loved a long the'. The 'riverrun' was a life force that joined all things together – or maybe not. The whole book is capable of 'commodius' interpretations. As Joyce wrote to Harriet Weaver, it would be 'the Muddest Thick that ever was made'. Once when asked why he had written it this way, Joyce replied, 'to keep the professors busy for three hundred years.'[12] When the same question had been asked earlier about *Ulysses*, he had given the same reply, except that book would only keep them busy for two hundred years. With *Finnegans Wake*, he was more ambitious. There was to be no respite for the professors. They would now be busy, *in toto*, for five hundred years.

At that first meeting in London in 1922, when Harriet Weaver had asked him about his next book, Joyce had told her that it would include the universal history of mankind. When he started writing, he had every intention of doing this. *Finnegans Wake* starts by concentrating heavily on Irish history, myth and legend. The ancient Irish hero, Finn MacCumhail, lies in death beside the Liffey and watches the history of Ireland and the world flow past him like flotsam on the river. He then creates an Irish Everyman character, but in no way similar to Leopold Bloom. This is no Hungarian Irish Jew, but a Dublin publican reincarnated from Celtic giants. His name is H.C. Earwicker. The initials stand for Humphrey Chimpden. He is often referred to in the book only by his initials H.C.E. which also stands for 'Here Comes Everybody' – the title of the sketch from which the book originated. 'Everybody' implies a mass Everyman, and has an even more universal ring to it. H.C.E. has a wife, Anna Livia

Plurabelle. They have twin sons, Shem the penman and Shaun the postman, his only daughter, Isabel, has a split personality – possibly Joyce's fearful premonition of what could be Lucia's fate, or maybe not. In the same conjectural way, Shem the penman is a writer, the Stephen Dedalus character of the book, and Shaun the postman, the more practical deliverer of things.

Harriet Weaver had always showed interest and been encouraging with all Joyce's work; now she bravely offered to type the opening chapters of *Finnegans Wake*. While she was typing, she became increasingly mystified as she followed Joyce's flotsam, with much jetsam, down the Liffey and into the sea. Joyce wrote her several letters explaining the book's more obscure symbolism. She typed on, without being any the wiser about where he was leading her. At one point, she made a constructive suggestion – that he consider publishing the book in an annotated form. Joyce, politely, did not consider it. In Paris, Joyce gave readings of finished chapters to interested admirers, and he grew used to defending his *Work in Progress*. After a reading he was often asked the same questions. Was he inventing a new language? Was the book a blending of literature and music? Joyce had replied, 'Pure music'. Aren't there different levels to be explored? 'No, no,' Joyce had replied, 'it's meant to make you laugh. I'm just an Irish clown, a great joker at the universe.' But after his readings, he often received letters of congratulations, sometimes even bouquets of flowers. To Lucia, who was showing a talent for drawing as well as dancing, he wrote, 'Lord knows what my prose means. In a word, it is pleasing to the ear. And your drawings are pleasing to the eye. That is enough, it seems to me.'[13]

Nora, however, regarded her husband with exasperation. She wrote to her sister Kathleen in Galway, 'He's on another book again.' She constantly asked him why he 'didn't write a book that people could understand.' Like many of their friends, Nora felt that his reputation was now such that if he would write a comprehensible novel, it would be a best-seller, and their future income would be assured. His brother, even more exasperated than Nora, had written him a long letter with some ferocious comments. Stanislaus called the portion he had read 'a drivelling rigmarole … witless wandering…a beginning of softening of the brain…. Is it written with the intention of pulling the reader's leg or not?'[14]

Joyce blithely ignored the criticism of his nearest and dearest, and of friends and foes. He pressed on, amply bearing out T.S. Eliot's encomium when they first met – 'Joyce I admire as a person who seems to be independent of outside stimulus, and who therefore is likely to go on producing first-rate work until he dies.'

At the end of 1923, in the midst of all this activity, Joyce still found time to come to the aid of a friend. He had received his copy of *The Confessions of Zeno*, with Svevo's covering letter, and the suggestion that he would come to Paris on his way to London. They arranged to meet, and Joyce went to the Gare de Lyon, but there was no Svevo. Next day he wrote to Svevo's London address.

30th Jan 1924

Dear Friend,

I went to the station but no train arrived, or was even expected at the time you mentioned. I was very sorry about this. When will you be passing through Paris again? Couldn't you spend the night here? Thank you for the novel with the inscription. I have two copies in fact, having already ordered one from Trieste. I am reading it with great pleasure. Why be discouraged? You must know that it is by far your best work. As for Italian critics I can't speak. But send copies to Valéry Larbaud, Benjamin Crémieux, T.S. Eliot (Editor Criterion), and Ford Madox Ford. I will speak and write to them about it also. I shall be able to write more when I have finished reading the book.

So far two things interest me. The theme: I should never have thought that smoking could dominate a man like that. Secondly, the treatment of time in the book. You certainly don't lack penetration and I see that the last paragraph of *Senilità*, 'Yes, Angiolina thinks and sometimes cries etc.' has been growing and blossoming in secret...

James Joyce.

P.S. Send to Gilbert Seldes, the Dial. New York.[15]

Svevo was delighted by Joyce's reaction, and enormously flattered that he had remembered the last paragraph of the book Svevo had written twenty-six years before. Svevo was a complex mix of someone who wanted recognition for his work, but had great reticence about promoting it himself. In Joyce, he found someone with no such conflicts. Joyce had total confidence in his work and absolutely no diffidence in promoting it. He had become, in the words of his new drinking companion – Ernest Hemingway, 'a sharp operator.' Yet Joyce was not solely self-interested; he would go to great lengths if he was convinced it was for a good cause. Svevo and his *Zeno* were definitely a good cause, and Joyce was as good as his word. He wrote to Svevo in February 1924:

> Dear Friend,
> Send the books without fear. I have already spoken about you to Larbaud and Crémieux. Make use of my name when you write to Seldes and Eliot. Also send a copy to Lauro de Bosis and to Enzio Ferrieri, the director of *Il Convegno*,via S. Spirito 24, Milan.
> Your book will certainly be appreciated. Who could not appreciate it....[16]

There is no record of Svevo seeing Joyce in Paris on his way home, but, in London, he abandoned his normal reticence and contacted T.S. Eliot. They had lunch together in a Fleet Street pub. In April Svevo, back in Trieste, received a letter from Joyce:

> Dear Friend,
> Good news. M. Valéry Larbaud has read your novel. He admires it very much, and will review it in the *Nouvelle Revue Française*. He has also written to a friend of his, Signora Sibilla Aleramo, of the *Tribuna*, about it.[17]

Joyce had set the ball rolling. A writer's success in Paris frequently depended on word-of-mouth and the number of mentions he received in the major literary magazines. Valéry Larbaud and Benjamin Crémieux were among the most influential critics in Paris. Larbaud edited a literary magazine, *La Nouvelle Revue Française,* and Crémieux had access to the columns of most of the others. They were also successful writers in their own right, and, very fortunately, both were great Italophiles. Crémieux had translated Pirandello's plays, with great success, into French. Joyce wrote again to say that Crémieux had also enjoyed and admired his novel and would write an article about him for *Le Navire d'Argent*. Joyce had well and truly shaken the tree. Now all Svevo had to do was sit and wait for the fruit to fall. He sat and waited in Trieste. Most writers know that finishing a book is only half the problem. It is the period afterwards that is most stressful. Svevo was sixty-three years old, his health was bothering him, and he worried that his 'afterwards' could be quite short. He waited for several months and, when no fruit fell, he became despondent. He felt it might all be a dream, or a joke that Joyce had dreamed up. Larbaud and Crémieux did sound very much like a French vaudeville act. Svevo tried to cope with the situation by writing and fictionalising what he was going through. A frustrated Triestine writer is tricked by a couple of malign practical jokers into believing that a visiting German publisher is going to offer him a large sum for the translation rights of a book that he had written forty years earlier. Svevo did eventually finish this short novel *Una Burla Riuscita* [A Perfect Hoax], and it was published two years later in an enlarged edition of the magazine *Solario* in Florence. In the U.K. and U.S. it was published under the title *A Perfect Hoax*.

This writing therapy did not work for Svevo. He finally lost patience and wrote to Joyce to find out what, if anything, was happening. Joyce immediately wrote to Larbaud;

> I had a letter from 'Italo Svevo' this morning. He is in despair about his book. If you could manage a short note on it somewhere, or as you suggested, give some pages of it in the second number of *Commerce*.....[18]

He then wrote to reassure Svevo, who replied:

Dear Friend,

Thank you for your letter of the 6th. I leave for London tomorrow. Thank Larbaud on my behalf and tell him he can do whatever he likes with my novel, even translate it *in toto* (a good idea?). I don't write to Larbaud myself only because of my experience, which is that men of letters in general are badly brought up (at least Italian ones are) and never answer letters. Of the three novels I sent to Italy none appears to have reached its destination. It is to my shame still to be worrying about my book; all the more, since I can only do it through you, and you, with your own great triumphs and anxieties (I mean about the operation) have plenty to occupy you already. When you have finished with these overtures to M. Larbaud, let's both leave the novel to its fate.

I've got hold of *Ulysses*. When I get back I will read it chapter by chapter, trying to live in it. Your brother has promised me that after I've worked through each chapter as thoroughly as I can, he will give me some help. Apart from you, I don't think I could have a better assistant....[19]

Svevo's 'experiences' made him want to avoid any further snubs from the literary world. Meanwhile he had *Ulysses* to read. He recorded later in an essay that, on a visit to Paris, he had nervously gone to see Joyce to talk about it:

I had applied myself thoroughly to the book and loved all the characters, but I had some questions to ask. For instance, in the famous dialogue between Bloom and Stephen, the element of water is studied in all its manifestations. It is analysed chemically, physically and geographically. I wanted to know why the author had not seen it in its humble, but all the same important, form of a human tear.[20]

There is no record of Joyce's answer, but the image of Svevo's 'human tear', in contrast to Joyce's 'water in all its manifestations' manages to encapsulate the difference between the two writers, the encyclopaedist and the miniaturist. At that particular meeting Joyce had put *Ulysses* behind him and wanted to talk about his *Work in Progress*.

However, Svevo's long vigil, waiting for Larbaud, did finally end. It is touchingly described in Livia's memoir of her husband:

However, in 1925, unexpectedly and suddenly, the sun rose gloriously and lit up his life. He was then sixty-three. I remember that day in January. We were sitting round the big table, where we had our meals with Letizia's family – she now had three children. Ettore absent-mindedly opened a letter from Paris. He began reading it aloud and even the way he was addressed took his breath away. It began: '*Egregio Signore e Maestro*

(Dear Sir and Master), Since I received and read *La coscienza di Zeno* I have done all I could to make this admirable book known in France. Propaganda by word of mouth only, but efficacious, as you will see....[21]

Larbaud goes on to give a list of publications which will mention the book and include translated extracts, which he will organise. He will then let a publisher see it. Meanwhile he is very interested in reading Svevo's two earlier novels. Since he has not been able to obtain them in France, could he please send them. He ends the letter:

Our friend James Joyce, as you will know, has had to undergo another operation on his eyes, but is now well and working again.

I beg you to excuse so many requests, and believe me, egregio Signore e Maestro.
Your devoted admirer
Valéry Larbaud[22]

Livia continues in her *Memoir*:

I do not remember ever having seen Ettore so radiant. It was to James Joyce, who had reappeared like a kindly star in his sky, that he owed this great satisfaction.[23]

Svevo, trepidatiously, sent his earlier two novels to Larbaud. After not too painful an interval, Larbaud replied, saying how excellent he had found the novels. 'I have read extracts to several friends, which were received enthusiastically: someone mentioned the name Marcel Proust.' Several pieces were scheduled to appear in several literary magazines, including a twenty-page extract from *Zeno*. He ended the letter:

We are impatient to start the campaign, but everyone of us has so much to do that things cannot go as fast as we should like them to; but your name is already known among the best young writers here. The rest will come gradually.

Believe me, dear Maestro, your most devoted admirer,
Valéry Larbaud.[24]

The 'someone who mentioned Marcel Proust' must have mentioned it all over the Left Bank, because Svevo was soon hailed as an Italian Marcel Proust, and *Zeno* was not even published there. In time even the Italians would realise there was a Proust in their midst. The 'Svevo campaign' was clearly underway. Svevo replied to Larbaud, and began:

> …If you knew what a revolution your two letters have made in my life. I have re-read *Senilità* and I am now seeing the book that I had regarded as worthless in the light of the judgement you have made of it; I have also re-read *Una Vita*. James Joyce always said that there is only room for one novel in a writer's heart, and that when one writes several it is always the same one disguised in other words. But in that case my one novel must be *Una Vita*. Only it is so ill-written that I would need to redo it. And for such a task I am not sure I have either the time or the health.
>
> All the same it has given me a more intense feeling of my life and my past….[25]

In May of that year, 1925, Svevo and Livia stayed in Paris for several days on their way to London. For both of them, it was a way of pinching themselves to make sure what was happening was real. On their first evening they saw Joyce and went out to dinner with him and Nora. Joyce had also invited, as if to prove they were not a French vaudeville act, Larbaud and Crémieux and their wives. The occasion was described in Livia's *Memoir*:

> A young Frenchman, Nino Frank, a writer and translator, was also there. Ettore, who as a rule was sociable, friendly and sweet-tempered with everyone, at once found himself perfectly attuned to his new friends, who showed an admiration that astonished him. Seized by what seemed like a slight intoxication, he talked a great deal that evening. He loved to be listened to, all the more when those he was speaking to were like himself.[26]

Svevo was not intoxicated; he was simply euphoric. His own enjoyment was enhanced by the presence of Mme Crémieux, who was also a novelist. Livia's *Memoir* continues:

The next evening we were invited to one of the most aristocratic literary salons, that of Princess Bassiano Caetani, the patroness of the magazine *Commerce*, at her house in Versailles. Larbaud and Crémieux were there too. During the long, brilliant conversation, my husband mentioned a new novel he was working on. It must have been the one later entitled *A Short Sentimental Journey*. During that remarkable and happy stay we also met M. Crémieux's wife, a woman of profound, sensitive intelligence. She was Corsican by birth, had studied in Florence, and spoke Italian with a perfect accent. We met every day either in her drawing-room or for lunch here and there. The lively sympathy between her and Ettore very soon became friendship, and a correspondence began between them which only ended with his death. To her he confided feelings which he liked to hide from others; always unsure of himself, he drew strength and comfort from her friendly presence.[27]

Svevo was old enough to be her father: he was 64, she 38, but he had found a kindred spirit. Judging by her *Memoir*, Livia, at least in retrospect, does not seem to have been jealous. Svevo was embarrassed when he thought of his behaviour in Paris, and in his letters of gratitude to Larbaud and Crémieux he asks them to excuse his exuberance: 'A baby 64 years old can't have such an experience with impunity.' Later, from Trieste, Svevo wrote to Marie Anne Crémieux that he was still living 'on the sounds that come from Paris.'

> … That unforgettable salon of yours, only spoilt by the photograph of Pirandello (to whom I sent my novel as well as a letter four months ago, without his deigning to reply, so that now I can't stand him: it isn't enough to write masterpieces you must be able to understand *La coscienza*) – that salon, I say, plays a part in my good fortune and I shall never forget it. There is not much chance that I will be passing through Paris again soon, since the firm considers I am too old to take on the Anglo-Saxons. I should be glad of this, if it weren't that it meant I can't thank you in person for all you have done, and wanted to do for me. It would be marvellous to come and see you as a real man of letters. To arrive in Paris and find a reception-party at the station. Then to live for a couple of months in that great city. Not too long ahead now though!

While I'm writing the sun outside is shining brilliantly. It is cold, but this only makes the air more transparent. So I sometimes think that instead of transporting me to Paris, we had better transport you to Trieste. When will M. Crémieux be free so he can travel?[28]

With 'Not too long ahead now though!' he was confiding to Mme Crémieux his increasing awareness of Time's winged chariot.

Meanwhile he had received an unexpected letter, not from Paris, but from Rome. The government wished to inform Ettore Schmitz that he had been awarded the honour of Cavaliere del Regno for his services to Italian industry. Clearly it should have gone to Olga, his mother-in-law, but women were not eligible for the award. Given his views on fascism, it was an honour of which he was more ashamed than proud. He comforted himself, however, with the fact that he was probably the only knight of the realm about to have a novel published in Paris that year.

In early January 1926 Svevo and Livia went to London, and while they were there they heard from Larbaud that the next issue of *Le Navire d'Argent* was virtually devoted to Svevo. There was a long article by Crémieux hailing him as 'the new Proust', and there were translations from *Zeno* and *Senilità* by both Crémieux and Larbaud. Svevo and Livia could not resist the temptation of a quick trip to Paris when the magazine came out. It was also an opportunity for them to see their new friends, and for Svevo to express his gratitude personally. They visited the Joyces and found him scarcely able to see after his seventh eye-operation. His play *Exiles* was about to open in London. It had still only had that one production in Munich in 1918 that had closed before Joyce could get there. Now Joyce was not well enough to travel, but even if he had been, his sight would not have been good enough to see it. Svevo promised to go to the opening night and report on the production. Joyce arranged for him and Livia to have complimentary tickets.

The opening night at the Royalty Theatre was on 14 February, missing Joyce's forty-fourth birthday by twelve days. Nonetheless there was a strange serendipity. It was an evening when Joyce's and Svevo's lives seemed to come full circle. Their earliest ambition had been to write plays. Their first published writings were dramatic criticisms,

Svevo's in Trieste on Shakespeare, Joyce's in Dublin on Ibsen. Now Joyce had a play on in London, and Svevo, his one-time pupil, was in the audience, writing a review to send to his friend, the playwright, in Paris. Next morning Svevo sent his review:

Dear Joyce,

…All the way through the evening I had the delicious sensation of being present at the unveiling of one of your major works, and one so different from all the rest. I read *Exiles* in manuscript some years ago in that precious calligraphy of yours, which I had a little difficulty in reading. Nor in fact did I get every word when I heard it acted. Particularly true when it comes to Rowan's last speech in Act One, which I imagine provides the essential clue to his behaviour. But we were rather far from the stage. Usually in London we sit so near the actors that when we say 'I beg your pardon', the actors, or at least the kinder ones, repeat themselves….

Miss Black-Roberts was unforgettable, I thought. It can't be an easy thing to do, to give that character something of the woman of the world, yet make her sincerity ring out like a bell, and without it seeming overdone. Instead of clapping I blew her a kiss, and hope it reached her….

Rupert Harvey gave me a start. I don't know if it was intended, but he moves, sits down, gets up and looks about him just like you. I should like to see him in another part now, to see if it was deliberate. He's certainly a powerful actor…. William Stack, who took the part of Robert Hand at the last moment, was also good.

…The audience was magnificent, though of course there had to be a few boors among them. A man next to me said 'They want to force on us Italian ways.' It's well known of course that Italians are jealous without even being in love.

A great deal of applause. Loudest after the first and second acts.

I hope to see you in Paris, at least for a moment, on the 25th.

Yours most affectionate

Ettore Schmitz[29]

Since the play has three acts, Svevo's penultimate sentence is a little loaded. Part of the audience would inevitably have been made uneasy by the play's morality, or lack of it. Harriet Weaver, also at the first night, reported favourably on the production to Joyce, but mentioned that at the end of Act One, when adultery is being discussed, a woman next to her got up and shouted 'I call this collusion' and walked out. A few days later there was a debate about the play, for which Svevo could not get a ticket. George Bernard Shaw spoke up for the play in the face of generally hostile reviews. Maybe if it had opened on Joyce's birthday.... Svevo was next in Paris in July 1926, to sign a contract with the prestigious publisher Gallimard. Like two benign French godfathers, Larbaud and Crémieux had arranged this, and the original plan was for Marie Anne Crémieux to translate the novel. Unfortunately, she suffered from migraine, and after a series of attacks had, very reluctantly, to back out. Svevo was very disappointed, but Crémieux found a replacement for his wife, a highly regarded young Swiss translator, Paul-Henri Michel. It was to be another year until the book was translated and published. Considerable cuts were requested en route. Svevo was not entirely happy about this demand coming from a French publisher:

> As if there weren't longer novels than mine in French. I was a bit long-winded, perhaps, but it is a painful business, for someone who *is* long-winded, to be cut off short – the sort of trauma, according to Freud, that is bound to cause repressions.[30]

Although denying the undue influence of Freud on his work, Svevo was not above quoting him to make a point. Meanwhile, the fact that the French had hailed Svevo as an 'Italian Proust' could no longer be ignored in Italy. The young poet Eugenio Montale had met Svevo briefly in Milan, and been very impressed by him. He went away and read all three of his novels and had been overwhelmed. He wrote a eulogistic article about Svevo and *Zeno* in the literary magazine *L'Esame*. Various others of Montale's literary peer group read *Zeno*, and wrote about it. By a younger generation of writers Svevo was now regarded as the sole pioneer of the modern novel in Italy. Svevo wrote an appreciative letter to Montale, and received a prompt reply:

> I have only expressed a part (and perhaps the least part) of my admiration for you in my articles. It was necessary, in addressing an

unprepared public and a timid and ignorant body of critics, to go very cautiously, or one might produce exactly the opposite of the effect one intended.[31]

Svevo reported to Marie Anne Crémieux:

The author of this letter is now a celebrity here. Every newspaper, has mentioned my name, in a more or less flattering way. As for actual criticism, there hasn't been any, but they say it will come…. I am still amazed at the way that one great kick of M. Crémieux's has opened the door of fame to me. I am known everywhere. Even in Trieste they are beginning (just) to be glad to have me among them. If I told you I was happier before all this, it would be a lie. I can remember my impatience and how I pestered my friends. What I will say is, I expected to be happier in my situation than I am. So you see, nothing is ever right in this world. They say it leads to progress….[32]

'They say it will come' – whoever 'they' were – they were right. As Montale suspected, the old guard of Italian literati were not going to surrender gracefully, and 'the timid and ignorant body of critics' were anything but timid. Fabio Caprin, an old established critic, wrote about Svevo's 'extreme poverty and style of language'. Montale's praise of Svevo was attacked in an anonymous piece in *The Times Literary Supplement* – at least Svevo was now international news:

Montale's defence of Svevo is not one that need necessarily be accepted; indeed in our view, it needs to be combated. It will certainly be combated in Italy, whose new and forcible political faith, yet to become an inspiration, will certainly not find that positive element on which it prides itself in the grotesque domestic vicissitudes of the gelatinous 'European' Zeno Cosini, the autobiographical hero of this book. [33]

The *TLS* must have gone to considerable trouble to find a pro-Italian fascist critic with the ability to construct ever longer sentences:

Italo Svevo has a restricted vision and a slipshod style, and his hero, either in his complacencies or in his indecencies, has no sublimity, and his recollections of an imaginary invalid's states of mind, far from being an effort, like M. Proust's, to arrange and fix valuable sensations of abnormal intensity, are nothing more than the voluble communications of a confessed futile and despicable person whose little desires and weaknesses are for him the centre of his interests....[34]

This battle between critics, generally the older versus the younger literati, became known as the 'Svevo Affair'. The basic conflict over *Zeno,* as with his first two novels, was always about its language, a literate Triestine against the classic Tuscan. Like Joyce, Svevo was comfortable with his style, and refused to change it merely because of ageing critics. The proof that they were right would be if their books survived longer than their critics' work. And they certainly did.

Svevo was being modest when he wrote to Marie Anne Crémieux that even in Trieste people were beginning (just) to be glad to have him among them. His literary friends at the Café Garibaldi were not just glad, they were delighted. One of them was the poet Umberto Saba. He had an international reputation as a poet, was Jewish, a Freudian and ran an antiquarian bookshop, where Svevo spent a lot of his time. He was also well-known for being cantankerous, and Svevo was the only friend who seemed able to charm him. Saba later said, and not begrudgingly, 'Perhaps there really never was a writer who so revelled in fame and remained so untroubled and uncorrupted by it.' But Svevo was troubled by it. In a letter to Marie Anne Crémieux, he wrote, 'Success (and I have had it for an hour or two, as you know) makes those who aren't used to it greedy and petulant.'

In the first 'hour or two' of his success, Svevo had accepted an invitation which he deeply regretted. He had agreed to give a lecture on James Joyce and *Ulysses* to a literary institution in Milan. Public speaking had always made him feel extremely nervous and insecure. He delivered the lecture in March 1927, and when he arrived he found – because it was in the late afternoon – that the audience was largely composed of women. They had clearly now heard of Svevo, and were interested in Joyce. This was the lecture in which Svevo defended Joyce from the accusation that he had been inspired by Freud to use interior monologue. He spoke with considerable insight of Joyce as a person and a writer, and of his association with Trieste –

... we Triestines have a right to regard him with deep affection as if he belonged in a certain sense to us. And as he was to a certain extent Italian. Trieste was for him a little Ireland which he was able to contemplate with more detachment than he could in his own country.[35]

With help from Stanislaus, Svevo had now read *Ulysses* very carefully. His view on the relationship of Stephen Dedalus and Leopold Bloom was of particular interest, although his audience would have had no idea that Bloom was partly modelled on their speaker:

At the close of a memorable day the scholar Dedalus comes to the point of feeling the Jew Bloom to be a kind of father to him, while Bloom for his part, amid dreams and adventures, is also aware of a sense of fatherhood. The incident is plausible because Bloom has lost his son, and Stephen would like to find some substitute for his own living father, whose tenor of life is enough to explain Stephen's mood of despair. This approach is rendered possible by other reasons. The Jews and the Irish are both nations whose languages are dead. Stephen, moreover, feels a relief in communion with one who eschews all the culture that obsesses Stephen.[36]

The lecture was well received, but Svevo had decided never to give another. He sent a transcript of it to Joyce. He continued his correspondence with Marie Anne Crémieux. She wrote to him:

2 February 1927
My Very Dear Great Friend,
I am very behindhand with you, but for two months I have been very ill. I am getting better at last, and one of the first smiles of my convalescence has come from *Zeno*, who is now expressed in limpid French after having charmed me in an Italian which only pedants found without grace. The translation is remarkable and I am now quite sure that you will receive the glory due to you, and that your *Zeno* will have an enormous success....Your book should appear in May or June.

You must certainly come to Paris to see that it is well-displayed in booksellers' windows. Do not sadden yourself by saying you will never be here again, you now have not only friends (and I claim to be in the front-rank of them, how presumptuous!), but a precious child, a child who has lost none of his novelty and charm through transportation, but who is in a country not his own and is in need, from time to time, of the warmth of your presence.

Au revoir, dear friend, best wishes to you and yours and to Zeno also.[37]

Nineteen twenty-seven was a fruitful year for Svevo. He heard that at last he was going to have a play produced. In April *Terzetto Spezzato* (Broken Trio) opened in Rome. It was a farce about an eternal triangle, which received good reviews and ran for a month. Svevo was suddenly too busy to go to Rome. It was a missed opportunity, because he was never to have another play produced. He had a drawer full of plays, which he occasionally took out and rewrote. He was a great theatre-goer in Trieste, London and Paris. In her *Memoir*, Livia writes that her husband once confided to her that the theatre was 'the form of forms, the only one where life can transmit itself directly and precisely.' Svevo had to console himself with a new edition of *Senilità* that was being published in Italian and French, before *Zeno*. It was because of editing this new edition that he missed seeing his play in Rome. He was grateful, however, to have this opportunity to write a new preface to the book:

> This second edition of *Senilità* was made possible by the generous word of James Joyce, who for me, as not long ago for an elderly French writer (Edouard Dujardin) was able to repeat the miracle of Lazarus. That a writer, whose own work makes such imperious demands on him, should have had the goodness of heart, on a number of occasions, to waste his precious time on behalf of his less fortunate brethren, is such an example of generosity as, in my view, explains his own extraordinary success; for all the other words he has spoken, all those making up his own vast *oeuvre*, are expressions of the same greatness of spirit.[38]

As well as its expression of gratitude, it was an appropriate gesture to the man who had suggested *Senilità's* English title – *As A Man Grows Older.*

After all the recent stresses, Svevo was concerned about his health, particularly his blood pressure. He went and wrote his will. He left most of his estate to Livia, and split the rest between his daughter, Letizia, and her husband, Antonio, whom he named his literary executor ('should my literary works, against all expectations, bring in any income.') He thanked the Veneziani Company and its directors for 'the happy and pleasant time he had spent working for it.' He ended the will:

> Please: no rabbis and no priests.
> Please: pierce my heart.
> And I say no goodbyes because I hope to see everybody this evening.[39]

At the time, piercing the heart was a quite a common custom in Italy to make sure it was really a corpse that was being buried. As well as being a hypochondriac, Svevo was also deeply claustrophobic.

He constantly pressed Marie Anne Crémieux to come with her husband and visit them in Trieste. He wrote: 'I don't know whether I shall see Paris again. I am struggling with all my might to stay on this earth which contains Paris.' But, finally, in October, *Zeno* was published in Paris, and Svevo and Livia were there and attended several parties and saw all their friends. The reviews were enthusiastic and overlapped the good reviews for *Senilità*. He had, within six months, had a play produced and two books published. He behaved as though a large weight had been lifted from his heart. It may even have helped his blood pressure.

Three months later he was back in Paris to be a guest of honour at a special P.E.N. dinner. Crémieux organised the dinner and Marie Anne sent out the fifty hand-written invitations. Jules Romains, a distinguished and popular novelist, was in the chair, the guests of honour were Svevo, the Russian novelist Isaak Babel and the Romanian poet Ion Pillat. Among the guests were the Joyces, George Bernard Shaw, Jean Giraudoux, André Gide, and the celebrated Russian writer and journalist, Ilya Ehrenburg. Livia sat next to Joyce, and records that he talked to her nostalgically about Triestine seafood, as well as the part that her hair played in his *Work in Progress*. Svevo was embarrassed talking to Jules Romains, whose work he had never read. Ilya Ehrenburg wrote a sardonic magazine piece about the occasion. One of his targets was Jules Romains:

> …in his welcome speech he talked about the foreign guests of honour as though the ultimate literary accolade was to have their books translated into French. But all was as it should be. After the speeches, everyone turned to their own concerns. All the writers talked with the publishers. The young ladies cast devoted looks at Joyce … the *ratés* (failures) and misanthropes sipped their acorn coffee. It was here that I got to know Italo Svevo. There was a twinkle in his eye. Despite the ghastly food and the world's applause, he was laughing at this select idyll. When I saw that twinkle, I saw that I had in front of me not an aesthete, but a man who was in love with life, and despite eulogies about him, an authentic living human. He smoked one cigarette after another. Then I remembered Zeno and smiled involuntarily. This man could make fun of things with kindness. Such meetings help one to live a little and hold up one's bored pen in one's hand.[40]

After the excitements of Paris, Svevo's return to Trieste and the world of maritime paint was inevitably an anti-climax. He was determined, however, not to let his recent experiences turn his head. He immersed himself in his old business routine, although he never stopped writing and entertaining his friends both at home and in the Café Garibaldi. One of his fables was written in this period, and later reproduced by Livia, who was finally resigned to his profound scepticism:

> The Lord God became a socialist. He abolished hell and purgatory, and set everyone in an equal place in Heaven, where they were in eternal happiness. A certain rich man then died and was amazed to find himself welcomed in paradise, but soon he got used to his new existence and even began to complain of it. 'What's the matter with you?' asked God in a huff. 'Oh Lord, send me back to earth, here you don't see anyone suffering.'[41]

His triumph in Paris, however, had given Svevo enough stimulation and confidence to start writing a new novel. If inspiration continued to strike, he vowed he would finally put the Venezianis' Moravia Anti-Fouling Composition behind him, and do what he had always wanted – write full-time. First, however, Livia insisted that they both needed a holiday. Svevo wrote telling Marie Anne Crémieux his plans:

Trieste, 19 August 1928
Dear Good Friend,
I have received your sweet letter of 28 July and all the news it contains....

For us to be together you must come to Trieste. I have so many things to show you, things I'm proud of. It is true I too am busy with my underwater paint, but in special cases I can make myself free of it. And there could be no more special case than the arrival of you and Signor Crémieux.... As the years pass, my gratitude to Signor Crémieux (and you who alone encouraged me before that lazy old fellow decided to write) increases.... In a few days I'm going off to the mountains, to Bormio for a fortnight. But I shall certainly be here after 10 September, and am expecting you here on my return.

I have a terrible fear that we shall not see each other again. I no longer go to London as travelling tires me, and it is very difficult for me to get to Paris. The railway makes me shudder. Ten hours by car gets me to Bormio....

You ask me what I am doing. I've written a few chapters of a new novel, *Il Vegliardo* (The Old Old Man), a continuation of *Zeno*.... If I manage to write a chapter I like, I'll send it to you.

From my wife, affectionate greetings to you and Signor Crémieux.

As for me, I kiss your hand devotedly,

Your very affectionate

Italo Svevo[42]

It is significant that in his letters to Marie-Anne Crémieux, he does not sign himself Ettore Schmitz. To her he wants to be the man she met and knew in Paris – the writer Italo Svevo. He had only really loved two women in his life, one was his wife Livia, and the other was M. Crémieux's wife, Marie Anne, and that, very discreetly and gallantly, in the pages of the many letters they exchanged.

At the end of August, Svevo, Livia and their six-year-old grandson,

Paolo, Letizia's second son, set off for Bormio, a spa in the Italian Alps, which they had visited the previous year. They were driven by a chauffeur. At the last minute, Svevo had slipped the opening chapters of *Il Vegliardo* into his suitcase – in case he found the time to do a little rewriting.

CHAPTER SIXTEEN

The Last Cigarette

IN PARIS, THE JOYCES' NOMADIC existence stopped. They had found a spacious apartment in a mid-nineteenth century block in the Square Robiac and were to stay in it for six years. It was their longest period in one place since Joyce and Nora had lived together. There were three bedrooms and a large study for Joyce. He spent long hours in there inventing his own unique language for *Work in Progress*. That was still its title, except to the privileged few, who included Nora and Svevo. The latter had first-hand experience of his friend's obsession with his new book. When he visited Joyce in Paris in 1924, Svevo had wanted to discuss *Ulysses*, but all Joyce wanted to talk about was *Work in Progress*. Its real title had slipped out when Joyce was explaining that his inspiration for a title came from the old Irish story of the hard-drinking hod-carrier Finnegan who, under the influence, falls off his ladder and is pronounced dead. His body is laid out, but in the middle of the wake the smell of whiskey is so great that Finnegan revives and grabs a passing glass.

Joyce had a particular literary problem of which he was very aware. It took him a long time to write a book – *Ulysses* had taken him seven years – and he had a premonition that *Finnegans Wake* would take even longer. It actually took seventeen. The notoriety of *Ulysses* combined with his being in Paris at the right time had turned Joyce into a literary celebrity. The problem was how to keep that reputation alive if he was not going to produce a new book in the near future. Everyone would ask if he had he run out of steam? Joyce had an innate flair for publicity, but, as a writer, he wanted to be celebrated for his work and not merely for himself. As well as the readings he gave, he knew enough editors of literary magazines to have them publish excerpts of chapters as he wrote them, rather as he had done with *Ulysses* and *The Egoist*. He had become friendly with Eugene and Maria Jolas, American expatriates who had been living in Paris for many years, and had started *transition*, a magazine for experimental writing. This suited Joyce perfectly, and the Jolases were now to play an important part in his life. They published the first chapters of *Work in Progress*. Joyce's title had the right ring to it, cleverly suggesting that here was an author important enough to have his creative process monitored. But this measuring out of his *Work in Progress* in teaspoonfuls ran the risk of being counter-productive. Of those who read it, as many might dislike as like it. As it turned out, the nays seemed to outnumber the ayes, both among friends and family.

The first of the nay-sayers was Stanislaus. His letter, in August 1924 (see note 13, Ch. 15) had spelt out very clearly and abusively his reaction to the three chapters he had read. Now at Easter 1926, Stanislaus came to visit his brother in Paris. It was the first time they had met since Joyce had left Trieste six years before. Stanislaus's criticism had inevitably led to a further coolness in their relationship. After a few days at Square Robiac, the puritan in Stanislaus asserted itself again. He felt his brother lived among admirers and sycophants, still drank too much, and had become obsessional about making puns. Nor did Stanislaus endear himself by telling his brother that he had written 'the longest day in literature, and now you are conjuring up the deepest night.'[1] Conversation was less combative when they discussed the family. They had both been very fond of their Aunt Josephine and had been saddened by her death the year before. It was a harder loss for Joyce than for Stanislaus – he had lost his main researcher of times past in Dublin. As for their father, now nearing eighty despite all the drink, John Stanislaus weighed heavily on Joyce's conscience. He felt he should go and see him before he died. In the end he never did get round to it, but at least he wrote to him from time to time. Stanislaus, more traumatised by his early home life, had no desire to see his father ever again. In all, his visit to Paris was not a great fraternal success.

As if Stanislaus's views were not discouraging enough, Joyce's normally supportive friends were also turning against the published excerpts they read of his *Work in Progress*. Ezra Pound did not mince his words:

> So far as I can make out, nothing short of a divine vision or a new cure for the clap can possibly be worth all the circumambient peripherization. There is not even the inkling of a joke there....[2]

Virginia Woolf had already argued with the admiring T.S. Eliot over *Ulysses*. She characterised it as the work of 'a queazy undergraduate scratching his pimples'.[3] Now she sent a copy of the 'Anna Livia' chapter to a friend with a covering note, in which she called it 'unintelligible' and added 'perhaps under morphia his meaning would swim to the surface, but it's a bloated drowned dog as likely as not, when you get it.'[4] Fortunately, Joyce did not see that letter. The one he did receive, and the most upsetting, was from Harriet Weaver. Because she had typed the first chapters of the book, she was the closest to it. She had had her misgivings about the content and the form it took from the beginning, but like the perfect benefactress she was, she was nervous about upsetting Joyce's creative processes. By February 1927, she was unable to sit on her unease any longer:

> ...Some of your work I like enormously – as I'm sure you know – especially the more straightforward and analytical parts and the (to me) beautifully expressed ghost-parts (for instance, the sentence in Shaun about the date and the ghost-mark.) But I am made in such a way that I do not care much for the output from your 'Wholesale Safety Pun Factory', nor for the darknesses and the unintelligibilities of your deliberately-entangled language system. It seems to me you are wasting your genius. But I daresay I am wrong and you will go on with what you are doing, so why thus stupidly say anything to discourage you? I hope I will not do so again.[5]

Joyce was so upset by this letter that he took to his bed for two days. Nora was not sympathetic. On the question of 'unintelligibility' she was at one with Harriet Weaver. Nora's view had always been that he should write sensible books that ordinary people could understand. Otherwise, he would have been better off as a singer. She was, quite naturally, worried that her husband was about to write himself out of their benefactress's generosity. But Harriet Weaver was not that sort of benefactor. She was generous enough to know that she could be wrong. Joyce was a genius, even while 'wasting it', and her philanthropy was not based on his merely pleasing her. And Joyce's attitude amply bore out T.S. Eliot's initial view that he was 'exceptional as he seems to be independent of outside stimulus.' Stimulus, of course, includes other people's criticism. When he went to the P.E.N. dinner in honour of Svevo, it must have seemed to Joyce that his old friend was receiving all the plaudits, while he was getting only brickbats. Later on that visit, Svevo and Livia had dinner with the Joyces, and Joyce told Svevo how touched he had been by his preface to the new edition of *Senilità*.

During this whole period Joyce had another crucial battle on his hands. He had discovered in 1925 that in the U.S. an eccentric magazine publisher, Samuel Roth, had started serialising *Ulysses* in *Two Worlds*, an early form of *Playboy* magazine that juxtaposed serious stories with titillating ones. For Roth, *Ulysses* fitted both categories, and its notoriety would sell magazines. Roth sent Joyce $100 and ignored his objections. Joyce, however, did not send it back, which was a mistake. He was not in the habit of returning money. This, however, enabled Roth to claim that Joyce had been paid for his work. The U.S. was not a signatory to the Berne Copyright Convention, and did not become so until 1988. This led to the more dubious American publishers pirating the works of foreign non-resident writers. Joyce was advised to go to law in the U.S. and fight for an injunction. Joyce's legal fees mounted and Roth continued publishing, claiming his magazine published at most five hundred copies.

On a trip to the U.S., Ernest Hemingway looked into the matter for Joyce, and found that Roth's magazine had a circulation of around ten thousand copies. Hemingway and others advised Joyce that the best way to deal with Roth was to organise a petition signed by well-known writers and have it circulated in the U.S. to attract publicity. Archibald MacLeish was an expatriate American, who had switched from a promising career as a lawyer in New York to become a poet in Paris. (He later became a leading American poet and Librarian of Congress.) He had recently attended a Joyce reading of *Work in Progress*, and next morning wrote Joyce a letter:

Dear Mr. Joyce,

I had not yesterday – nor have I today for that matter – words to tell you how the pages you read us moved and excited me. This pure creation that goes almost beyond the power of the words you use is something I cannot talk about. But neither can I keep silence. Of this I am sure – that what you have done is something even you can be proud to have written.
Faithfully yours,
Archibald MacLeish[6]

These were the very words that Joyce wanted to hear – the very words he would have chosen himself. Now he sought out MacLeish for legal advice, and it was he who wrote Joyce's protest in the correct legal, but rousing, language:

Roth's piracy is a matter of the gravest import not only to all writers but to all honest men, against which American law offers no protection. The undersigned protest to American publishers and readers is not primarily in the name of an esoteric masterpiece but in the name of common honour and decency and of that security of the works of the intellect and the imagination without which art cannot live.[7]

Writers are always passionate about their copyright, and the protest was signed by 168 internationally known authors. Joyce's case eventually came before the New York Supreme Court and an injunction was issued preventing Samuel Roth from using any more of Joyce's work. The damages granted Joyce were small and did not even cover his legal bills. He only ever paid half of them. Despite the royalties coming in from *Ulysses*, via Sylvia Beach, money still seemed to be an ever present problem for Joyce. He wrote to Harriet Weaver:

My position is a farce. Picasso has not a higher name than I have, I suppose, and he can get 20,000 or 30,000 francs for a few hours' work.

I am not worth a penny a line… I am more and more aware of the indignant hostility shown to my experiment in interpreting 'the dark night of the soul'…. I cannot understand why they cannot understand that the night world can't be represented by the language of the day.[8]

Joyce survived this 'hostility', and the long legal process with Roth, but the strain of it, on top of his work, according to his ophthalmologist, exacerbated his eye problems and Joyce went for his tenth eye operation. Before he went into hospital there was at least some good and most surprising news from Trieste. After forty-two years as a bachelor, Stanislaus had written that he was going to marry Nelly Lichtensteiger, an Austrian former student of his, fourteen years his junior. Joyce was not fit enough to attend the wedding, but sent a cheque that would have more than covered the debt he still owed Stanislaus. In August 1928, he was well enough to go with Nora to Salzburg to meet Stanislaus and Nelly at the end of their honeymoon trip. There is no account of how they all got on, but marriage must have already mellowed Stanislaus – the only remark he made about his brother's book was that he should hurry up and finish it.

On his return to Paris in September, Joyce received some very sad news. He immediately wrote about it in a letter to Harriet Weaver:

I have some very bad news. Poor old Italo Svevo was killed on Thursday last in a motor car accident. I have no details yet only a line from my brother and so I am waiting before I write to his widow. Somehow in the case of Jews I always suspect suicide though there was no reason in his case especially since he came into fame, unless his health had taken a very bad turn. I am very sorry to hear of it, but I think his last five or six years were fairly happy.[9]

Wherever Joyce got his strange idea that Jews were more prone to suicide than others is unclear. Svevo was certainly not a suicide. He was returning from his holiday in his car from Bormio with Livia and their six-year-old grandson, Paolo, and the chauffeur was driving. In a heavy rainstorm the car skidded on a mountain road, swerved, and crashed into a tree. The chauffeur was unhurt. Paolo's face was covered with blood, but only from superficial facial cuts, and Livia suffered a fractured forehead. She and the chauffeur hauled Svevo out of the car. He was clutching his leg and groaning. Local cars soon arrived and they were driven to the hospital in the nearest town, Motta di Livenza. A doctor examined them and immediately saw that Svevo was in the most serious condition. It was not his broken femur that was critical, but the effect of the shock on his heart. The hospital did what they could for him, but next morning it was clear that he was dying. Letizia arrived at dawn with her husband, Antonio Fonda, and Svevo's nephew, Aurelio Finzi, who was a doctor. They all sat in the room around Svevo's bed.

There have been various accounts of Svevo's last hours. It was expected that a man, renowned for his *witze* all his life, would produce some memorable last words. The most reliable account and quotes have to come from Livia's *Memoir*, who was there beside his bed.

When he saw Letizia was weeping, he said gently, 'Don't cry, Letizia, dying is nothing'. A little later, he saw his nephew lighting a cigarette, he made a sign asking for one. Aurelio refused him. Then Ettore said, his voice already muffled: 'That would have been my last cigarette'.

A nurse came in and asked me quietly if it was necessary to send for a priest. Although I was very religious, I did not think it was right. Ettore heard me, and I saw he was joining his hands together. I asked him: 'Ettore, do you want to pray?'

'When you haven't prayed all your life, there's no point at the last minute.'

Then he said no more. Two hours later he was dead. It was half past two on Thursday, 13 September 1928.[10]

Svevo had finally found the cure both for smoking and hypochondria.

Thus an accident ended his life. Our time together on earth was over. The man who had for so many years held me sweetly by the hand was no more. I remained alone to face the terrible storms hanging over me, without his comfort, to bear the appalling horrors which the war was to pile up for our family.[11]

The letters of condolence began to arrive. Joyce's arrived two weeks after Svevo's death, when he had ascertained more about the facts.

Dear Signora Schmitz,

A Trieste newspaper has been forwarded to me from Le Havre in which there is a paragraph about the fatal accident to poor Schmitz and the injuries to yourself.

I telegraphed you at your Trieste address although I did not know where you then were.

We are all greatly shocked to hear of his death. A very sympathetic notice by Madame Crémieux appears in the *Nouvelles Littéraires* and I am having a copy sent to you. I am also asking the editor of *transition* to reprint, by permission of the same paper, M. Nino Frank's article written when you were last here which is the best literary portrait I can recall of my old friend. I, at least, can see him through the lines of it.

Later on, when time and remembrance of your own devotion to Italo Svevo have in some way reconciled you to such a loss, will you please let me know what success he has had with the English and American publishers to whom I had recommended him. I spoke to his German publishers in Zurich last month and he told me they would bring the book out this autumn.

I hope you have recovered from your shock and your injuries. It is perhaps a poor, but still some, consolation, to remember that our last meeting in Paris was so pleasant to us all.

Please remember me if at any time my help can serve to keep alive the memory of an old friend for whom I had always affection and esteem.

To yourself, dear Signora Schmitz, and to your daughter, all our sympathy.

Sincerely yours,

James Joyce[12]

Letters came from all Svevo's artistic friends at the Café Garibaldi, from all his admirers and business friends in Trieste, from his many friends in London, particularly from Charlton, and his new literary friends in Paris. Numerous Italian and French newspapers and magazines wrote columns about him. In one, Valéry Larbaud lamented that Svevo had to wait so long to receive his just reward, and that he regretted not having read Svevo's work sooner and faster. This was a feeling shared in many of the obituaries and memorial pieces. Larbaud wrote of Svevo's distinctive and colourful language, and of Trieste itself – 'Where a disenchanted comic muse, subtle and kind, dwelt for some time.'[13] Benjamin Crémieux wrote to Livia of his own guilt at not seeing more of Svevo when he was in Paris, and of that last memorable dinner at P.E.N.:

…where he was so happy, alive, for all that he was under no illusions. He left all the other writers who were there with a charming remembrance. No one has forgotten him; they all ask for news of him every time we meet.

The longest and most heartfelt letter came from Marie Anne Crémieux. A letter of profound condolence is addressed to Livia, but included another letter addressed to the departed Italo Svevo.

Dear Great Friend,

I have collected all your letters. I have looked at them all again. Who should I consult but you yourself? I see that in every one of them there is the same plea: 'Dear friend, you must both come to Trieste. If you do not come, it is clear that I shall never see you again.'

You were right! You knew. With your sweet and wise obstinacy you were preparing for departure…. And we let you go without seeing you again. Poor deaf people that we are! You had such need of your friends. Glory – that glory that came to you so late – meant a lot to you, certainly; but it was only as dear as it was because of your friends, who helped you, and for whom I know you would have sacrificed it if need be.

Dear Italo Svevo, you who slew all the vanities…. We got to know each other very quickly. We exchanged great pledges of loyalty and friendship. Should I not have kept you company always? You did me the honour of believing yourself safe when I was with you. How is it I do not keep your company today, and how shall I voice my sorrow?

To that smile that I send you over there, where you no longer are, the smile that dares to express admiration and tenderness that one finds so hard to express to the living – to that smile, dear friend, you will not respond. But your smile will never be absent from our house.

Marie Anne Crémieux[14]

In fact, this was a much longer letter, and the less personal parts of it appeared in both the *Nouvelles Littéraires* and the Italian literary magazine *Solario*. Marie Anne Crémieux was clearly distraught, but Livia seems to have had no qualms about including most of the letter in her *Memoir*.

Svevo's funeral was attended only by close family and the Veneziani employees. He was buried in the family chapel in the Sant'Anna Church in Trieste, without any religious ceremony. There is a mosaic reproduction of the Sassoferrato Madonna on the wall of the chapel, and underneath it is a memorial plaque with an epigraph composed by Svevo's cantankerous poet friend, Umberto Saba:

Fortune
was to him as far as it can be to any man
favourable
… … …
From his own consciousness and that of his race
from all that unsuspectingly surrounded him
he drew
the matter for three novels and one
gentle fabled-blossomed
tale.
He lived
His last years' thousand and one days
As in a dream a sunset
of gold.

Later, and less formally, Saba wrote a short reminiscence of Svevo. He recalled with affection how Svevo would come into his bookshop to chat with their friends. Svevo liked to talk of his business *coups*. Everybody's favourite was the one about how he had gone to the Admiralty and, in five minutes and in English, have his cherished underwater paint adopted by the most powerful navy in the whole world. He was a man 'who seemed to be, and was, full of humanity, and after his unexpected literary success, of an affecting *joie de vivre*.'[15] Saba was much impressed when told, not entirely accurately, about Svevo's last words: 'Is this all there is to dying? It's easy, very easy. It's easier than writing a novel.'[16] However, he thought Svevo's finest *witze* was 'That would have been my last cigarette'.

Saba wrote finally: 'I've always thought (and these words uttered by that man at that moment confirm my belief) that humour is the highest form of kindness.'[17]

CHAPTER SEVENTEEN

The Final Border

JOYCE OUTLIVED SVEVO BY THIRTEEN years, but the shadows were growing, quite literally, for the rest of his life. His sight continued to deteriorate, and there were periods when he was dependent on people to read to him and take dictation. Despite this, he continued to write his *Work in Progress*. He publicised the book, and often found himself defending it, when extracts were published. Increasingly, Lucia's mental state was a source of anxiety. She was very much closer to her father than to her mother, and it was Joyce who accompanied her to a string of Parisian doctors and psychiatrists. At one point, they travelled to Zurich together, Joyce went to visit a highly regarded ophthalmologist, Lucia saw Dr. Jung, who decided she was not a suitable subject for psychoanalysis. Jung believed that the core of Lucia's problems lay in the father-daughter relationship, and that they both had schizoid tendencies, which Joyce managed to release creatively in his writing. Lucia, talented but not a genius, had found no such outlet. Jung had read *Ulysses* and written about it. Many years later, he told Richard Ellmann, in an interview, that he had found father and daughter were like 'two people going to the bottom of a river, one falling and the other diving.'[1]

Ill health now dogged the Joyce family. In 1929, Nora was suspected of having cancer and given radium treatment, which was ineffective. A short time later she was back in hospital for a hysterectomy. On both occasions a camp bed was provided by the hospital so Joyce could sleep beside her. He showed how profoundly he depended on Nora's loyalty and toughness.

Between his trips to the hospital, Joyce had time to have lunch with H.G. Wells, who was passing through Paris. Joyce had not met Wells before, and found him friendly and stimulating. Wells moved on for a holiday on the Riviera, and wrote to Joyce from there. The letter was like receiving a warm embrace before being banged on the head:

My Dear Joyce,

I've been studying you and thinking over you a lot. The outcome is that I don't think I can do anything for the propaganda of your work. I've an enormous respect for your genius dating from your earlier books and I feel now a great personal liking for you, but you and I are set upon absolutely different courses. Your training has been Catholic, and insurrectionary; in stark opposition to reality. Mine, such as it is, was scientific, constructive and, I suppose, English. Your mental existence is obsessed with a monstrous system of contradictions. You really believe in chastity, purity and the personal and that is why you are always breaking into cries of cunt, shit and hell....

...Your two last works have been more exciting to write than they will ever be to read. Take me as a typical common reader. Do I get much pleasure from this work? No. Do I feel I am getting something new and illuminating? No. So I ask: who the hell is this Joyce who demands so many of my waking hours of the few thousand I have left to live for a proper appreciation of his quirks and fancies?

All this from my point of view. Perhaps you are right and I am all wrong....

My warmest good wishes to you, Joyce. I can't follow your banner any more than you can follow mine. But the world is wide and there is room for both of us to be wrong.

Yours,

H.G. Wells[2]

Wells was declining the invitation into Joyce's maze. Joyce might question the proposal to take Wells 'as a typical common reader', but, uncharacteristically, Joyce did not take offence at the lengthy criticism in his letter. He had liked Wells and they agreed to meet again. With Jung's implication that his work was schizoid and now with Wells calling him a deluded Catholic, the nay-sayers' list was growing longer.

In December 1930, Giorgio, who now called himself George, married Helen Fleischman, a wealthy New York divorcée, ten years older than him. It was the possibility of his becoming a grandfather that decided Joyce to plan a most surprising event. He and Nora, now in very good health, went to London and were married in a registry office in Kensington on 4 July 1931, chosen because it was his father's birthday. After seventeen years, Joyce felt that his father would be pleased that he was no longer living in sin. He had finally succumbed to the idea of legitimising their children, and avoiding problems with any inheritance he might leave his family. They had hoped to keep the event quiet, but their marriage, with photograph, was on the front page of the *Evening Standard.* A grandson duly arrived in 1932. He was named Stephen James Joyce. There was big family argument about whether he should be christened or circumcised because Helen was Jewish. Joyce was against both courses. In the end, the baby was christened but nobody dared to tell Joyce.

This birth had just been preceded by a death in the family. John Stanislaus Joyce died on 29 December 1931. He had been ill for some time, but even though his eldest son never came to see him, he still remained his favourite. Joyce wanted to avoid emotional farewells, but another potent reason for not going to Dublin was his hatred of his jealous 'enemies' there – Gogarty and Cosgrave, and a host of lesser fry – not to mention the publishers. Shortly after *Ulysses* was published, W.B. Yeats had written about Joyce being 'in flight from the object of his hatred…the Dublin that he hated but would never forget.' Ten years later, Joyce's feelings were unchanged. His fears had been confirmed when Nora and the two children had been fired at on that Galway-Dublin train. Joyce preferred the Dublin of his own reality, created with pen and paper in front of him – in Trieste or in Paris.

Despite being thoroughly neglected, John Stanislaus was clearly proud of his son the writer living in Paris. That had a glamorous ring to it. John Stanislaus must have read some of *Ulysses*, because he called his son 'a blackguard' for writing it. He had heard about *Finnegans Wake* from others, as well as from Joyce in his letters. Just before he died, he ventured another gem of literary criticism – 'I hope his night thoughts are better than his day thoughts.' However, Joyce was deeply upset by his father's death. On 1 January 1932, in a letter to T.S. Eliot, he wrote: 'He had an intense love for me and it adds anew to my grief and remorse that I did not go to Dublin to see him for so many years.'[3] In a letter to Harriet Weaver, shortly afterwards, he wrote:

> ... He was the silliest man I ever knew and yet cruelly shrewd. He thought and talked of me up to his last breath. I was very fond of him always, being a sinner myself, and even liked his faults. Hundreds of pages and scores of characters in my books came from him. His dry (or rather wet) wit and his expression of face convulsed me often with laughter.... I got from him his portraits, a waistcoat, a good, tenor voice, and an extravagant and licentious disposition (out of which the greater part of any talent I may have springs).[4]

None of John Stanislaus's other eight surviving children ever remotely felt like that about their father. 'Being a sinner myself' is not very explicit. It is more like a nod, a euphemism from one heavy drinker to another across the generations. John Stanislaus had made James his sole heir. There was one small property left. To mark his sadness at his father's passing, Joyce invented a new weekday calendar – Moansday, Tearsday, Wailsday, Thumpsday, Frightday, Shatterday.

In 1932, the publishers Random House bought the rights to *Ulysses*, and an appeal against its banning was lodged in the Federal Court in New York. In early 1933, a liberal judge, John M. Woolsey, lifted the ban. Joyce was delighted, and said that now England 'would follow suit in a few years and Ireland a thousand years hence'. *Ulysses* was published in the U.S. in 1934, and in England in 1936. In fact the book had never been banned in Ireland, but was never available since booksellers feared prosecution. It did, however, become available in somewhat less than a thousand years. Sylvia Beach, after some persuasion, had agreed to hand over her rights in exchange for a small percentage of royalties. These financial arrangements and Joyce's constant nagging for advances led to an estrangement between them. Beach's partner, Adrienne Monnier, whose magazine *Le Navire d'Argent* had been so helpful to Joyce, was the first to take direct issue with him about his financial habits. André Gide had remarked to Monnier that Joyce's courage in carrying his literary experiments to the limit, indifferent to success or money, had something saintly about it. This remark was reported to Joyce. For Monnier this was the last literary straw. She wrote to him:

> …What Gide doesn't know – and like the sons of Noah we put a veil over it – is that you are, on the contrary, very concerned about success and money. You wish others also to go to the limit; you lead by rough stages to some Dublingrad or other place, which they're not interested in, or rather, you try to lead them. My personal opinion is that you know perfectly well what you are doing, *in literature,* and that you are quite right to do it, especially if it entertains you; life isn't so funny in this vale of tears, as Mrs. Bloom says, but it's folly to try and make money at any cost with your new work. I won't say you can't make any, everything is possible, but it is most unlikely….Times are hard and the worst isn't over. We're travelling now third class and soon we'll be riding the rods.
>
> Give my best regards to Mrs. Joyce and Lucia, and be assured, dear Mr. Joyce, of my very great and faithful admiration.
> Adrienne Monnier[5]

Clearly, Sylvia Beach and Adrienne Monnier still thought Joyce was a genius, but he was not their genius any more. They turned down the possibility of playing any part in the publication of *Work in Progress*.

The hard times to which Adrienne Monnier referred were the Great Depression. It had hit the U.S. first. The dollar was down, and returns on investments and dividends nosedived. Many American expatriates went home, and several very rich ones were ruined. Political tensions in Europe were rising, and the carefree, rich days of Paris were nearly over. One of Joyce's American admirers, who remained a drinking companion, was Ernest Hemingway. He was a hard drinker with a hard head, and enjoyed Joyce's company. In certain circumstances, Hemingway was very useful. According to him,

> We would go for a drink, and Joyce would fall into a fight. By then, he couldn't even see the man so he'd say: 'Deal with him, Hemingway. Deal with him.'[6]

Hemingway finally left Paris in 1936 to report on the Spanish Civil War.

Now Joyce was even more dependent on loyal friends. Eugene and Maria Jolas published almost everything he wrote in their magazine *transition*. Eugene Jolas would take Joyce to the cinema, and have to sit in the front row so Joyce could see the film. Another helper was Samuel Beckett, a brilliant linguist and aspiring poet, who was a great admirer of Joyce's work. He first met Joyce in 1928 and the two men got on well. Beckett was never Joyce's secretary, as has sometimes been claimed, but he was soon taking Joyce's dictation for *Work in Progress*, an extraordinary linguistic challenge. At the time, Beckett himself was writing poetry and a novel. He went back to Dublin to take up a teaching post in French at Trinity College, but stayed only for a year. He disliked academia and, like Joyce, found literary and social life in Dublin conservative and constrictive. He returned to Paris and continued his visits to Joyce. These visits created a highly embarrassing situation for Beckett and the Joyces, for it soon became clear that Lucia was in love with Beckett. She was two years younger than him, and they had gone out together several times, but he did not reciprocate her feelings. He was forced to make it clear to her that he came to the apartment only to help her father. Lucia's mental state was immediately affected. She became seriously depressed and then uncontrollably angry. Joyce and Nora, who were both fond of Beckett, agreed that the only course was for him not to see her. They apologised, but banned him from coming to the apartment for a year. Beckett went off travelling in Europe, but still saw Joyce when he returned to Paris. Later, he admitted Joyce's influence on him, but added, 'Joyce was a synthesiser, bringing in as much as he could. I am an analyser, trying to leave out as much as I can.'[7]

The person who did become Joyce's secretary, and looked after all his affairs, was Paul Léon. He was an admirer of Joyce's work, became a close friend, and refused to take any pay. He and his wife, Lucie, were both Russian Jews who had emigrated from Russia to Paris just after the revolution. Lucie became a correspondent for the *New York Herald Tribune*. In Russia, Léon had been trained both in law and literature. He had published several scholarly books in French, and was fascinated by linguistics. Joyce always felt most at home with people who were linguists and etymologists – Beckett, Jolas, Stuart Gilbert and now Paul Léon. They would sit around, usually with a bottle of wine, and discuss words and ideas in several languages.

Léon and Joyce shared a caustic sense of humour, and Joyce was always happy to let Léon sign his letters. An example of their collaboration is their reply to a questionnaire from the International Union of Revolutionary Writers in Moscow, which asked 'What significance has the October Revolution had on you as a writer?' and was signed by H. Romanova. They replied:

> Dear Sir/Madame,
> Mr. Joyce wishes me to thank you for yours of the 17th instant from which we have learned with interest that there has been a revolution in Russia, in October 1917. On closer investigation, however, he finds that the October Revolution happened in November of that year. From the knowledge he has collected up to now, it is difficult for him to judge the importance of this event, and he wishes only to say that judging from the signature of your secretary the changes cannot amount to much.
> Yours sincerely,
> Paul Léon[8]

As Joyce's sight got ever worse and Lucia's mental state increasingly unstable, the Léons became very protective about Joyce and Nora. Léon was enormously stimulated by Joyce, but had the ability to treat him with a certain wryness. Early in their association, he wrote to his brother in London:

> Lately I've been spending a lot of time with literature. I have been working with James Joyce. The name probably means nothing to you, but it is that of the great, the greatest, writer of our time. And yet he is writing in a way that nobody understands or can understand. I've found it wonderfully amusing to translate simple ideas into incomprehensible formulas and to feel it is a masterpiece.[9]

Joyce's fiftieth birthday was on 2 February 1932, and all his friends had gathered at the Jolas's apartment to celebrate it. There was a birthday cake with fifty candles, and a smaller one in the shape of a copy of *Ulysses* with ten candles on it. That afternoon, Lucia had an argument with Nora. She became hysterical and hurled a chair at her mother. George, who was there, called a taxi and took her to a nearby psychiatric clinic. Joyce was in no mood for his party that evening. A slightly calmer Lucia came home, but her return was only temporary. From now on she was to receive treatment in various clinics and sanatoria. In one of these she set fire to her own and a neighbouring room. The cost of this took a large chunk out of Joyce's royalties and Harriet Weaver's cheques.

Meanwhile Joyce kept in touch with Svevo's widow, Livia, sending the annual Christmas card with a note attached, enquiring about the sales of her late husband's books. In March 1932, Joyce received a request from Livia. She had remembered his promise to let him know if he could ever do anything to help with Svevo's literary affairs. She told him that *Senilità* was going to be published in English, under Joyce's suggested title *As a Man Grows Older,* and asked him if he would write an introduction. Under considerable family stress and the prospect of another eye operation, Joyce's spirits were at a low ebb. He wanted to devote any remaining energy to the semantic challenge of his *Work in Progress.* He apologised to Livia and suggested Ford Madox Ford, but he was not acceptable to the publishers in London. Joyce then had a brainwave – he suggested his brother. The idea was welcomed by the publishers and Stanislaus agreed to their offer. It was a delicate task for him – to write about his brother against whom he held many grievances, personally and artistically, and about an older man whom he had taught and respected. However, it was an opportunity to demonstrate his own talent as a writer. He began his introduction by tracing the course of the friendship of Joyce and Svevo from their first meeting at the Berlitz School to their admiration of each others' work, the encouragement they gave each other, and the many frustrations before either of them had any success. Stanislaus tried to be objective about the characters of both men:

Perhaps more than his sincere admiration for Svevo's work, the example of my brother's overweening confidence in himself was useful to Svevo. His self-respect as an artist had received so deep a wound that he never altogether recovered.... They both had to struggle with the scarce believable shiftiness of publishers, but at no time did my brother ever lose faith in his work or consent to any changes in it. His inflexibility was firmly rooted in failure. Prosperity was as near to being fatal to Svevo's artistic conscience as indigence was to my brother's. Svevo's outlook is far simpler than my brother's, his humour more urbane. On the other hand, my brother has a way of observing without appearing to observe; and it may not be too far-fetched to see in the person of Leopold Bloom, Svevo's mature, objective, peaceable temper reacting upon the younger writer's more fiery mettle.[10]

A new addition to Joyce's small circles of friends and helpers was Herbert Gorman, an American journalist and writer who was working in Paris. He had already written a book about Joyce –*James Joyce, his First Forty Years*, published in 1924. At first they met socially and Joyce decided that it was time for a full-scale biography – his first fifty years. He talked to Gorman about the project, and agreed to cooperate. It would be an authorised biography, a genre that can often inhibit a biographer. Joyce told him, only half-jokingly that he wanted to be treated as a saint with an unusually protracted martyrdom. Gorman was to deal sympathetically with Joyce's early life, its later hardships and sacrifices, and the courage he had shown in pursuing his private vision. The book was not a hagiography, nor intended as a critical study of his work.

In 1934, Joyce and Nora took a holiday in Denmark. They went to Elsinore and then Copenhagen, where he gave one of his very rare interview to a local journalist, Ove Vining. Joyce was unable to resist the temptation to conduct the whole interview in Danish. (He had learned Dano-Norwegian years before in order to read Ibsen in the original.) Vining obviously asked the usual journalistic questions about how Joyce worked. He received a very personal and illuminating reply:

It is a wonderful thing to live with a book. Everything gives way to it. Since 1922, when I began *Work in Progress,* I have not led a normal life. My book has been a greater reality to me than reality.[11]

Gorman's biography was meant to be published by 1935. Joyce hoped it would help the sales of *Ulysses* and pave the way for *Finnegans Wake*. Disappointingly, it was not to come out until 1940, when the potential readership had other things on its mind. Joyce, however, caused some of the delays himself. When he read the manuscript, he was upset that Gorman had dealt with certain details of his life – his father's life-style, Lucia's illness and his marriage. He insisted on the deletion of any mention of these, as well as a myriad of smaller corrections. The world did not need to know about the skeletons in the family cupboard – drunkenness, madness and living in sin. Gorman considered his work had been butchered and had no more to do with Joyce.

In April 1936, with Lucia in a sanatorium, George (Giorgio), Helen and their son now living in New York, and the prospect of another eye operation, Joyce expressed his deep gloom to Harriet Weaver:

> ...although I have the faithful support of my wife and Léon's loyal friendship, to say nothing of your own patience and sympathy, there are moments and hours, when I have nothing in my heart but rage and despair, a blind man's rage and despair. On many sides I hear that I have been an evil influence on my children. But what are they doing away from that influence? On the other hand what can I ask them to come back to? Paris is like a haughty ruin, or a decaying reveller. Any time I turn on the radio I hear some British politician mumbling inanities or his German cousin shouting and yelling like a madman. Perhaps Ireland or the U.S. are the safest places. And perhaps this is where the gas is really going to be turned on. Well so be it. The motto under my coat of arms is *Mors aut honorabilis vita*...[12]

In view of what was soon to happen to several of Joyce's friends, the colloquial mention of gas was unknowingly, but chillingly, unfortunate.

Joyce may have thought Paris now 'a haughty ruin' with nothing to offer his children, but he was overstating his case. Some expatriates still lived there, art was still created, visitors still came, and Joyce himself was regarded very much as an object of pilgrimage. His sight was poor enough for him not to be aware of the people who pointed him out and stared at him in restaurants and cafés. Nora, however, found it irksome and embarrassing. In mid-1938 Joyce finally had some positive news. His friend T.S. Eliot, now an editor at Faber and Faber in London, admired *Finnegans Wake,* was enthusiastic about the title, now divulged, and made an offer for the book. Joyce promptly accepted, and it was scheduled for publication early the following year.

Joyce finally had something to celebrate, but he was rarely lucky with his major publication dates. His first book, *Dubliners*, had been published in June 1914, two months before the Great War; his last book, *Finnegans Wake*, in May 1939, four months before World War II. That left the British and Irish critics just enough time to have a field-day with *Finnegans Wake*. A few, a very few, praised its originality, its poetic command of language with 'many moments of beauty'. The majority, however, had sharpened knives – except for the *Sunday Times*, which did not review it at all, on the grounds that it was 'irrelevant to literature'. The *Daily Express* called it 'An Irish stew of verbiage… with unexpected beauty arriving now and then....'[13] The *New Statesman* wrote that it was 'like having to learn Chinese, but, for a patient reader, where the meaning fades the music tides one over.'[14] The *Daily Mail* critic settled for 'reading it is like spending a night in the tower of Babel.' Having savaged it in the *Daily Telegraph*, Harold Nicolson[15] wrote in his diary, 'I truly believe that Joyce has this time gone too far in breaking all communication between himself and his reader. It is a very selfish book.' Richard Aldington, in the *Atlantic Monthly,* was almost the nastiest with 'The boredom endured in the penance of reading this book is something one would not inflict on any human being....'[16] Joyce's erstwhile friend Oliver St. John Gogarty wrote in the *Observer* that 'In some places the reading sounds like the chatter during the lunch interval in a Berlitz School.... This is the most colossal leg-pull in literature.'[17] It was the practical and kindly Paul Léon who gave the most balanced verdict on the book in a letter to Harriet Weaver:

> I can easily understand how anyone concerned with the grave political and social problems of this oppressive period will be painfully affected by its colossal triviality, its accumulation of words, meaningless, I suppose for the ordinary intelligent reader of today.... But it is

impossible to deny that he has acted according to his conscience and that he has actually consumed all his substance, physical and spiritual, moral and material in the writing of a book likely to be received with derision by his ill-wishers and with pained pleasure by his friends. And in this attitude he has remained true to himself.[18]

Joyce always claimed that politics were of no interest to him. He had spent the Great War in neutral Switzerland and the Irish Troubles in Zurich, Trieste and Paris, but on 3 September 1939 politics finally caught up with him.

Germany invaded Poland on 1 September and, two days later, Britain and France declared war on Germany. The so-called phoney war lasted from September 1939 until May 1940. Then Hitler launched his blitzkreig through Holland and Belgium and into France. The Joyces all had British passports, but they stayed in Paris for the moment. Joyce was trying desperately to find a safe haven for Lucia, and eventually found Dr. Delmas's clinic at Ivry outside Paris. Her moods were increasingly unpredictable and, on occasion, when she became violent, she had to be restrained in a straitjacket. Dr. Delmas moved his clinic to a safer location south of La Baule on the Atlantic coast, and Lucia was to stay there for the duration of the war.[19]

Their friends were anxious for the Joyces to leave, but Joyce was reluctant. Paris was his home and, in addition to his sight, his digestion was troubling him. He had convinced himself that Lucia was getting better, and he could not bear to leave her. It was different for Nora whose relationship with Lucia had completely collapsed. As they waited to see what the Germans would do next, another family misfortune hit them. George and Helen were having marital difficulties, and Helen had an acute nervous breakdown. She was admitted to a clinic. If the Germans captured Paris, Joyce and Nora, with their British passports, would be interned as enemy aliens.

Eugene Jolas left for the U.S. to launch an American version of *transition*. Before joining him, his wife Maria evacuated her bilingual school to Saint-Gérand-le-Puy, a small town in the Auvergne, near Vichy. She persuaded the Joyces to join her there. George arranged for Helen's brother to come from the U.S., collect his sister and take her back to a sanatorium in New York. On 22 December, Joyce, Nora, George and the six-year-old Stephen left for the Auvergne. It was the last time Joyce and Nora saw Paris. There was not much to celebrate that Christmas. In the New Year, Joyce was sick, probably with an ulcer, and finally demoralised. He called the reception of *Finnegans Wake* in Europe 'a complete fiasco', he was bored by village life, and mourned for his daughter and daughter-in-law, now both in psychiatric institutions. Joyce never saw either of them again.

The German Army entered Paris on 14 June 1940. On 22 June, the Germans made the French sign the Armistice in the same railway carriage at Compiègne that the French had used in 1918 to sign their victory over the Germans. France was divided into occupied and unoccupied zones, and Vichy was made the capital of the new collaborationist regime. In late June, the Joyces, back in Saint-Gérand-le-Puy, woke up to find a company of German soldiers encamped in the town square. They had arrived there by error, having strayed over the demarcation line from occupied France. They stayed for six days before withdrawing north, and the Joyces stayed indoors. In mid-June the Italians acted as they had done in the Great War, entering the war on what they thought would be the winning side – this time it was Germany's.

In Saint-Gérand-le-Puy, the Joyces watched the world they knew breaking up around them. For Joyce there was yet another pressing problem. Owing to wartime exchange controls, Harriet Weaver could not send Joyce his monthly cheque to France. It was possible to send the money only through Ireland, and it must not exceed £30 a month. It was now clear to the Joyces that the war would continue for the foreseeable future, its outcome too frightening to contemplate. Many of their friends had also left Paris and were scattered round the country, or had gone to the U.S. Beckett came to visit them at Saint-Gérand-le-Puy with his girlfriend, later wife, Suzanne Dumesnil. They were heading for the Spanish border to try and leave the country. They never made it to the border but stayed in France and fought with the Resistance. Beckett had strongly advised Joyce to leave the country before it was too late. The Joyces' thoughts now turned to Zurich, which had been a home from home for them during the Great War. They knew a great many people there, and it turned out to be as well that they did. For the next four months their battle with bureaucracy was a nightmare. They needed exit visas from the Vichy French authorities, as well as entry visas from the Swiss. Their British passports had to be renewed, and there was no British consul in Vichy. They managed to persuade the American consul to put an extension stamp in them. They then required a declaration of their financial assets, which at that point were fairly minimal and difficult to muster. Just as the French exit visas came through, they discovered that the Swiss demanded 50,000 Swiss francs as a financial guarantee. Joyce had virtually no money left, but he still had something just as useful – many rich friends and admirers. A Swiss banker, Paul Ruggiero, negotiated with the Swiss authorities to bring the sum down to 20,000 francs. Then, with the help of the Swiss Society of Authors, rallied by his friend Jacques Mercanton, the authorities were persuaded of Joyce's pre-eminence as a writer.

The Zurich cantonal authorities now raised one final obstacle. Without giving any reason, they rejected the visa application. Another Zurich friend, the art critic Carola Giedion, who had arranged accommodation for the Joyces, now went to the authorities and demanded to know why their applications had been rejected. With some embarrassment, they explained that it was because the Aliens' Department of the Zurich police had discovered that Joyce was a Jew. Mme Giedion was appalled. When Joyce, waiting in Saint-Gérand-le-Puy, was informed of this, he said, '*C'est le bouquet, vraiment.*' Even in this surreal predicament, Joyce was still able to pun bilingually. He told Mercanton to tell them – '*que je ne suis pas juif de Judée mais aryen d'Erin.*' [20] Less wittily, Mercanton signed a deposition saying that Joyce was not a Jew, and that they were probably muddling him up with a character in *Ulysses* – Leopold Bloom.

Emotionally and physically exhausted, Joyce and Nora, George and Stephen arrived in Zurich on 17 December 1940. They spent Christmas with the Giedions. Joyce was very quiet, and spent a lot of time walking by the lake with his grandson in the snow. Early in the New Year, he received a letter from Stanislaus telling him the Italian authorities had forced him to leave Trieste and he was now having a difficult time in Florence. Joyce sent him a postcard with a list of names of people who might be of help to him. It was the last postcard he ever wrote. After dinner on 9 January, Joyce complained of acute stomach pains. He was rushed into hospital where X-rays showed that he had a perforated duodenal ulcer. An emergency operation was performed. Afterwards, he rallied briefly, and then went into a coma. He died at 2 a.m. on 13 January 1941.

Joyce was buried on 15 January at the Fluntern cemetery on the outskirts of Zurich, next to the Zoological Gardens, which he liked and compared to the zoo in the Phoenix Park. There were worldwide obituaries and tributes to Joyce, but like so many 'prophets', he was not, in his lifetime, appreciated in his own country. His fellow Irish novelist, Elizabeth Bowen, tried to rectify this in the last paragraph of her obituary in *The Bell*:

> …Let us strip from Joyce the exaggerations of foolish intellectual worship he got abroad, and the notoriety he got at home, and take him back to ourselves as a writer out of the Irish people, who received much from our tradition and was to hand on more. [21]

Those words might have pleased Joyce most. After all, his young alter ego, Stephen Dedalus, as he left Dublin for Paris, had grandiloquently proclaimed, , , 'I go to experience for the millionth time the reality of experience and to forge in the smithy of my soul the uncreated conscience of my race.'[22]

Nora stayed on in Zurich, living frugally off Joyce's royalties. *Finnegans Wake* did not greatly add to them. Harriet Weaver's cheques were much reduced by the post-war exchange controls. She did, however, pay for Joyce's funeral. Nora often took visitors up the hill to the cemetery beside the zoo to see Joyce's grave. She said to one of them, pointing at the simple tombstone, 'Jim was awfully fond of the lions – I like to think of him lying there and listening to them roar.'[23]

In 1942, still living in Trieste, Svevo's wife Livia had to travel to Rome to register her status under Mussolini's new race laws. Through her mother's family, the Moravias, she was a quarter Jewish. An observant Catholic with two grandsons serving in the Italian Army on the Eastern front, she assumed that she would be classified as Italian Catholic. Her assumption was wrong. Livia and her daughter, Letizia, were going to be classified as Jewish. She objected strenuously, and was then told quietly that there was a way out of this problem. 'The way out' entailed handing over an enormous bribe. Livia was outraged. In a fury, she said that under these circumstances she would prefer to be classified as a Jew. Svevo would have much appreciated the irony of his Catholic wife, who had always wanted him to convert, ending up, officially, a Jew. Livia and Letizia went back to Trieste, but soon realised that, classified as Jews, life there might no longer be safe for them. They quickly packed up all Svevo's enormous collection of manuscripts and papers and, with Letizia's youngest son, Sergio, they went to live in Arcade, a remote village in Treviso near the mountains. Letizia's husband, Antonio Fonda, stayed behind in Trieste to help run the Veneziani company.

In early 1943, the family heard that Letizia's older two sons, Piero and Paulo, had been captured and were in a Russian prisoner-of-war camp. They both died there, within a month of each other, in March 1943. In February 1945, the Villa Veneziani and the factory were destroyed by American bombs. In April, there was an uprising against the Germans, now occupying Trieste. One of the leaders of the uprising was Antonio Fonda. He had been joined by Sergio, now just nineteen, who had come down from Arcade. He was killed in the street fighting, almost under his father's eyes. It would never be possible for the surviving three members of the family to recover entirely from these losses. Livia, however, had saved nearly all her husband's work, and now, with Letizia's help, devoted herself to guarding and promoting it. In her remaining years she researched and wrote a touching memoir of her husband. It was published under the name she finally took – Livia Veneziani Svevo. Despite her official classification as a Jew, she remained a devout Catholic, and in the last paragraph of her Memoir wrote, 'Letizia and I live on memories, until the day when Ettore, with his grandsons around him, welcomes us at the gates of eternity.'[24]

Livia died in Trieste in 1951, at the age of 77 and Nora died in that same year, aged 67. Unlike their husbands, Livia and Nora both had Catholic rites at their funerals. Nora had stayed on in Zurich. Her friends were there, and there were occasional visitors from Paris and London. She always tried to avoid journalists intent on interviewing her about her life with Joyce. In an interview she did not manage to avoid, the journalist asked about her memories of literary Paris in the twenties and thirties. Had she met Proust, Cocteau or Gide? She thought for a few moments before replying, 'Sure, if you've been married to the greatest writer in the world, you don't remember all the little fellows.'[25] Apart from Proust, Cocteau and Gide, among those 'little fellows', forgotten in Nora's memories, were also five Nobel Prize winners – W.B. Yeats, G.B. Shaw, Ernest Hemingway, T.S. Eliot and Samuel Beckett.

Neither Joyce nor Svevo ever won a literary prize. In Trieste, there is a statue of Italo Svevo in the Piazza Hortis, opposite the Museo Sveviano. Half-a- kilometre away, on the bridge that crosses the Canale Piccolo, is a statue of James Joyce, with a cane, bow-tie and jaunty straw hat. A plaque reads: '*...la mia anima è a Trieste...' Lettera a Nora, 27 ottobre 1909*. Dublin was slow to recognise their prodigal son who had never returned. A statue of Joyce was finally erected in 1990 in North Earl Street. There is also a sculpture that subtly connects Joyce and Svevo. It is the elongated figure of Anna Livia, the symbol of the River Liffey in *Finnegans Wake*. Joyce had asked Svevo and Livia for permission to use her hair as the model for Anna Livia's. Now it is memorialized in bronze. The figure was originally to be seen emerging from a small waterfall and pool in the middle of O'Connell Street. It was, most disrespectfully, referred to by Dubliners as 'the floozie in the jacuzzi'. More disrespectfully, and less amusingly, many Dubliners threw their rubbish and empty bottles into the pool. Dublin Council decided to move Anna Livia to a new site. In 2011, it was installed in a Memorial Park on Wolfe Tone Quay,[26] resting serenely beside its true home, the River Liffey.

The last words on Joyce and Svevo should rest with Stanislaus Joyce, who knew both men so well. On May 27 1955, at the University of Trieste, he delivered a lecture on his brother and their mutual friend, Italo Svevo. This lecture also concluded his own academic career.

The happy chance that brought these two remarkable men together was a literary event that is likely to increase rather than decrease in interest in years to come.

Although it had no political significance, the meeting was a link between two cultures, between two cities. Both of these men arose at the close of epochs in the lives of their respective cities to impress the memory of them on history. As there was a Dublin that has passed away, but still lives in the pages of Joyce, so there was a Trieste of Svevo that has gone with the wind and the blasts of war, but that we can now regard with better understanding and with greater affection because of the love and understanding with which Svevo wrote.[27]

Three weeks after giving this lecture, as if to round off the circle of endings, Stanislaus died – on 16 June – Bloomsday.[28]

Endnotes

CHAPTER 1

1 S. Benco, Preface to *La coscienza di Zeno* (Milan, 1930), p.6.

2 L. Veneziani Svevo, *Memoir of Italo Svevo* (Evanston, Ill., 1990), p.35.

3 R. Ellmann, *James Joyce* (London, 1982), p.156.

4 G. Bowker, *James Joyce, a biography* (London, 2011), p.121.

5 B. Maddox, *Nora* (London, 1988), p.36.

6 R. Ellmann, *James Joyce*, p.156. Whoever did what and to whom on the evening of 16 June 1904 at Ringsend has long been a matter of controversy among Joyceans. Both Ellmann and Maddox have been criticised for weaving 'fact from fiction'.

7 P. Costello, *James Joyce, the Years of Growth. 1882-1915* (London, 1992), p.235.

8 To Stanislaus Joyce, 11 October 1904, *Letters of James Joyce*, vol. 2 (London, 1966), p.65.

9 To S.J., 28 December 1904. Op. cit., p.75.

10 I. Svevo, *The Confessions of Zeno* (London, 1930), p.108.

11 Cited in Jan Morris, *Trieste and the Meaning of Nowhere* (London, 2001), p.65.

12 J. Joyce, *A Portrait of the Artist as a Young Man* (London, 1916), p.222.

13 M. and P. Colum, *Our Friend James Joyce* (New York, 1958), p.39.

14 Lady Isabel Burton, *Life of Sir Richard Burton* (London, 1893), p.553.

15 Op. cit., p.109.

16 Elio Schmitz, extracts from his diary are included in vol. 5 of I. Svevo *Opera Omnia*. ed. B.Maier (6 vols. Milan, 1972).

17 Op. cit., p.24.

18 Op. cit., p.32

19 P.N. Furbank, *Italo Svevo: The Man and the Writer* (London, 1966), p.34.

20 I. Svevo, *Una Vita* (London, 1966), p.56.

21 I. Svevo, *Opera Omnia*, vol. 3, p.813-14.

22 L. Veneziani Svevo, *Memoir*, p.35.

23 S. Benco, Italo Svevo (Milan, 1960), p.48.

24 Op. cit., pp.50-2.

25 Op. cit., p.53.

26 I. Svevo, *The Confessions of Zeno*, p.71.

27 P.N. Furbank, *Italo Svevo*, p.82.

CHAPTER 2

1   J. Joyce, *A Portrait of the Artist as a Young Man* (London, 1916), p.217.

2   S. Joyce, *My Brother's Keeper* (London, 1958), p.119.

3   Op. cit., pp.92-3.

4   Op. cit., From Stanislaus's diary, Sept 1903. Quoted in Richard Ellmann's introduction to *My Brother's Keeper*, p. 17. Ellmann spent considerable time with Stanislaus in the last two years of his life and gained vital information and documents not available to his fellow scholars. Stanislaus certainly conveyed to Ellmann his own, and often acid, view of the fraternal relationship, although always acknowledging his brother's genius.

5   Op. cit., p.18.

6   Op. cit., p.161.

7   R. Ellmann, *James Joyce* (1982), p.74.

8   S. Joyce, *My Brother's Keeper*, p.180.

9   Ibid., p.98.

10 R. Ellmann, quoted in *James Joyce*, p.101.

11 J. Joyce, *A Portrait of the Artist as a Young Man*, p.228.

12 S. Joyce, *My Brother's Keeper*, p.228.

13 Op. cit., p.231.

14 Op. cit., pp.233-5.

15 J. Joyce, *Ulysses*, p. 4 (first published Paris: Shakespeare and Company, 1922). All the quotations and page numbers here refer to the Penguin Annotated Edition, edited and with notes by Declan Kiberd (London, 1992).

16 Op. cit., p.8.

17 G. Bowker, *James Joyce* (London, 2011), p.115.

18 J. Joyce, *My Brother's Keeper*, p.244.

19 J. Joyce, *Ulysses*, p.704.

CHAPTER 3

1   From Joyce to Italian journalist, quoted in R. Ellmann *James Joyce* (London, 1982), p.561.

2   Svevo's *Betrothal Diary* is contained in I. Svevo, *Opera Omnia*, vol. 3, p.768.

3   J. Gatt-Rutter, *Italo Svevo: A Double Life* (London, 1988), p.140.

4   Op. cit., p.160.

5   Op. cit., p.165.

6   M-A Commène, *Italo Svevo in Europe* (Paris, 1960).

7   L. Veneziani Svevo, *Memoir*, p.114.

8   Op. cit., p.49.

9 J. Gatt-Rutter and B. Moloney, *This England is so Different: The London Letters of Italo Svevo* (Market Harborough, 2003), p.7.

10 Umberto Saba in I. Svevo, *Opera Omnia,* vol. 1, pp.152-4.

11 J. Gatt-Rutter and B. Moloney, *This England,* pp.22-3.

12 I. Svevo, *Saggi* (Essays) *Opera Omnia,* vol. 3, p.182.

13 L.Veneziani Svevo, *Memoir,* p.23.

CHAPTER 4

1 R. Ellmann, Introduction to S. Joyce, *My Brother's Keeper* (London, 1958), p.10.

2 To Mrs. Josephine Murray, *Letters of James Joyce,* vol. 2 (ed. R. Ellmann, London, 1966), p.128.

3 Mrs. Josephine Murray to S. Joyce, *Letters of James Joyce,* vol. 2, p.215.

4 S. Joyce, *Dublin Diary,* 29 March 1904 (London, 1962), p.25.

5 After his lecture about Joyce in Trieste, Francini Bruni published his pamphlet, *Joyce: Stripped Naked in the Piazza* in both Italian and English (Trieste, 1922).

6 Letter to S. Joyce. *Letters of James Joyce,* vol. 2, p.210.

7 Op. cit., p.218.

8 Op. cit., p.153.

9 Op. cit., p.162.

10 Op. cit., p.225.

11 Op. cit., p.216.

CHAPTER 5

1 I. Svevo, letter quoted in R. Ellmann, *James Joyce,* p.272.

2 S. Joyce, Introduction to I. Svevo, *As a Man Grows Older* (London, 1932), p.vi.

3 L. Veneziani Svevo, *Memoir,* p.67.

4 S. Joyce, Introduction to I. Svevo, *As a Man...,* p.vii.

5 P.N. Furbank, *Italo Svevo,* pp.94-5.

6 E. Settanni, quoted in *Il Giornale della Sera* (Trieste, 8 August 1949).

7 J. Joyce, *Ulysses* (London, 1992), pp.776-7.

8 Letter to Letizia Veneziani Svevo, 10 April 1908. Quoted in P.N. Furbank, *Italo Svevo,* pp.94-5.

9 Op. cit., p.96.

10 S. Solmi, *Ricordi di Svevo* (*Solario,* Florence. 1929), p.79.

11 I. Svevo, *The Confessions of Zeno,* trans. Beryl de Zoete (London, 1930), p.354.

12 I. Svevo, *The Confessions of Zeno,* trans. William Weaver (New York, 2001), p.407.

[13] J. Joyce, *Ulysses,* pp.430-2.

[14] Ibid., pp.444-8.

[15] R. Ellmann interview with Jacques Mercanton, *The Hours of James Joyce* (Zurich, 1950).

[16] J. Joyce, *Ulysses,* p.73.

[17] L. Hyman, *The Jews of Ireland* (Dublin and Jerusalem, 1972), p.185.

CHAPTER 6

[1] J. Joyce, *Ulysses,* p.173.

[2] R. Ellmann, *James Joyce,* p.268. Ellmann quotes this from Stanislaus's Diary entry, 6 February 1908. There has always been considerable mystery about Stanislaus's *Triestine Diary* (*Book of Days*). It was never published. In his personal dealings with Stanislaus, Ellmann had access to it, and took a photocopy. The diary covers a period from January 1907 to February 1909, and therefore Ellmann uses it only in chapter 14 of his Joyce biography. See Laura Pelaschiar, *James Joyce Quarterly* vol. 36. no. 2 (Winter 1999), pp. 61-7.

[3] S. Joyce, from *James Joyce in Context,* ed. John McCourt (Cambridge, 2009), p.229.

[4] I. Svevo, *Saggi* (Essays) *Opera Omnia,* vol. 3, pp.187-8.

[5] P.N. Furbank, *Italo Svevo,* p.59.

[6] J. Joyce, *A Portrait of the Artist as a Young Man* (London, 1916), p.1.

[7] Quoted in R. Ellmann, *James Joyce,* p.273. This and the letter to Letizia containing Svevo's story of the wardrobe-makers is part of the Joyce collection at Yale University. Yale was Ellmann's alma mater and his preferred resting place for more of the Joyce archive, but they were eventually to be outbid by the libraries of numerous high-spending universities, Cornell, Harvard, Buffalo, Tulsa, and, of course, the University of Texas at Austin.

[8] Op. cit., p.274.

[9] Letter from Stanislaus Joyce to Herbert Gorman, 8 August 1931, *Letters of James Joyce,* vol. 3, p.225.

[10] I. Svevo, 'James Joyce', trans. S. Joyce, published as appendix in L. Veneziani Svevo, *Memoir,* p.152.

[11] R. Ellmann, *Selected Letters of James Joyce* (London, 1975), p.76.

[12] Francini Bruni, see note 5, chapter 4.

[13] B. Maddox, *Nora* (London, 1988), pp.146-7.

[14] R. Ellmann, *James Joyce,* p.300.

[15] J. Joyce to Nora, 9 December 1909. *Letters of James Joyce,* vol.3, p.174.

[16] I. Svevo to J. Joyce, *Letters of James Joyce,* vol. 2, p.286.

[17] J. Joyce, *Dubliners* (London, 1914), p.121.

CHAPTER 7

1. J. Joyce to S. Joyce, February 1907, *Letters of James Joyce*, vol. 2, p.113.
2. Tullio Silvestri was known among Yiddish speakers in the Jewish community as a *schnorrer*. By managing to borrow from Joyce, he became celebrated as the *schnorrer's schnorrer*.
3. For I. Svevo's review in letter to J. Joyce, see note 29 in chapter 15.
4. I. Svevo, trans. S. Joyce, in appendix of L. Veneziani Svevo, *Memoir*, p.158.
5. Op. cit., p.171.
6. R. Ellmann, *James Joyce*, interview with Dr. Daniel Brody in 1954, p.628.

CHAPTER 8

1. This postcard is in the Museo Sveviano, Biblioteca Civica, Trieste.
2. J. Joyce to Grant Richards, 4 March 1914, *Letters of James Joyce*, vol. 1, p.75.
3. J. Joyce, *Gas from a Burner,* first published privately in Trieste and Dublin 1914, and then reprinted in *Critical Writings of James Joyce* (London, 1959).
4. W.B. Yeats, letter written by him in 1923, quoted in R. Ellmann, *James Joyce* ,with no accreditation.
5. E. Pound, *The Letters of Ezra Pound to James Joyce*, ed. Forrest Read (New York, 1967), pp.17-18.
6. R. Ellmann, *James Joyce*, p.350.
7. P. Hutchins, *James Joyce's World* (London, 1957), p.102.
8. I. Svevo to L. Veneziani Svevo, *Epistolario, Opera Omnia*, vol. 1.
9. I. Svevo, 'James Joyce', published as appendix in L. Veneziani Svevo, *Memoir*, p.150.
10. J Joyce, *Giacomo Joyce*, hand-written in 1914 on 16 pages (London, 1968), p.2.
11. Op. cit., p.10
12. Ibid.
13. Op. cit., p.13.
14. Op. cit., p.3.
15. Op. cit., p.15.
16. I. Svevo, 'James Joyce', in L.Veneziani Svevo, *Memoir*, p.149.
17. Op. cit., p.151.

CHAPTER 9

1. J. Morris, *Trieste and the Meaning of Nowhere* (London, 2001), p.38.
2. I. Svevo, *The Nice Old Man and the Pretty Girl* (published posthumously, Milan, 1929), English trans. by L. Collison-Morley (Leonard & Virginia Woolf, Hogarth Press, London, 1930), p.39.

[3]   Op. cit., p.25.

[4]   J. Joyce, *Critical Writings,* eds. Ellsworth Mason and R. Ellmann (London, 1959), pp.68-72.

[5]   R. Ellmann, *James Joyce*, p.399.

[6]   Op. cit., p.413.

[7]   Op. cit., p.481.

[8]   Op. cit., p.510.

[9]   F. Budgen, *Myselves When Young* (Oxford, 1970), p.170.

[10]   Op. cit., p.184.

[11]   T. Stoppard, *Travesties* (London, 1975), p. 65.

CHAPTER 10

[1]   I. Svevo, *Epistolario, Opera Omnia*, vol.1, p.725.

[2]   I. Svevo, *Saggi e pagine sparsi, Opera Omnia*, vol. 3, pp.92-3.

[3]   Quoted in M. Thompson, *The White War* (London, 2008), p.316.

[4]   E. Hemingway, *Farewell to Arms* (London, 1929).

[5]   E. Hemingway, *Toronto Star,* 27 January 1923.

[6]   M. Thompson, *The White War*, p.324.

[7]   L. Veneziani Svevo, *Memoir*, p.73.

[8]   Quoted in M. Thompson, *The White War*, p.361.

[9]   Archive, Museo Sveviano, Trieste.

[10]   I. Svevo, *Saggi* (Essays), *Opera Omnia,* vol.3.

[11]   I. Svevo, *The Confessions of Zeno*, p.1.

[12]   Op. cit., p.33.

[13]   Op. cit., p.51.

CHAPTER 11

[1]   S. Joyce to J. Joyce, 25 May 1919, *Letters of James Joyce,* vol.2 (London, 1966), p.442.

[2]   I. Svevo, Appendix to L. Veneziani Svevo, *Memoir*, p.172.

[3]   J. Joyce to F. Budgen, 14 February 1919. *Letters of James Joyce*, vol. 1 (London ,1966), p.134.

[4]   M. Colum, *Life and the Dream* (London, 1947), p.383.

[5]   J. Joyce to E. Pound, 31 May 1919, *Joyce-Pound Letters,* ed. Forrest Read (New York, 1967).

[6]   J. Joyce, *Ulysses*, p.452.

7 Op. cit., p.463.

8 Ibid.

9 Op. cit., p.478.

10 Ibid. pp.478-9.

11 J. Joyce to H.Weaver, *Letters of James Joyce*, vol. 1, p.137.

12 E. Pound to J. Quinn, *Pound-Joyce Letters* (New York, 1967), p.178.

13 H. Weaver to J. Joyce, 6 July 1919, *Letters of James Joyce*, vol. 1.

14 F. Budgen, *Myselves When Young* (London, 1970), pp.260 and 268.

CHAPTER 12

1 I. Svevo, *Epistolario, Opera Omnia*, vol.1, p. 779.

2 E. Montale to I. Svevo, *Carteggio, Opera Omnia*, vol.6.

3 I. Svevo, *The Confessions of Zeno*, p. 74.

4 Op. cit., p.80.

5 Op. cit., p.81.

6 Op. cit., p.88.

7 Op. cit., p.89.

8 Op. cit., p.98.

9 Op. cit., p.108.

10 Op. cit., p.91.

11 Op. cit., p.111.

12 Op. cit., p.122.

13 Op. cit., p.129.

14 Op. cit., pp.133-4.

15 Op. cit., pp.137-8.

16 Op. cit., p. 93.

17 C. Duggan, *The Force of Destiny: A History of Italy since 1796* (London, 2007), p.413.

18 M. Macmillan, *Peacemakers* (London, 2002), p.289.

19 Op. cit., p.288.

20 Op. cit., p. 311.

21 G. d'Annunzio, quoted in C. Duggan, *The Force of Destiny*, p. 411.

22 B. Mussolini, quoted in C. Duggan, p. 400.

23 Op. cit., p.417.

24 I. Svevo to E. Montale, September 1927, *Epistolario, Opera Omnia*, vol. 1.

CHAPTER 13

1 J. Joyce, *Ulysses*, p.698.

2 To Italo Svevo from J. Joyce, 5 January 1921, *Selected Letters of James Joyce* (London, 1975), p.275.

3 To Carlo Linati, 21 September 1920, *Letters of James Joyce*, vol. 1, pp. 146-7.

4 Op. cit., p.148.

5 S. Beach, *Shakespeare and Company* (London, 1957), p.35.

6 Op. cit., p.36.

7 T.S. Eliot to Ezra Pound, 3 July 1920. *Letters of T.S. Eliot 1898-1922* (London, 1988), p.388.

8 T.S. Eliot to Robert McAlmon, 2 May 1921, ibid. pp.563-4.

9 T.S. Eliot to John Quinn, 9 May 1921, ibid. p.452.

10 E. Hemingway, 'A Tribute to Ezra Pound', *Poetry Magazine* (London, Autumn 1925).

11 S. Beach, 'Ulysses in Paris', *Mercure de France*, May 1950, p.24.

12 Ernest Hemingway letter to Sherwood Anderson, 9 March 1922. Quoted in R. Ellmann, *James Joyce*, p.695.

13 S. Beach, *Shakespeare and Company* (London, 1957), p.52.

14 G.B. Shaw, letter to *Picture Post* magazine, 3 June 1939, London. (Footnote in R. Ellmann's *James Joyce*, p.576.)

15 W.B. Yeats to J. Joyce, September 1932, *Collected Letters of W.B. Yeats* (Oxford, 1986), p.600.

16 J. Joyce to W.B.Yeats, 5 October 1932, *Collected Letters of W.B. Yeats*, vol. 1, p.325.

17 V. Larbaud, 'James Joyce', *Nouvelle Revue Française* xviii (April 1922), pp.385-405.

18 U. O'Connor, *James Joyce and Oliver St. John Gogarty: A Famous Friendship*, *Texas Quarterly*, iii (Summer 1960), p.191.

19 S. Joyce to J. Joyce, 26 February 1922, *Letters of James Joyce*, vol. 1, p.110.

20 S. Joyce to J. Joyce, 1 March 1922, *Letters of James Joyce*, vol. 1, p.122.

21 J. Joyce to Nora Joyce, April 1922, *Letters of James Joyce*, vol. 3, p.63.

22 R. McAlmon and J. Boyle, *Being Geniuses Together* (New York, 1930), pp.167-8.

23 Giorgio was still dining out on it when Ellmann interviewed him in 1953. R. Ellmann, *James Joyce*, p.535.

24 Ellmann interview with Harriet Weaver, 1956. R. Ellmann, *James Joyce*, p.537.

25 J. Joyce to H. Weaver, 23 November 1923, *Letters of James Joyce*, vol. 3, p.82.

26 P. Hutchins, *James Joyce's World* (London, 1957), p.139.

CHAPTER 14

1   *This England is so Different: Italo Svevo's London Writings,* ed. and trans. by J.Gatt-Rutter and B. Moloney. 'Kindness' (*La Nazione,* Trieste. 25 December 1920), p.229.

2   Op. cit., p.232.

3   Op. cit., p.237.

4   I. Svevo, *The Confessions of Zeno,* p.151.

5   Op. cit., p.154.

6   Op. cit., p.380.

7   I. Svevo, *Corto Viaggio,* p.96.

8   I. Svevo, *The Confessions of Zeno,* p.191.

9   Op. cit., p.196.

10 Op. cit., p.228.

11 Op. cit., p.229.

12 Op. cit., p.231.

13 Op. cit., p.350.

14 Ibid.

15 Op. cit., p.359.

16 Op. cit., p.377.

17 Ibid.

CHAPTER 15

1   P.N. Furbank, *Italo Svevo,* p.110.

2   B. Mussolini, *Opera Omnia,* vol. 18, September 1922, p. 412.

3   C. Duggan, *The Force of Destiny, Italy since 1796* (London, 2007), p.432.

4   Ibid.

5   L. Pirandello to Mussolini by telegram, 17 September 1924, C. Duggan (London ,2007), p.453.

6   L. Veneziani Svevo, *Memoir,* p.35.

7   J. Mercanton, *Les Heures de James Joyce* (New York, 1952), p.46.

8   F. Budgen, *Further Recollections of James Joyce* (London, 1938), p.10-11.

9   S. Gilbert, interview with R. Ellmann, quoted in R. Ellmann, *James Joyce,* p.714.

10 S. Joyce, *Dublin Diary,* ed. G.H. Healey (London, 1962), p.15.

11 J. Joyce, *Finnegans Wake* (London, 1939), p.1.

12 Letter to H. Weaver, *Letters of James Joyce,* vol. 2 (London, 1966), p.187.

[13] R. Ellmann, *James Joyce* (London, 1982), p.703.

[14] Ibid., quoted from unpublished letter in library of State University of Buffalo, N.Y.

[15] P.N. Furbank, J. Joyce letter to I. Svevo, 30 January 1924, *Italo Svevo*, p.117.

[16] Ibid.

[17] Op. cit., p. 119.

[18] J. Joyce to V. Larbaud, 6 June 1924, *Letters of James Joyce*, vol. 2 (London, 1966), p.214.

[19] P.N. Furbank, letter I. Svevo to J. Joyce, 10 June 1924, *Italo Svevo*, p.118.

[20] I. Svevo, *Saggi* (Essays), *Opera Omnia*, vol.3, p.231.

[21] L. Veneziani Svevo, *Memoir of Italo Svevo*, p.79.

[22] Op. cit., p.83.

[23] Op. cit., p.79.

[24] Op. cit., p.84.

[25] Ibid.

[26] Op. cit., p.85.

[27] Ibid.

[28] Op. cit., pp.89-90.

[29] P.N. Furbank, *Italo Svevo*, p.127.

[30] Op. cit., p.135.

[31] J. Gatt-Rutter, *Italo Svevo: A Double Life*, E. Montale to I.Svevo, p. 334.

[32] L. Veneziani Svevo, *Memoir*, p.107.

[33] Review in *The Times Literary Supplement*, 20 May 1926, quoted in P.N. Furbank, p.139.

[34] Ibid.

[35] I. Svevo, lecture on Joyce, Milan, 1927. Appendix to L. Veneziani Svevo, *Memoir*.

[36] Ibid.

[37] L.Veneziani Svevo, letter from M.A. Crémieux to I. Svevo, 2 February 1927, *Memoir*, p.107.

[38] I. Svevo, preface to 2nd ed. *Senilità* (Milan, 1927).

[39] J. Gatt-Rutter, *Italo Svevo*, p.347.

[40] I. Ehrenburg, *Solario*, Florence 1929, p.35, quoted in P.N.Furbank, *Italo Svevo*, p.145.

[41] L.Veneziani Svevo, *Memoir*, p.117.

[42] Op. cit., p.125.

Endnotes

CHAPTER 16

1 J. Joyce to J. Weaver, *Letters of James Joyce,* vol. 3, p.140.

2 E. Pound to J. Joyce. *The Letters of Ezra Pound,* ed. Forrest Read (New York, 1966), p.202.

3 V. Woolf, *A Writer's Diary*, ed. Leonard Woolf (London, 1954), p.50.

4 Op. cit., p.55.

5 H. Weaver to J. Joyce, 4 February 1927, *Letters of James Joyce,* vol. 2, p.206.

6 A. MacLeish to J. Joyce, undated, *Letter of James Joyce,* vol.2, p.187.

7 A. MacLeish, protest letter sent out to writers, dated 2 February 1927, Joyce's birthday.

8 J. Joyce to H. Weaver, 14 August 1927, *Selected Letters of James Joyce,* p.326.

9 J. Joyce to H. Weaver, 20 September 1928, *Selected Letters of James Joyce,* p.334.

10 L. Veneziani Svevo, *Memoir,* p.128.

11 Ibid.

12 Op. cit., p.135.

13 V. Larbaud, *Nouvelles Littéraires,* Paris, November 1928.

14 L. Veneziani Svevo, *Memoir,* pp.132-4.

15 Umberto Saba, *A Recollection,* published in translation as an appendix to *A Perfect Hoax* (London, 1993), pp.79-81.

16 Ibid. Many celebrated last words have been attached to activities that dying is 'easier than'. The original quote is most likely the actor David Garrick's farewell, after a performance at Drury Lane –'dying is easy, comedy is difficult'.

CHAPTER 17

1 Interview with R. Ellmann in 1953, quoted in *James Joyce,* p.679.

2 H.G. Wells to J. Joyce, 23 November 1928, in P. Hutchins, *James Joyce's World* (London, 1957), p. 159.

3 J. Joyce to T.S. Eliot, 1 January 1932. *Letters of James Joyce,* vol. 1, p.311.

4 J. Joyce to H. Weaver, 11 January 1932, *Letters of James Joyce,* vol. 1, p.312.

5 R. Ellmann, *James Joyce,* p. 651. An unpublished letter that Ellmann traced to Monnier's legal executor in Paris.

6 'An American Storyteller', *Time Magazine,* 13 December 1954, p.75.

7 S. Beckett, conversation with Arthur Power, *New York Times,* 19 April 1981.

8 P. Léon, letter 17 September 1932, *A James Joyce Yearbook* (New York), p. 119.

9 P. Léon to A. Léon, 3 June 1930, quoted in R. Ellmann, *James Joyce,* p.630.

[10] S. Joyce, Introduction to I.Svevo, *As A Man Grows Older* (London, 1932).

[11] O. Vining, *James Joyce in Copenhagen* in collection *Portrait of the Artist in Exile* (Seattle, 1979), pp.139-52.

[12] J. Joyce to H. Weaver, 1 May 1935, *Letters of James Joyce*, vol. 1, p.365.

[13] Beachcomber, *Daily Express*, 11 May 1939.

[14] G.W. Stonier, *New Statesman*, 29 May 1939.

[15] H. Nicholson, *Daily Telegraph*, 5 May 1939.

[16] R. Aldington, *Atlantic Monthly*, June 1939.

[17] O. St. J. Gogarty, *The Observer*, 7 May 1939.

[18] P. Léon to H. Weaver, 10 December 1938, *Dear Miss Weaver*, ed. Lidderdale and Nicholson (London), p.373.

[19] After the war and several attempts to live with relations or friends, in 1951 Lucia was admitted to St. Andrew's psychiatric hospital, Northampton. Harriet Weaver had become her guardian and paid for her care. Lucia died there in 1982 at the age of seventy-four.

[20] Letter to Jacques Mercanton, 29 October 1940, *Letters of James Joyce*, vol. 3, p.492. These *bon mots* only work in the original French. There are various not so effective versions in translation.

[21] E. Bowen, Obituary in *The Bell* (Dublin, March 1941), p.16.

[22] J.Joyce, *A Portrait of the Artist as a Young Man*, p.228.

[23] Too good a line for Nora not to have said. She apparently said it to a Zurich friend, John Prudhoe, who passed it on to Richard Ellmann in 1953.

[24] L.Veneziani Svevo, *Memoir*, p.146.

[25] S. Campbell, *Mrs Joyce of Zurich*, *Harper's Bazaar*, October 1952, p.171.

[26] Slightly remodelled by its sculptor, Eamonn O'Doherty

[27] S. Joyce, Lecture given on 27 May 1955. Published in *Joyce in Svevo's Garden* (Trieste, 1995), pp. 77-94.

[28] The sixteenth of June 1955 was also the first anniversary of the celebration of Bloomsday in Dublin, started by a group of Irish writers in 1954 on the 50th anniversary of the day on which the events of *Ulysses* took place – an annual celebration still going strong.

Sources and Bibliography

PRINTED PRIMARY SOURCES

WORKS – JAMES JOYCE

Chamber Music (London: Jonathan Cape, 1971 ed.)

Dubliners (London: Jonathan Cape, 1968 ed.)

A Portrait of the Artist as a Young Man (London: Penguin, 1960 ed.)

Ulysses (New York: Random House, 1934)

Ulysses Annotated Edition. ed. Declan Kiberd (London: Penguin Books, 2011)

Finnegans Wake (London: Faber and Faber, 1989 ed.)

Collected Letters of James Joyce ed. Stuart Gilbert vol. 1 (London: Faber and Faber, 1957)

Collected Letters of James Joyce ed. Richard Ellmann vols. 2 & 3 (London: Faber and Faber, 1966)

Selected Letters of James Joyce ed. Richard Ellmann (London: Faber and Faber, 1975)

Occasional, Critical and Political Writing ed. Kevin Barry (Oxford University Press, 2000)

WORKS – ITALO SVEVO

A Life trans. Archibald Colquhoun (London: Penguin Classics, 1982 ed.)

As A Man Grows Older trans. Beryl de Zoete (London: Penguin Modern Classics, 1982 ed.)

The Confessions of Zeno trans. Beryl de Zoete (London, Penguin Modern Classics, 1984 ed.)

The Confessions of Zeno trans. William Weaver (New York: Everyman, 2001)

The Nice Old Man and the Pretty Girl trans. L. Collison-Morley (London: The Hogarth Press, 1930. New York: Melville House, 2010 ed.)

A Perfect Hoax trans. J.G. Nichols (London: Hesperus Press, 2003)

This England is so Different: The London Writings of Italo Svevo trans. John Gatt-Rutter and Brian Moloney (Leicester: Troubador Publications, 2003)

Carteggio Inedito Italo Svevo-James Joyce trans. Harry Levin (Florence: *Inventario* anno 2. No.2. 1949)

James Joyce (Svevo's Milan lecture of 1927) trans. Stanislaus Joyce (New York: New Directions. 1950. London: Hesperus Press, 2003).

SELECTED SECONDARY SOURCES

BOOKS

Arnold, Bruce, *The Scandal of Ulysses: The Life and Afterlife of a Twentieth-Century Masterpiece* (Dublin: The Liffey Press, 2004)

Beach, Sylvia, *Shakespeare and Company* (London, 1957)

Bowker, Gordon, *James Joyce, a biography* (London:Weidenfeld & Nicolson, 2011)

Budgen, Frank, *James Joyce and the Making of Ulysses* (Oxford University Press, 1934)

---------- *Myselves When Young* (Oxford University Press, 1970)

Burgess, Anthony, *Here Comes Everybody -- James Joyce for the Ordinary Reader* (London: Arena Books, 1987)

Colum, Mary and Padraic, *Our Friend James Joyce* (New York: Doubleday, 1959)

Costello, Peter, *Leopold Bloom, a Biography* (Dublin: Gill and Macmillan, 1981)

---------- *John Stanislaus Joyce,* with John Wyse Jackson (London: Fourth Estate, 1997)

Crivelli, Renzo, *James Joyce, Triestine Itineraries,* trans. John McCourt (Trieste: MGS Press, 1996)

Davidson, Neil R., *James Joyce, Ulysses and the Construction of Jewish Identity* (Cambridge University Press, 1996)

Duggan, Christopher, *The Force of Destiny. Italy since 1796.* (London: Penguin Books, 2007)

Ellmann, Richard, *James Joyce* (Oxford University Press, 1982)

Fennell, Conor, *A Little Circle of Kindred Minds:Joyce in Paris.*(Dublin: Green Lamp Editions, 2011)

Furbank, P.N., *Italo Svevo. The Man and the Writer* (London: Secker and Warburg, 1966)

Gatt-Rutter, John, *Italo Svevo: A Double Life* (Oxford University Press, 1988)

Gibson, Andrew, *Joyce's Revenge. History, Politics and Aesthetics in Ulysses* (Oxford University Press, 2002)

Gross, John, *James Joyce* (London: Fontana, 1971)

Hughes-Hallett, Lucy, *The Pike, Gabriele d'Annunzio* (London: Fourth Estate, 2013)

Hutchins, Patricia, *James Joyce's World* (London: Methuen, 1957)

Jackson, Kevin, *Constellation of Genius* (London: Hutchinson, 2012)

Joyce, Stanislaus, *My Brother's Keeper*, Preface, T.S. Eliot, Introd. Richard Ellmann (London: Faber and Faber, 1958)

---------- *Joyce in Svevo's Garden* (Trieste: MGS Press, 1995)

---------- *The Complete Dublin Diary*, Edited by George H. Healey (Ithaca, New York: Cornell University Press, 1971)

Kiberd, Declan, *Inventing Ireland* (London: Jonathan Cape, 1995)

---------- *Ulysses and Us. The Art of Everyday Living* (London: Faber and Faber, 2009)

Maddox, Brenda, *Nora* (London: Hamish Hamilton, 1988)

McCourt, John, *The Years of Bloom. James Joyce in Trieste* (Dublin: Lilliput Press, 2000)

Morris, Jan, *Trieste and the Meaning of Nowhere* (London, 2001)

Nadel, Ira, *Joyce and the Jews* (Iowa City: University of Iowa Press, 1989)

O'Brien, Edna, *James Joyce* (London: Weidenfeld and Nicolson, 1999)

Ó'Grada, Cormac, *Jewish Ireland in the Age of Joyce* (Princeton University Press, 2006)

Smith, Mack, *Mussolini* (London: Weidenfeld and Nicholson, 1981)

Stoppard, Tom, *Travesties* (London: Faber and Faber, 1975)

Svevo, Livia Veneziani, *Memoir of Italo Svevo*, trans. Isabel Quigly (Evanston, Illinois: Northwestern University Press, 1990)

Thompson, Mark, *The White War. Life and Death on the Italian Front. 1915-1918.* (London: Faber and Faber, 2008)

ARTICLES

Bailey, Paul, 'Svevo, Comic Genius', *The Independent*, 24 September 1999

Bowen, Elizabeth, 'In Memory. James Joyce', *The Bell*, No.10, 1941

Burgess, Anthony, 'In the Footsteps of Joyce – Trieste', *New York Times*, April 1982

Di Biase, Carmine, 'Svevo, Work of a Golden Sunset', *Times Literary Supplement*, 4 January 2013

Gorman, Herbert, 'James Joyce. Obituary', *The Spectator*, 14 February 1941

Lasdun, James, 'Saving Svevo', *The Guardian*, 24 August 2002

Ó'Grada, Cormac, 'Lost in Little Jerusalem', *Journal of Modern Literature*, Indiana University Press, 2004

Parks, Tim, 'Joyce and Company', *London Review of Books*, 5 July 2012

Staley, Thomas F., 'The Search for Bloom', *James Joyce Quarterly*, 3, Summer 1966

Wood, James, 'Mixed Feelings – Zeno's Conscience', *London Review of Books*, 21 October 2013

Index